MENOTTI

MENOTTI

A BIOGRAPHY

John Gruen

MACMILLAN PUBLISHING CO., INC.
NEW YORK

COLLIER MACMILLAN PUBLISHERS
LONDON

Macmillan Publishing Co., Inc.
866 Third Avenue, New York, N.Y. 10022
Collier Macmillan Canada, Ltd.

Library of Congress Cataloging in Publication Data

Gruen, John.
Menotti.

Includes index.
1. Menotti, Gian Carlo, 1911–   2. Composers—
Biography.
ML410.M52G8   782.1'092'4 [B]   77–9304
ISBN 0–02–546320–9

First Printing 1978

Printed in the United States of America

CONTENTS

FOREWORD

"There once lived a Man in a Castle
and a strange man was he."

(The Unicorn, the Gorgon and the Manticore)

As I sped toward Yester House on the train, it seemed inconceivable at first that Gian Carlo Menotti would choose to live in Scotland —would want to spend the rest of his life in the moist, green, and turbulent land of Robert Burns, and on the very spot that once held Yester Castle, built in the thirteenth century by Hugo Gifford. And yet it was consistent with his passion for the theatrical and bizarre that Menotti should wish to live in a house whose original owner was believed to have been in league with the devil, using Satanic powers to build the sunken "Goblin Hall," Yester's most celebrated room. (Sir Walter Scott himself used this myth as a dramatic episode in "The Host's Tale" in *Marmion.*) Menotti's temperament, leaning toward the fantastic, would respond to every aspect of Yester's spectacular history and setting.

Traveling through sun and through the crisp geometry of lush farmland, I anticipated no change in the perfect weather. The clouds floating over the landscape were large, billowy, and snow white, like cushions thrown on the azure sheet of the Scottish sky. But minutes before the train's arrival at Edinburgh, an ominous darkness enveloped the countryside and distant thunder could be heard. Suddenly a flash storm, with loud and heavy rains, obscured the approach to the city. Its majestic castle could barely be seen. Its ancient buildings, its wide streets were blurred by the onrush of the fierce summer wind and relentless downpour. The train stopped in the station. Passengers began to stream out onto the platform as the thunder roared. It had been arranged that a car would meet me in Edinburgh, and with my baggage at my feet, I stood looking around me. A moment later, a uniformed chauffeur inquired whether I was the gentleman looking for Maestro Menotti. The car was waiting, and would I follow him?

Menotti himself suddenly alit from an enormous black Rolls-Royce—actually a hired taxi. (Menotti's own cars are generally delapidated, second-hand contraptions, as he considers it a waste to spend money on automobiles.) It was a warming surprise, for I had not expected the composer to meet me at the train personally. After an effusion of greetings and a warm embrace, we settled back into the spaciousness of the Rolls and began driving through the city. As the car drove out of the station, the storm miraculously ceased, and we soon found ourselves traveling in clear sunlight on an empty road, flanked by the gentle slopes that soon became the hills of Lammermoor.

Gian Carlo Menotti looked fit and handsome. At sixty-three he looked to be in his mid-forties. The pressures and marks of age seemed to have eluded him. His face, with its prominent nose, light brown eyes, and high brow, was relatively unlined. Menotti had gained a bit of weight, but this did not alter his general appearance of trimness and buoyancy. The hair, graying at the temples, was full and wavy. He was dressed in brown slacks, tweed jacket, and tie. Menotti is a formal person, not given to overly casual attire.

An undercurrent of excitement attended the light banter we were exchanging. He was obviously looking forward to my reaction to Yester House but would tell me nothing about it, despite my inquiries. "You'll see," he kept repeating. The ride, I learned, would last approximately an hour, and the hour was nearly over. The car was beginning to slow down. Its pace was now so slow that I thought at any moment Yester would come magnificently into view. Instead, the car stopped altogether, and through the pane of glass that separated us, the chauffeur informed Menotti that, to his regret, the Rolls had broken down. We found ourselves on a road conspicuous for its lack of traffic. Menotti, crestfallen, asked the driver to seek help. The driver walked off into the emptiness, while the composer and I sat bewildered.

After some fifteen minutes a car approached. We waved it down, explaining the situation. A middle-aged couple, on their vacation, and clearly impressed by the Rolls, offered to drive us on to Yester. Just then, the chauffeur reappeared. Bidding us farewell, he said he would attend to the broken-down car. Menotti and I, now driven by two perfect strangers, approached the Yester estate. A tall, prominent gate, flanked by two small gate-houses and topped by an elaborate golden crest, gave entry into the private grounds. An arbor of old and stately trees lined the road. A new atmosphere enveloped us. A sudden silence seemed to descend upon this sequestered stretch of land. The sense of privacy became intense.

This was Menotti's new domain. The car, its windows rolled down, moved slowly. The faint murmuring of water broke the green stillness as we crossed a bridge beneath which a small stream wandered. In a moment Yester House came into view. Shafts of sunlight streamed against its pink stone. This Italianate color came as something of a surprise, for I had envisioned a noble gray, commensurate with what I had heard and seen of Scottish manors. But the house was devoid of any such allusions. No turrets, no gothic arches, no elaborate decorative details disturbed its façade. What met the eye was simple and perfect symmetry—Palladian in aspect and design. Yester, completed by James Adam in 1789, followed the architectural dictum of Leon Battista Alberti: nothing could be added or taken away without impairing the whole.

"Welcome to Yester House," said Menotti with a broad grin, as our wide-eyed escorts and I exclaimed over the extraordinary vision. The car stopped in front of a *porte cochère*. Awaiting us at the entrance stood two dark-skinned young men in uniform (two imports from Ceylon, I later learned). The boys bowed, took my bags, and disappeared. Menotti led the way into the entrance hall, a mammoth columned vestibule with marble floors and coffered ceilings, from which hung an elaborate crystal chandelier. Against the walls hung large paintings—portraits of Yester's ancestral owners, the Fourth Marquess of Tweeddale and Lady Tweeddale, surrounded by their children and relatives. A magnificent clock graced the opposite wall, and beneath it stood a long, lavishly inlaid marble table.

The perfect host, Menotti asked our rescuers into the library and offered them something to drink. Menotti had not quite expected my visit to Yester to proceed in this fashion, but with characteristic graciousness, he sat and chatted with his guests, who were full of questions about the house and obviously curious about the gentleman with the slight Italian accent. They did not know that Gian Carlo Menotti was one of the day's most celebrated composers, or that I had come to Yester to gather material for a biography.

We were sitting in what was formerly called the Yellow Ante Room, now a magnificent drawing-room, with a large William Kent fireplace, over which hung a life-size portrait of a courtier by Van Dyck.

Although extremely imposing, the room was surprisingly welcoming. Huge windows allowed for brilliant light and looked out on a vast stretch of lawn. Menotti soon offered a brief tour of the downstairs quarters. He led us into a huge dining room at least three times the size of the anteroom. Its interior, designed by William Adam, was of neoclassic proportion, with elaborate stucco decorations portraying the Four Seasons. A miraculously delicate eighteenth-century chandelier hung from the intricate ceiling. In every way, the dining room suggested aristocratic splendor, without seeming oppressive.

We moved on to what was an even larger room—this one devoid of any furnishings at all. Menotti explained that this would ultimately be Yester's living room, which the previous owners had emptied. Huge French windows looked onto a distant, rolling landscape. And again, even in this very formal empty room, one felt the warmth of shared living. Adjacent to the dining room was a large library, its walls a series of overcrowded bookshelves that ran from ceiling to floor (Menotti is a voracious reader). Here too, as in the other rooms, the furnishing had—in spite of the occasionally over-sumptuous draperies—inherited a casual elegance, both formal and inviting, from the previous owners.

Menotti's serendipitous guests announced they had to depart, and we escorted them to their car. Upon parting, they said, "This has been the part of our vacation that thrilled us most!"

Menotti, obviously pleased, now took me to my quarters, which were reached by ascending a truly regal staircase situated at the end of the columned hallway, executed with dazzling details by Joseph Enzer in 1736. Overhead, the sun streamed onto the staircase through an ornate skylight set in a superbly decorated vaulted ceiling. At the upper landing, one faced another enormous portrait—this one of the Eighth Marquess of Tweeddale, painted by Raeburn.

On this second floor, which I had assumed to be devoted solely to bedrooms, I was ushered into Yester's largest room of all—the ballroom. It took one's breath away. Not one, but two crystal chandeliers of an extraordinary balance and delicacy hung from the vaulted ceiling, quite overpowering with its neoclassical design of huge medallions. Three tall windows, facing north, looked out on an endless vista of trees. A mammoth table, covered with a floor-length velvet cloth, stood on a magnificent carpet. Here the walls held six panels depicting scenes of romantic ruins. There was another huge fireplace, remarkable for the delicacy of its design. A door, framed by two columns and a lintel, led from the south end of the ballroom into Menotti's studio. Of all the rooms, this was perhaps the simplest: a grand piano, a desk, a few easy chairs. Two fireplaces, one at each end of the room, provided most of the heat. Three enormous windows faced miles of uninterrupted landscape. From his studio Menotti could enter his bedroom, dressing room, and bath.

There are eight main bedrooms at Yester House. One of these—the Red Bedroom—would be mine for a period of nearly four weeks. Spacious and comfortable, it contained a four-poster, a desk, fireplace, and assorted antique furnishings, as well as several roomy closets. My adjoining bath was draped and papered in a red-and-green tartan design. The bedrooms, each named for the color in which it was decorated, were all studies in comfort and luxury.

Menotti told me about the regimen observed at Yester. One did not meet for breakfast. The morning meal would be served in bed. He pointed to a house telephone resting on one of the night tables. It bore ten blue buttons. Upon waking, I was to press the one marked Kitchen. The cook would take my breakfast order, and one of the young Ceylonese servants would bring it up on a tray, which would also bear the daily papers, the mail, and a bouquet of flowers. I had been told that my time would be my own until around eleven, at which time I was to join Menotti in his studio for a second cup of coffee. There we would discuss the plans for the day. The daily chat with the composer would last less than an hour. I would again be on my own until approximately half-past one, when we would meet in the downstairs library. We would have a prelunch drink, and at the appointed hour one of the houseboys would announce lunch.

Our luncheons, served by one of the elegantly uniformed Ceylonese boys, were not eaten in the main dining room, but in a smaller one. The food, prepared with consummate care, would always be ample and delicious. But during my visit Menotti had decided to diet—at least for luncheon. He would eat yogurt and honey and a fresh salad. Lunch over, the afternoon would be devoted to work. From approximately three until seven, Menotti and I would meet in his study for long hours of conversation and taping. At the conclusion of this work period, we would again retire to our rooms and would not reappear until eight-thirty, meeting once more in the library for our predinner drinks.

When Menotti entertained other guests (an infrequent occurrence during my visit), we would all meet in the library and spend a pleasurable hour exchanging stories, most of these instigated by

Menotti, who is a splendid listener, as well as a superb raconteur, with a most endearing, if often wicked, intuition about his friends' foibles. Dinners were usually sumptuous, and lovingly prepared by Yester's chief factotum, Mr. Pearson. A typical meal would consist of Scotch salmon, beef broth, lamb, beef or fish, an ample salad picked from Yester's five-acre garden, and to conclude, an outrageous dessert. Coffee and liqueurs would then be enjoyed in the library.

The summer days in Scotland are very long. The sun usually sets at nine or nine-thirty. It must be admitted that Scottish weather does not include a generosity of warmth or of sunshine. During August (the period of my stay), one was obliged to wear heavy sweaters against the chill. On a battled sky, sun and rain would succeed each other several times within one day. At night the winds would often howl. Grayness would be the order of most days. When the sun did appear, it was invariably looked upon as a gift to be treasured, if only for a few hours. Menotti was often asked by his visitors why, of all places, he had chosen to live in a country where the weather was so erratic and turbulent. He was, after all, an Italian, and Italians thrive on warmth and sunshine. His answer was that he did not particularly like warmth and sunshine, but was far more drawn to a moodier, more tempestuous climate. He liked his weather cold, brisk, changeable.

If it did not rain, Menotti would take a long walk after dinner. On my very first evening at Yester, he invited me to accompany him for a turn around the grounds. In a vestibule near the entrance hall hung a variety of coats and capes, as well as walking sticks and umbrellas. My host donned one of the voluminous capes and invited me to wear one as well. He drew two walking sticks from the stand, and, handing me one of these, asked me to follow him. Like two figures in a nineteenth-century novel, we proceeded into the gloomy outdoors, walking on soft, moist grass and on paths leading away from the house.

The huge trees around us formed ominous shadows. Neither moon nor stars were visible. The sky formed a low, opaque ceiling, as we moved toward the sound of water flowing under Yester's small bridge. After a while Menotti asked me to stop and turn around. There, in a flood of light, stood Yester House. Menotti had arranged to have all the lights turned on inside the house, while spotlights, coming from several directions, illuminated the exterior. It was a most dramatic and theatrical vision. Yester House suddenly looked like a noble set out of some romantic opera. It was a regal, dazzling stage setting, with chandeliers ablaze—a scene full of dramatic possibilities and expectations. This was Menotti's latest production, something of a dream come true, a fantasy fulfilled.

This is where Menotti claimed he would end his days. This is where he would compose his last works, where he would rework his earlier compositions. This is where he might write new librettos, where he would continue to study, and where he would reflect upon his life. It would also be at Yester that he would destroy all of his notebooks, and all of the first drafts relating to his works. As he told me, "I don't want people looking into my dirty laundry." And it would be at Yester that he would, at last, completely relish solitude.

Years before the purchase of Yester House, Menotti made these jottings: "Only very rarely does solitude yield new thoughts or new emotions. Its real value is in revealing and clarifying for ourselves the confused and unconscious impressions we have received from our contact with people. Even when we think that our solitude has nurtured in us new creative impulses, we end by realizing that they are but the reactions to previous emotions. Therefore, the artist must seek solitude only after having deserved it."

Menotti had now reached a point in his life where he had indeed deserved his solitude. As he told me during one of our many conversations, his move to Scotland was prompted by this desire for merited seclusion: "I've chosen to live here, so that I could be completely cut off from my past. It was a desire to find a place where I could hide. I feel it is now time to take stock of my past. It is time for reflection. Both in America and in Italy I know too many people, and I have too many ties. Solitude is almost impossible there. You could put it this way: Italy created me; America nourished me; and Scotland will bury me. Italy is my unicorn; America is my gorgon; Scotland is my manticore."

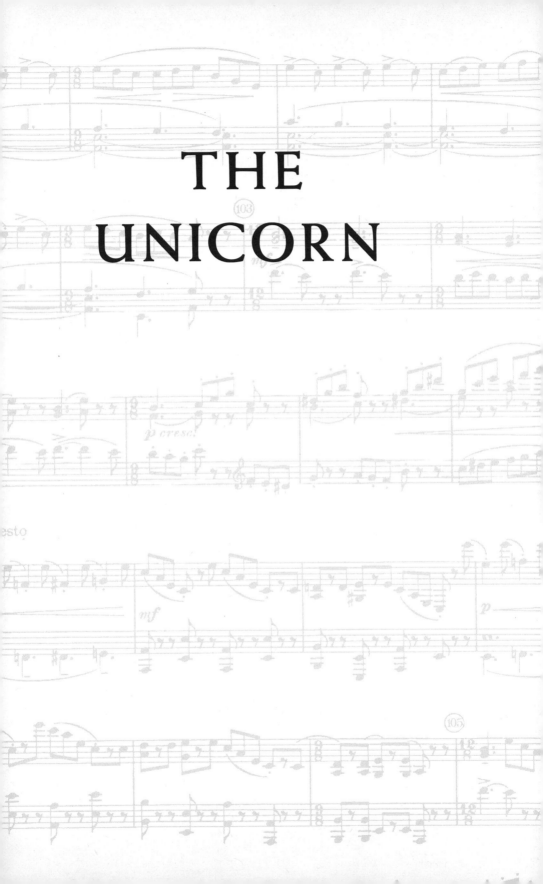

THE
UNICORN

Unicorn, Unicorn,
My swift and leaping
Unicorn,
Keep pace with me, stay close to me,
Don't run astray,
My gentle rover.
Beware of the virgin sleeping
Under the lemon tree,
Her hair adrift among the clover.
She hides a net under her petticoat
And silver chains around her hips;
And if you kiss her lips
The hidden hunter will pierce your throat.
Unicorn, beware, beware!
Her crimson lips are hard as coral
And her white thighs are only a snare.
For you who likes to roam
A kiss is poisoned food:
Much sweeter fare
Is the green laurel;
Much safer home
Is the dark wood.

(*The Unicorn, the Gorgon and the Manticore*)

CHAPTER
1

"It was a different world, the gentle world in which we grew . . ."

(*Maria Golovin*)

Lombardy, 1915.

Imagine a cool and verdant path in the mountains—a road perfumed by a thousand flowers from nearby gardens and the pungent smell of pines. Think of a soft breeze and of sunlight streaming through endless high branches. A small caravan of people slowly wends its way upward amid the greenery, just now moving toward a clearing. There are eight young children, each dressed in white, led by a group of men and women. The youngsters, boys and girls of assorted sizes, dart toward an appointed spot. Following at a more leisurely pace are servants carrying large baskets filled with food and drink. A huge, restless St. Bernard moves among them all, contentedly sniffing the cool ground. The group is settling down for an afternoon picnic. The servants spread blankets and cloths in the chosen shady spot. There is laughter and conversation. The children's white outfits will soon bear the marks of dust and sand. Their faces will become smudged and flushed by their games and exertions. The women will shake their heads over the difficulties of keeping the youngsters clean or in tow, but will proceed with their own amiable chatter and the ritual of their summertime outing.

These are the Menottis, a small tribe of aristocratic-looking people, residents of Cadegliano. And with them are their relatives, the Pellinis, the Bianchinis, the Righinis, aunts and uncles, nephews and nieces. But the children all dressed in white are the sons and daughters of Ines and Alfonso Menotti. From the eldest to the youngest, they offer the image of well-being, vivaciousness, and affectionate rapport. They are named Pier Antonio, Amalita, Giosi,

Domenico, Francesco, Gian Carlo, Tullio, and Maria Rosa. These children have lived in Cadegliano all their lives, going to school, attending the local church, and, upon occasion, making a trip to the largest nearby city, Milan. Many years ago their maternal grandfather was mayor of Cadegliano, and since that time the small village nestling in the mountains and overlooking Lake Lugano has become dotted with numerous villas, each containing a Menotti or a Pellini or a Bianchini or a Righini. It is a village of relatives who gather together during the summer months, open their villas, tend their gardens, and lead a life of charmed conviviality. The children visit their aunts and uncles, and the Alfonso Menotti villa, a large pink stucco house flanked by huge pines and a garden filled with camellias and roses, is often the scene of happy summer disorder.

There would be much music-making at the Menotti villa. The piano would be in constant use. Ines Menotti, an imperious and flamboyant woman, had seen to it that her children were taught piano, violin, and cello. She herself loved the piano and would play it for hours with passion and élan. Amalita and Giosi joined her in duets or accompanied their brothers, Pier Antonio and Domenico, each adept at the violin and cello. There would be chamber music evenings, and although the youngest children would have to be in bed by 9:00 during these occasions, a special little mattress was placed in the music room so that Ines' favorite son, four-year-old Gian Carlo, could be part of the music-making and fall asleep with the sound of music in his ears.

Thus it was that Gian Carlo Menotti grew up in a milieu where music was central to his life. But there were other meaningful diversions. Pier Antonio, the oldest brother, introduced Gian Carlo as he grew older to the world of books. Pier Antonio would read passages out of Dostoyevsky, Tolstoy, or the great French classics. He was the potential intellectual of the family. But more than that, Pier Antonio loved the theater. Frequently he would set up his puppets and give performances that included elaborate scenery with special lighting effects. All the children would gather round and watch the puppets and marionettes enact strange and often violent tales. In time, Pier Antonio attended the University of Pavia, near Milan. On holidays he would return with extraordinary accounts of having been at the city's great opera house, La Scala, and he would give fantastic descriptions of operas he had seen. These vivid and dramatic stories inflamed Gian Carlo's imagination. Pier Antonio's tales were so marvelously descriptive that when young Gian Carlo actually saw his first opera—*Rigoletto*—he could not help but find it disappointing.

Of all his brothers and sisters, Gian Carlo's favorite was Amalita, some years older than himself. She was a complex and extremely shy girl, suspicious of people, and very loyal and possessive. The two would talk for hours and share confidences. Gian Carlo also enjoyed being with his sister Giosi but never felt very close to her. There was, however, a rapport with Domenico, whom the family called Minuccio. He was the cellist in the family and adored music. Gian Carlo was not particularly close to his brother Francesco, called Cecchino, who was very secretive and kept to himself. On the other hand, Gian Carlo's younger brother, Tullio, shared his room and was his inseparable friend, and it was with him that Gian Carlo invented ritualistic mysterious games that only the two of them could understand. The two loved each other profoundly. The youngest of the children was Maria Rosa, who seems to have been very neurotic and spoiled by her mother. Gian Carlo had already left for the United States when, at the age of thirteen, she developed tuberculosis, incurable in those days, and died of the disease.

A tight-knit family, the Menottis were dominated by their mother, whose quixotic nature caused even her husband to be in awe of her. "My mother was an impulsive woman," recalled Menotti, "and a very handsome one. She had a domineering personality, and many people in the town found her high-handed and a bit of a snob. I think my father was terrified of her. All of us children, however, adored her. My father struck me only once, and I remember it vividly, because the punishment was so cold and deliberate. My mother, on the other hand, spanked me practically every day, and I don't remember it at all, because it was always so spontaneous and emotional.

"Mother was a very imaginative woman. She always found things for us to do and was never at a loss for projects. I remember how she would throw my father into fits because, on an impulse, she would decide to replant the whole garden. She would cut down all the camellias and put mimosa in their place. A recurring subject of their constant bickerings had to do with mother's wanting to move to Milan during the winter. She thought it was unfair to keep us in the country all the time. She was especially anxious for me to come into contact with the artistic activities of a big city. Most of all, she was eager for me to attend the music conservatory because I had already started to compose by the age of five."

The influence of Gian Carlo Menotti's mother would color his entire life and career. Young Gian Carlo could never quite understand his father, however. He was a shadowy figure who seemed more devoted to hunting than to his family. He lived the life of a country gentleman, supported by an income from an import-export firm based in South America.

As the story goes, it was Francesco Menotti, Alfonso's older brother, who had the idea of starting a business in Colombia. Francesco, who had been destined for the priesthood, seemed to have an impulsive streak. On the very day of his ordination, and upon the occasion of delivering his first sermon, he suddenly became so terrified of his calling that he fled from the pulpit and made straight for South America.

Settling in Colombia, Francesco Menotti established wide business contracts and in a relatively short time founded an export firm that dealt mainly in coffee. The success of his company was such that he decided to enlist the help of his brother Alfonso. The younger Menotti had just married Ines Pellini in Cadegliano, and the two considered a trip to Colombia an exciting adventure. The brothers managed the business, to continuing success. In time, Ines Menotti gave birth to her first child, but it died in infancy. A year later a second child was born, and it too was not destined to live. The young wife soon began to long for her homeland. She persuaded her husband to return to Cadegliano with her. A decision was made to hand over Alfonso Menotti's affairs to an assistant, who would continue to work with Francesco. Business thrived, and when Alfonso and Ines Menotti returned to Cadegliano, they could retire on a handsome income arriving regularly from South America. Alfonso Menotti was never to set foot in South America again.

As for Uncle Francesco, not only had he turned his back on the priesthood, but, upon settling in Colombia, he had fallen passionately in love with an exotic mulatto woman, whom he took as his mistress. When he met her, this handsome dark-skinned woman was already the mother of two grown daughters. One day, after Francesco and his mistress quarreled, he, in an impulsively conciliatory moment, declared that he would give her whatever she wanted. To his shock, she demanded that he marry one of her daughters. Hopelessly in love with his mistress and afraid of losing her, Francesco agreed to the extraordinary request. The marriage took place, although, according to Francesco, it was never consummated. Gian Carlo met this odd trio when, some years later, they too came to live in Cadegliano. As it turned out, the Menotti children adored their uncle's mistress, whom they affectionately called Mameta. As for Francesco's young wife, she seemed content with the arrangement.

The psychic panorama of the Menotti family was to strongly affect and color the life of Gian Carlo. As time went on, Francesco Menotti's mistress died in Cadegliano, while he grew to be an old man in his native city, progressively changing from an eccentric into a neurotic, incapable, for example, of falling asleep unless someone sat up all night beside him. Gian Carlo recalled how young people had to be hired for this odd duty.

The young Gian Carlo Menotti was equally intrigued by tales of his maternal grandmother. Much to the displeasure of her husband, she had borne six daughters, of which Menotti's mother was the last. When all these daughters had married, the old woman became something of a Tolstoyan character. It was her desire to return to the earth, and much to the consternation of her children, who had all made chic marriages, she was often found working the fields.

Of the six Pellini sisters, Gian Carlo's mother was the object of her father's greatest scorn. As she was the last of a long succession of girls, he would barely look at her. It was a slight that Ines Pellini would carry throughout her life.

The Pellini sisters led an active life in Cadegliano. Most of them married and bore children, populating the small village. Among the most beautiful of Gian Carlo's many aunts was Emma, a woman of great charm and personal warmth. Gian Carlo likened her to the character of Anna Karenina, for while married to a stiff and proper gentleman, she fell madly in love with a dashing young man, who happened to be one of her brothers-in-law. It was a hopeless affair. Later, when both her husband and beloved brother-in-law died, she grew into a huge and endearing old woman whom everyone adored. All the Menotti children would run to her whenever they had problems. Aunt Emma would always be there to lend a sympathetic ear.

In recalling his youth, Gian Carlo Menotti touched on the fact that a bit of madness ran in his family. One of his Pellini aunts—zia Ida—was feebleminded and developed an obsession about germs. Another relative, Liline Bianchini, who early on had taught Gian Carlo to play the organ, developed a religious mania and suffered from hallucinations. She was placed in an institution for a period of time. Upon her release, she committed suicide. A nephew, Amalita's son, was a schizophrenic. This strain of madness in the Menotti family would place Gian Carlo in touch with the strange and disquieting factors upon which he would draw during his creative life.

Menotti's Cadegliano childhood was filled with future source material. The long, long winters spent in his tiny village—the heavy snowfalls, the farmers' huts that dotted the landscape, the cold starry skies—would ultimately find themselves as the setting for *Amahl and the Night Visitors*. And there were other strong and lasting influences. Menotti describes himself as having been something of a "goody-goody"—a mamma's boy. He was a very obedient child, finding comfort in his mother's protective attention. Ines Menotti pampered her young son; he was a sensitive boy, delicately built, with serious eyes and slightly stooping shoulders, and his family was fond of calling him *"il camellino,"* the little camel. Under his mother's adoring gaze, Gian Carlo would delight in pleasing her, but he could also be mischievous and full of fun. He loved organizing games. Like his brother Pier Antonio, who introduced him to the staging of puppet shows, Gian Carlo adopted this pastime for his own. Every Christmas or birthday he was given new puppets, finally amassing nearly a hundred of them. All the younger children would help in making their costumes. They would write special plays with music, then call the family together, as well as all the children of the village, for the performances. They had discovered how to produce marvelous lighting effects, with sulphur for the apparition of, say, the Devil. Gian Carlo's little brother Tullio, forbidden to operate the speaking puppets because of his stuttering, and mainly condemned to handling the stage effects, would emerge from under the stage at the end of the show, all blackened and with eyebrows and hair singed by the flashing sulphur.

Life in Cadegliano also included faithful visits to the local church. Its curate, Don Rimoldi, proved another meaningful figure in Menotti's life. Menotti recalled that Don Rimoldi, known throughout the region, was something of a mad priest, who ruled his parish with a strong and domineering hand. A man of outrageous imagination and filled with strange obsessions, he took a special interest in young Gian Carlo.

"He was one of the great forces of the town," Menotti recalled. "He was a sort of genius, passionately fond of astronomy, and obsessed about machinery and progress. His house was full of buttons and switches. He was one of the first people to have what would correspond to a Murphy bed: you pushed a button and the bed would plop out from the wall. If children were very good at Sunday School, they would be allowed to enter his room and press the button. He was also obsessed about sex. All over the house were signs reading 'Woman is the Devil,' or 'Woman is unclean.' An old peasant woman was his servant, but he could not bear to be in her presence. In order not to have to see her, he had installed an intercom system, something unheard of at the time. Don Rimoldi would talk to this woman on the intercom and would tell her when to serve his meals. She would then bring food to the table and disappear. Only then would the priest come in to eat."

Don Rimoldi resented the powerful, well-off people of his parish. When one of the Bianchinis presented the church with a new organ, he did not relish the idea of having it played by the more genteel members of the community. He wanted the ignorant peasants to be able to play it, and to that end he devised a method of teaching them how to read music. Menotti remembered it as a most ingenious system. Don Rimoldi divided each octave of the keyboard into different colors and had special signs for certain chords. For the melodic lines he employed pictures: a bird flying would mean a short note, while a bird on a pole was a long note. "Mad as it seems, he was able to teach a couple of peasant girls how to accompany the whole Mass, and all with the right harmonies!"

Don Rimoldi's contempt for Cadegliano's upper crust did not prevent him from becoming interested in Gian Carlo, whose musical abilities were becoming more and more apparent. Upon many occasions, the priest would permit the boy to play the organ during Mass. Gian Carlo was often given to improvising and thus deviating from the required musical solemnities. When this happened, Don Rimoldi would stop the Mass, turn to him and shout, "*Musica sacra, Gian Carlo! Musica sacra!*" Gian Carlo would obediently turn to a more sober rendition.

As a young boy, Gian Carlo Menotti was deeply religious, having been raised in the Catholic Church and guided by the religious zeal of Don Rimoldi. But even here his sense of seriousness was tempered by the unusual methods practiced by this odd and imaginative parish priest. For example, Don Rimoldi strongly disliked hearing confession. In order to avoid listening to the endless litanies of sins brought to him by his parish, he drew up a list of the most popularly perpetrated transgressions. He would hand these out and ask his parishioners to check which of the sins they had committed during the week. "Of course," said Menotti, "everybody hated that, because they loved to go and confess everything at great length."

Another vivid memory was Don Rimoldi's allowing the children of Cadegliano to come and play games in the church. Approaching the heretical, the priest boldly set up a gramophone near the altar and would encourage the children to dance and sing. Gian Carlo was also riveted by Don Rimoldi's sermons, which would center on the mysteries of astronomical phenomena and would have little bearing on more conventional religious matters. Don Rimoldi would also think nothing of insulting various members of the Menotti clan during his sermons, making fun of a hat that Gian Carlo's mother might be wearing, or generally bringing discomfort to any of the assembled people. If Menotti would later look upon religious matters with a certain jaundiced eye, if he would become progressively aware of certain foibles and inconsistencies in the Catholic scheme of things, it could probably be traced back to his exposure to the mildly heretical personality and curious practices of Don Rimoldi.

Throughout his life Menotti would always be fascinated with the Church and its protagonists—the saints, the martyrs, and the religious philosophers—who instilled in him an ambiguous yearning for spiritual knowledge and revelation. Miracles, the mysteries of the stigmata, the shadowy world of rite and ritual, the ethos and ethics of religious consciousness, and the grappling with the unknown would years later make themselves evident in such works as *The Island God, The Saint of Bleecker Street, The Death of the Bishop of Brindisi,* and *Martin's Lie.* A preoccupation with the occult or the miraculous workings of dreams would strongly color *The Medium* and *The Consul.* A strain of the fantastic and the magical would subtly tinge all of Menotti's works.

CHAPTER

2

"Don't cry, Mother dear, don't worry for me.
If I must go begging, a good beggar I'll be."

(Amahl and the Night Visitors)

Gian Carlo Menotti's earliest musical training was fostered by his mother. She noted how her boy would sit for hours at the piano, improvising and composing little songs. He would find some poetry —perhaps some verses by Giovanni Pascoli or Gabriele D'Annunzio —and set them to music. He would sing these songs, in a sweet soprano voice, to the delight of his family. All the Menottis began to take it for granted that Gian Carlo would become a musician.

Ambitious for her son, Ines Menotti engaged a piano teacher to give the boy lessons. Menotti recalled his very first piano teacher: "She was a dwarf. Not only was she a dwarf, but she was also an epileptic. However, she was the only one who was willing to take the train from Milan and make the long trip to Cadegliano. Actually she gave lessons to me, my mother, and my sisters. I remember she was a woman of very modest means, who used to arrive wearing the same old coat and the same hat. It was a hat covered with cherries and birds. One day my little brother Tullio decided to take the whole hat apart. He wanted to see what was inside the birds and the cherries. Poor Signorina Lisa! My mother had to buy her a new hat. Anyway, she came for a long time, and although she was a very sweet woman, she turned out to be a rather poor piano teacher. My mother finally thought that we should have someone who was less limited."

In time, a certain Signora Bertini came to teach—a far better musician than the much-loved Signorina Lisa. It was this new teacher who introduced Menotti to the marvels of Scarlatti. He recalled that if a lesson had gone particularly well, Signora Bertini would reward him by playing a Scarlatti sonata. A new one would be played after each successful lesson. As it turned out, this teacher of Menotti's childhood lived long enough to come to one of the Spoleto Festivals. "She came to Spoleto the year before she died," said Menotti. "She had become very poor and lived in the country. Shortly after she died I received a package containing a single cowbell that had belonged to the only cow on her farm. A note accompanied the gift: 'I have nothing to give to you except this cowbell.' And it was signed by my old piano teacher."

One additional teacher made his appearance in Cadegliano. This was another discovery of Ines Menotti, brought into the household for the sole purpose of writing down Gian Carlo's compositions. In keeping with the bizarre assortment of teachers surrounding the boy composer, this gentleman turned out to be blind. Menotti's little songs—his very first compositions, all done between the ages of five and thirteen—were thus set down in Braille.

For years, Ines Menotti decried the fact that her family was tied to the confines of Cadegliano. Her repeated complaints finally induced her husband to move the family to Milan, at least for the winter months. Ines' highest trump card in this argument was Gian Carlo's growing talent. By the age of eleven, he had already written his first opera, *The Death of Pierrot*. She felt his gifts were being stifled under such circumscribed conditions. She wanted Gian Carlo to attend the Milan Conservatory of Music.

Thus the Menottis moved to Milan and took up residence at Via Canova, 14. Gian Carlo was duly enrolled in the conservatory. He took private lessons with Ettore Pozzoli, a teacher well known at the time for his books on *solfege*. As it turned out, Menotti was an unresponsive pupil. The technical part of music bored him. He hated *solfege* and the study of harmony and counterpoint, but he continued to compose. The young Menotti soon wrote his second childhood opera, *The Little Mermaid*, based on Andersen's fairy tale.

Ines Menotti, inflamed by her son's productivity, now sought the advice of the celebrated composer Umberto Giordano, who had scored a triumph with his opera *Andrea Chenier*. Giordano was encouraging. He invited Gian Carlo to his villa on Lago Maggiore and listened to *The Little Mermaid*. He advised the boy to continue going to the conservatory and also introduced him to his niece, who taught piano in a new fashion. At the time, piano-playing technique emphasized raising the fingers high before striking a note. Giordano's niece belonged to the new school which involved movement of one's wrists. Menotti took Giordano's advice and returned to the conservatory, while also taking private lessons in this new technique.

If Menotti did not make any real technical headway at the conservatory, his compositions continued to show a marked lyric and melodic gift. Simple, forthright, unencumbered by harmonic complexities, the line of Menotti's music was as flowing as it seemed inevitable.

He was an *enfant prodige,* rivaled only by his fellow student Nino Rota, who would become an important film composer, notably for Federico Fellini. At the conservatory Rota was the avant-gardist of the school. "Nino wrote a very sophisticated oratorio when he was around twelve or thirteen," said Menotti. "He played his compositions for Igor Stravinsky and was very much taken up by everyone. He was much, much more clever than I, musically, except that I had my revenge: I could sing and he could not. Also, it was thought that I possessed a more marked melodic gift. So we were great rivals. Now we have become good friends." Signora Menotti and Signora Rota were quite jealous of each other's sons, and Signora Rota one day remarked, "I know that my Nino is going to be the next Beethoven, and your Gian Carlo is going to be the next Mascagni." Their friendship came to an abrupt end.

For three years Gian Carlo Menotti lived and studied in Milan, with periodic visits to Cadegliano during the summer and at Christmas time. He threw himself into the artistic bustle of the city, going to see countless operas at La Scala, and still today vividly remembers some of Toscanini's performances of the time—particularly his celebrated interpretation of *Falstaff*. The theater fascinated him no less. "I adored going to the theater, and especially remember an experimental group which had started in Milan. It was called 'Gli Arcimboldi.' They gave one-act plays in continuous sequence, from four in the afternoon until nine at night. Every hour a new play would be put on, and these would be changed every week. I remember sneaking out of school early to see these marvelous short pieces and having to find an excuse almost every day for getting home late. Mostly I was hungry for a different life from the one I had been leading in Cadegliano.

"It was exciting to be in a big city; it was wonderful to be exposed to painting and music and theater and films and to see a lot of people rushing around the streets. Of course, by then I had developed a voracious appetite for reading. I was particularly mad for

fairy tales. I loved them and collected them from all over the world
—Indian, Persian, Russian. I loved that fantastic world. It was very
important to me. I could lose myself in those stories and be miles
and miles, and ages and ages away. I also loved to dress up. I loved
masquerades. I'd never lose an opportunity of going to a masquerade
party. I was a country boy of fifteen, avid for the exotic, the theatrical, the occult and the decadent. Even though the family often went
back to Cadegliano during the holidays, they would just as often go
to the seashore. They would go to Venice and stay in the Grand
Hotel des Bains—the hotel Visconti used as the setting for his film
Death in Venice." Those were enchanted days for Gian Carlo.

"One summer—I don't know why—my mother couldn't take us
to the seashore herself, but she sent me and two of my brothers to
Varazze, a small sea town near Genoa. In fact, she rented a little
apartment for us in an old villa. The proprietors turned out to be
spiritualists. They were an old couple who would hold seances. It
was my first contact with spiritualism, and I was fascinated."

Menotti's studies at the conservatory, while fairly intense, did not
hold the sort of promise Ines Menotti had envisioned. Once again
she sought the advice of a major musical figure of the time. On her
own she had made the acquaintance of Arturo Toscanini and his
wife. She went to see them in the hope that they might give her
some concrete suggestions for focusing her son's musical direction
more fully. Toscanini, already world famous, had been to America
and heard that a music school had recently opened in Philadelphia
—the Curtis Institute of Music. An Italian, Rosario Scalero, had
been hired as teacher of composition. Toscanini felt that the boy
would benefit greatly by being sent to America to study under
this brilliant teacher. Ines was stunned by this piece of advice. It
had never entered her mind to send her young son to a foreign
country, let alone to leave him there on his own.

While Menotti was in his teens, his father fell ill. As Menotti put
it, his father had become something of an alcoholic and developed
cancer of the liver, and the disease ultimately killed him. Menotti
was not present when his father died, nor was he greatly bereaved
by the loss. The two had never been close. Alfonso's passion for
hunting had not been shared by his young, sensitive son, who could
not bear the thought of killing animals.

"I cannot say that I really knew my father," said Menotti. "We
had very little in common. He was completely uninterested in the
arts. He did not care much about music. He was a man of few

words. The fact is, I was a bit afraid of him. Also, he showed little interest in me. If he was attached to any of his children, it was to his firstborn—my step-brother, Bartolomeo. You see, my father was married once before, but his first wife was never discussed in our house. Anyway, Bartolomeo and my father would go hunting together and generally had a very close rapport. My father was also quite attached to my brother Cecchino. As I said, I was more my mother's son."

With her husband's death, Ines became aware that his share of the business had been irrevocably absorbed by his former associate, who was loath to continue sending money to Alfonso Menotti's large family. Ines had prudently insisted that Alfonso acquire some property in Milan, as well as a house, so the Menottis were by no means poor, although their situation had altered considerably. The South American income had suddenly stopped. Ines Menotti, terrified by this turn of events, took it upon herself to travel to South America in the hope of saving the situation. The trip, with several of the children but not Gian Carlo, proved a lost cause. As she returned to Italy, the future seemed grim for her. In the meantime, some of her older children had married and were leading their own lives. She could not resign herself to the complete failure of her business trip to Colombia, and planned to return for another attempt to straighten out her late husband's complicated business affairs. She did not, however, relish the thought of being parted from Gian Carlo, nor of leading a life of solitude. She was still an attractive, energetic woman. Finally she decided to make another trip, this time accompanied by Gian Carlo, to see if she could make better arrangements for the support of her family.

As chance would have it, Ines Menotti's personal life changed dramatically at that time. During the last year of her husband's illness she had made the acquaintance of a certain doctor from the region of Abruzzi, Alberto Trozzi, who was considered a brilliant physician. Although fifteen years her junior, he had fallen in love with her. She was flattered by his attention but deemed it inappropriate to see him while her husband lay ill or during her period of mourning. Still, Trozzi was an eager suitor. When Ines Menotti embarked on her voyage to South America, she was stunned to find Trozzi on the same ship. He had come to persuade her to marry him.

Menotti recalled the event:

"This affair with Trozzi became the biggest scandal in my family.

As long as they were not married, everything was all right. But when mother married him, the entire family became outraged. Perhaps it was the fear that she might have another child, and that all the money and all the properties my father had left her would go to this eventual child and not to us. I was particularly shocked when my favorite sister, Amalita, who had since married, joined in the outcry against our mother. But my two older brothers were also dead set against the marriage.

"Anyway, a lawyer was appointed to administer our family's finances. Those of us who were minors could continue to live with our mother, but she was not permitted to touch our money. Of course, mother suffered terribly over this state of affairs and was deeply hurt that her children should have taken such drastic measures against her. At any rate, mother and her new husband ultimately settled in South America. My three eldest brothers and my sister Amalita continued to be convinced that Alberto Trozzi had married my mother for her money. I, on the other hand, sided completely with my mother. I was, and still am, very fond of my stepfather, a very sweet and very cultured man."

Although Menotti's mother had found a new life for herself, she by no means abandoned her ambitions for Gian Carlo. She brooded over Toscanini's advice to send the boy to the United States to study at the Curtis. The thought of being separated from her adored son troubled her, but so auspicious a recommendation by so revered a man as Toscanini could not be taken lightly. With good judgment overriding personal anguish, she decided to undertake the long voyage to the United States, fully convinced that the land of opportunity would justify her unswerving belief in Gian Carlo's talent. Leaving her new husband in South America, she undertook the long journey into the future. For his part, Menotti had his own fears and trepidations.

Toscanini had written ahead to Philadelphia. The letter to Scalero said that a seventeen-year-old boy would be arriving, and anything Scalero could do to help would be appreciated. Scalero answered that entrance into the Curtis was entirely dependent on a student's merit and talent—that only after having looked at the boy's compositions would he be able to judge his qualifications. So Menotti went to Philadelphia not knowing whether he would be allowed to stay. This sense of insecurity, Menotti's inability to speak English, and his having to live on his own without the guidance or protection of his mother, caused the boy great anxiety. But in the fall of

1928 he and his mother arrived in New York, then boarded a train to Philadelphia, and the two made their way to Rittenhouse Square, where the Curtis is located. Rosario Scalero looked at the boy's manuscripts and listened to him play some of his piano pieces. What he heard convinced him that Gian Carlo Menotti, while clearly in need of serious study, showed unique talent in composition. He informed the trembling boy that he would be allowed to stay, and that if he worked hard, there would be no reason why he should not develop into a fine musician.

Deeply relieved but saddened, Ines Menotti prepared to leave her son to make his life in America. She did not depart without first installing Gian Carlo with a family of Italian-Americans. She did not want her son to lose contact with his heritage. The Riccis seemed to fill the bill. There was a pleasant room in their house, and the atmosphere seemed congenial. Some days later, mother and son bid each other farewell.

"I'll never forget that awful rainy afternoon," recalled Menotti. "It was late afternoon and the rain seemed particularly sad. I'll never forget it. There was just nobody on the sidewalks. The streets were deserted. I walked my mother to the train station holding an umbrella. We hardly dared speak to each other. Finally we reached the station, and we had to say goodbye. Both of us burst into terrible sobs. Finally she entered through the gates where her train was waiting. I saw her depart. She could not look back. And so, off she went. I was on my own.

"I returned to my little room with the Ricci family, bringing with me lots of photographs of my family and Italian friends, which I wanted to hang on the wall. As I couldn't find enough nails in the house, the next morning I went into a hardware shop. As I entered it, I realized that I had forgotten the English word for nails. I did know that the French word was *clou* and the Spanish was *clavos*. In my anxiety, I simply mixed and anglicized the two words, and told the astonished shopkeeper that I wanted to buy some clouds. That was the first thing I tried to purchase in America."

CHAPTER

3

"Can one be happier than gathering stones and
twigs to make a fire by the Brandywine?"

(Landscapes and Remembrances)

The Curtis Institute of Music was founded in February, 1924. Its
founder and president was Mary Louise Curtis Bok, a wealthy
patron of the arts. Daughter of Cyrus H. K. Curtis, the publisher,
she had envisioned a school that would bring together the finest
musical talent available, in order to establish a conservatory dedicated to the highest standards of musical training.

The first director was John Grolle, who was succeeded in 1925 by
William E. Walter. In 1927 Mrs. Bok appointed Josef Hofmann to
the post of director. He had been the head of the piano department
from the beginning. Hofmann resigned as director of the Curtis in
1938, although he continued in his capacity as head of the piano department. Among those who have taught at the Curtis and who conducted the Institute Orchestra were Leopold Stokowski, Artur
Rodzinski, and Fritz Reiner. Also on the faculty were such well-
known musicians as Leopold Auer, Moriz Rosenthal, and Marcella
Sembrich, as well as Efrem Zimbalist, who, upon Edward Bok's
death, married the school's founder, Mary Louise Curtis. Rosario
Scalero was head of the composition department. Courses were
offered in all branches of applied music and theory. At the time
Gian Carlo Menotti entered Curtis, its director was Josef Hofmann.

Menotti, surrounded by an ambiance of high artistic and creative
activity, took courses with Scalero and studied piano with Vera
Resnikoff, who had been a pupil of Josef Hofmann. The Italian newcomer proved an industrious student; he was shy, due to his difficulties with the English language, but already evincing the charm
that would become a major asset throughout his life.

Menotti recalled working with Scalero: "The one thing Scalero taught me was how to learn things on my own. Although he was considered a rather pedantic teacher, and very severe, he actually worked on very revolutionary principles. For example, he always refused to examine any of the exercises we submitted to him (be it a simple contrapuntal exercise, a canon, a fugue), if he found that the thematic material was inexpressive or lacked rhythmic vitality. Many were the times when, after having glanced at the initial measures of a composition, he would throw it aside saying, 'With such a boring theme, what do you expect to achieve? Go home and start all over again. I can't be bothered with this.' Nor did he ever give us a rule. He would simply say, 'For your next lesson, bring me a two-voice fugue.' On my asking him, 'But how does one go about writing a fugue?' he would reply, 'Find out for yourself.' I would desperately scout around and bring what I thought was a fugue. Only then would he begin to teach you, pointing out your mistakes, dismissing you at the end of the lesson with a 'Now go back and write a *good* fugue.' I remember asking him, 'Why didn't you tell me to begin with how to write a good fugue?' And he would answer, 'Because I want to sharpen your wits and teach you how to find things out for yourself.' It was a marvelous principle, but it was a painful way to learn."

For his part, Scalero initially found Menotti to be something less than fully committed to his work. Some years prior to his death he recalled his young pupil: "The boy had some stuff in him, but he was most undisciplined and raw. Early on, I told him, 'Gian Carlo, if I am to teach you, we must come to an agreement, you and I. I promise you that I will be uncompromisingly severe. Do you promise me to put in some very hard work, something you have never done before?' Well, Gian Carlo promised, and he abided by his agreement."

Menotti's first and only piano teacher at Curtis was the highly spirited Vera Resnikoff, who many years later would become a central character in Menotti's children's opera *Help! Help! The Globolinks!* She also remembered her young pupil:

"Gian Carlo was as tall as he is now, and as sweet as he is now. He came to me because I was the only one who could speak some French, which Gian Carlo spoke reasonably well. He really couldn't play the piano at all. I had to teach him all about the keyboard. His lessons were always perfectly prepared. I looked at my old Curtis ledgers the other day and saw what I wrote down about him.

'Menotti is very intelligent and very temperamental.' In three months' time he improved incredibly. I had taught him only for two semesters, when he already handled well all his scales, chords, octaves—whatever had to be learned. Then he began playing. Easy things to begin with: Clementi, Bach Inventions, and the simpler sonatas of Mozart. Still, it was amazing because although he was not intending to be a pianist, he showed an enormous affinity for the instrument.

"I remember one little incident. One day Gian Carlo came to me and said, 'Miss Resnikoff, I'm going to ask you to do me a favor. I've composed a ballade for the piano and I have to play it for some society. Would you listen to it and tell me whether I should play it or not?'

"So he began to play, and when he was done, I began working with him on it, from the first bar to the last. Finally he said, 'I see that I haven't understood anything at all about composing for the piano.' You see, he had composed something much more difficult than he was able to perform. As a pianist I could show him what passages were important in the piece, what should be brought out or not. Already his gift as a composer seemed to supercede his abilities as a pianist."

Shortly after his arrival at Curtis, Menotti met Samuel Barber, a fellow student. It was their composition teacher, Rosario Scalero, who thought the boys should meet. Barber spoke French and agreed to help Menotti through the difficult first months in America. For over forty years they have remained friends.

"Sam was the very first friend I made in America," recalled Menotti. "I was seventeen at the time and Sam was eighteen. I had learned he was the absolute idol of the Curtis Institute of Music. He too studied composition with Scalero, but also piano with Isabelle Vengerova and voice with Emilio de Gogorza. He was considered a genius in all three courses. Not only was Sam enormously gifted, but he was very handsome and very intelligent. I, on the other hand, was rather ugly and scrawny, with a long nose, and awkward in many ways. I was still terribly naïve and clung defensively to my religious beliefs. The fact is, I felt lost in Philadelphia and needed a guide. When Scalero introduced me to Sam, I immediately thought him to be marvelous. He knew so much more than I did. He had already written a string quartet, which everybody loved. He was terribly nice to me and took me under his wing. I became his special friend. He was amused by me and thought I was funny and charming. Sam always loved foreigners—he thought them very exotic. He taught me a great deal about music, especially about Brahms, whose music was at that time little known in Italy— and it was through his lovely baritone voice that I heard for the first time many of Schubert's songs—a revelation which influenced my music for ever after."

Menotti studied at Curtis for one semester, and then returned to South America for the summer. He had missed his mother, although with good work behind him and a good friend to keep him company, the thought of returning to Philadelphia was not unpleasant. He and Sam Barber corresponded throughout the summer months, and when Menotti returned to the Curtis, their friendship blossomed.

"A new term was beginning at the Curtis and Sam and I saw each other constantly. Ours became an intense friendship. Those were marvelously happy days."

Samuel Barber had been brought up in a more or less puritanical environment, in West Chester, Pennsylvania. He was born there on March 9, 1910 and spent a childhood in which music was an all-encompassing factor. His aunt was the famous contralto Louise Homer, wife of the composer Sidney Homer, and there was music-making in the Barber household. Barber became a charter pupil of the Curtis Institute of Music, entering it in 1924. A man of enormous wit and culture, Samuel Barber remembered with affection his meeting Menotti:

"He was very, very thin. He had a large nose, which I think he's grown up to. And he was scared. He had settled down to a nice existence with the Ricci family and soon got over his intense grief over being away from home. He went to the movies three times a day, because it was the time when the movies started to talk and he thought it was the quickest way to learn English. So he did that, and he did his work with Scalero, which were all private lessons, and the two of us became friends. It took about a year and he began coming to my house in West Chester, about thirty miles from Philadelphia. He was immediately adopted by my family. He was like a young gentleman and behaved very well. He was fascinated by everything around him, and was trying desperately to learn English.

"I remember one time my sister and I meeting him at the train station. Driving to our place, we pointed out the local high school. He asked, 'Tell me, please, what is the difference between I-school and ice cream?' His English was really nonexistent then.

"People liked him at Curtis. He was very amusing. Also he was much more intelligent than people gave him credit for. He was a voracious reader."

Except for his friendship with Samuel Barber, Menotti's six years at the Curtis were not strikingly eventful, at least in a social sense. Intense study was the order of those years. In time, Rosario Scalero imbued him with the most rigorous precepts of compositional techniques. He plunged Menotti into the vast complexities of counterpoint. Skeptical of precociousness, he insisted that Menotti learn the fundamentals and guided him through the history and theory of past musical forms. The two would study, analyze—in other words, would "murder to dissect"—works of such Italian polyphonic masters as Palestrina, Di Lasso, Monteverdi—composers Scalero venerated.

And so Menotti's earliest work at Curtis consisted of motets, madrigals, and canons, music involving techniques that he would put to highly inventive use in later years. It was Scalero's philosophy that the role of a teacher was to supply the future composer with the tools of composition. A composer's inspiration would have to have its own source. Scalero, who had known Brahms and worshiped his music, was clearly a man of highly conservative tastes. He admired Wagner, but was not truly interested in opera per se. Menotti's future emergence as an operatic composer owed little debt to Rosario Scalero. The greatest lesson Menotti learned was the lesson of thoroughness. Scalero was not interested in easy solutions. In fact, the slightest deviations from his own methodology would find him unsympathetic. He would say, "I must cut your wings *now*, so that when they grow back, you can fly farther." Menotti profited immensely by this remark. In later years even his greatest detractors would credit him with a flawless technique.

CHAPTER

4

"If one can stroke the cat and kick the dog;
If one can pluck the peacock and flee the bee;
If one can ride the horse and hook the hog;
If one can tempt the mouse and swat the fly,
Why, why
Would a man both rich and well-born
Raise a Unicorn?"

(*The Unicorn, the Gorgon and the Manticore*)

For four consecutive summers, beginning in 1929, Gian Carlo Menotti and Samuel Barber visited Menotti's birthplace, Cadegliano. Barber recalled one such visit:

"There was no one in the house, except a couple of servants. It was a charming old Victorian house—perhaps pre-Victorian—looking over Lake Lugano. I met Gian Carlo's family—not his mother, who by then lived in South America—but some of his older brothers and sisters who had married and settled in Cadegliano, and would come to the house and fuss, or have a wonderful time, as Italians generally do.

"I did meet Gian Carlo's mother some years later. She was very beautiful—perhaps not really beautiful, but imperious. Gian Carlo takes after her somewhat. He has her qualities of imperiousness, strong will, and capriciousness. His mother was very fascinating. She was made to be the heroine of a Puccini opera. She was intelligent, she loved music."

In 1931 Barber was working on his Overture to *The School for Scandal,* and by 1932 he arrived in Cadegliano with his Cello Sonata well under way. In 1933, Barber decided that he had derived all the benefit he was to receive from the Curtis, and left the school. (He ultimately received his Bachelor of Music degree in 1934;

Menotti would graduate with honors in 1933). With a $1,200 prize Barber had received for his Overture to *The School for Scandal,* and a like sum from Menotti's family abroad, the two young men decided to travel to Europe.

Their trip began auspiciously with a visit to Toscanini at Lake Maggiore. In a letter Barber wrote his parents in 1933, he described the visit:

"It is the most romantic place you could imagine; the Toscaninis have the whole island to themselves, and their villa is up on the crest of the rocks. . . . We got out of our boat and trembled up the footpath to the house, not having the slightest idea whether they would receive us or not, for we had not written or phoned that we were coming. Not daring to ask for the maestro himself, we timidly asked if Mme. Toscanini was at home . . . then a long nerve-racking wait, while the servant seemed to be hunting in the garden for her, and our hearts sank. And then he returned saying 'Madame Toscanini is much too busy to see you now, but the Maestro has nothing to do and is coming to receive you.' Our wildest thoughts were that we would have a formal brief visit, but here he was telling us how glad he was we came, and treating us like old friends. . . . We made a tour of the island, up and down through the gardens. . . . Back at the house, he took Gian Carlo and me into his studio and showed us some of his treasures—among them an unpublished fragment Wagner wrote at the end of his life. . . . He had a portrait of Beethoven in his youth, the only one in the world. He picked up two volumes which he said he was never without— Beethoven's string quartets. (Owing to his extreme myopia, the poor Maestro did not realize that one of the cherished volumes he was showing us happened to be an *English Grammar Simplified for Beginners.*) Then . . . we had tea and talked some more, and left in a daze of enthusiasm for him and his house."

In the summer of 1933 Menotti and Barber decided to move to Vienna.

"In those years the thing to do was to go to Paris," recalled Barber. "But when we finished the Curtis, we chose—I don't really know why—to go to Vienna. Of course there were many important creative people in Vienna at the time, but we didn't know them. Mostly we spent our time ice skating. We met a pleasure-seeking group of irresponsible but amusing people (mostly English), and wasted a lot of time going to wild parties. Now, I think how much I would like to have known Alban Berg, who was in Vienna at the same time, or Schoenberg. They were not yet *that* famous, and it would probably have been easy to meet them. I *did* meet Ernst Krenek, whom I didn't like very much."

The two friends took up residence in an apartment house at Brahmsplatz, 4, which belonged to a Czechoslovakian baroness, an immense old woman, who would prove instrumental in Menotti's composing his first major work, the opera *Amelia al Ballo*. Installed in their quarters, Menotti and Barber were swept up in Vienna's social whirl. Young, handsome, and productive, they moved easily and with panache among artists, intellectuals, and high society. They attended the city's concerts, given by Toscanini, Bruno Walter, Lotte Lehmann, Maria Jeritza, and Elisabeth Schumann. Lawrence Tibbett, the baritone, whose acquaintance they made that year, often provided them with tickets to the Salzburg Festival.

Even as Hitler was rising to power in Germany, the city's upper echelon and its large enclave of artists and bohemians seemed unconcerned with or unaware of the threat of Nazism.

Vienna's social arbiters took up Barber and Menotti, inviting them to a round of endless parties and introducing them to the city's *haute monde*, its decadence, and the internationally known artists accepted by them.

"It was all very amusing for me," said Menotti, "because I had come from straight-laced Milan and from Philadelphia, which, God knows, is not a very wild city. Suddenly I was plunged in the middle of the most sophisticated group of people. They all seemed very mad. There was one mad party after another. There was a tremendous use of drugs, and there were a few extraordinary characters who did everything to 'epater les bourgeois.' One of them was Baron Waldek (he remains a good friend to this day), one of the biggest social lions of Vienna. Waldek would give huge dinners in his charming palace, and afterwards would take all of his guests to some village inn on the city's outskirts, wake up the innkeeper, order tons of champagne, and improvise a supper dance to the accompaniment of a gypsy orchestra which he had brought along. He was, needless to say, very, very rich, and a terrible snob. But he loved the arts. His was the only house in Vienna where artists and the aristocracy mingled. There was hardly a famous artist in the city who didn't claim his friendship.

"I was very naïve, very wide-eyed. Vienna was my very first contact with so-called international society. Sam, who was much more sophisticated than I, never seemed to enjoy himself as much as I did in this world. And one did meet very strange people. I recall a boy called Robin Thomas, who was the son of Michael Strange, the poetess, and (he claimed) John Barrymore. He was a very handsome boy who lived in a large studio where he kept two pet geese named Ugo and Camilla. Robin Thomas was fond of giving breakfast parties, which he held around his bed. He would lie there, covered by black silk sheets, dispensing fresh gossip and stale epigrams á la Oscar Wilde, while people would come and go between nine and eleven in the morning. Two butlers served delicious breakfasts on small scattered tables. Later, Robin Thomas killed himself."

It was at Brahmsplatz, 4, in the Czechoslovakian baroness' apartment, that Menotti found the object that would inspire him to write *Amelia al Ballo.* The baroness, whose highly ornate apartment was in the same house, would often invite the two young composers into her boudoir. "She was so fat that she could hardly move," recalled Menotti. "She lived in her bedroom and seldom left her bed. She loved food and stayed in bed all day, eating. She was so lazy that she had a contraption designed which enabled her to lock her bedroom door without having to move from her bed. She tugged on a chain, and a piece of wood would fall over the handle, locking the door.

"Every once in a while she would call me down, and I would go to her bedroom and sit on her bed. We would talk. She would order champagne and *pâté de foie gras,* and a wonderful dish, still popular in Vienna, called *Garnierte Liptauer,* which is a kind of cottage or cream cheese dish, with all kinds of seeds and condiments around it, which you then mixed all together. The baroness would tell me wonderful stories of great balls being given in Vienna, about the great names of an earlier period, about the emperor, and about how she made her debut as a young girl.

"I was so amused to see this huge, fat woman gorging herself, and talking about the beautiful girl she must have been. Anyway, in one corner of her bedroom there was the most incredible dressing table made of porcelain, and full of little cupids and ribbons and flowers. It was the dominant object in the room—the most coquettish thing I'd ever seen. It was this dressing table which gave me the idea for *Amelia al Ballo,* and in my libretto that dressing table plays a prominent part."

In the spring of 1934, Samuel Barber received an offer from Mary Louise Bok to come back to America and stay at her estate near Rockport, Maine, where many musicians congregated and worked.

There followed a period of successes for Barber: a performance of his *Music for a Scene from Shelley,* by the New York Philharmonic; G. Schirmer's publication of his *Dover Beach,* the Cello Sonata, and several songs, and in 1935 the Prix de Rome, which entitled him to a stipend of $2,500 and free living quarters in Rome at the American Academy, which he disliked intensely for its "somewhat expatriated Harvard Club atmosphere."

Menotti, in the meantime, divided his time between stays with his family in Cadegliano and preparatory work on his opera-in-progress, *Amelia al Ballo,* and other, smaller pieces, one of which, *Poemetti* (piano pieces for children) was published in 1937.

In May of 1936, the two young composers joined up in Lugano and together began a vacation trip to Salzburg and Grenoble. To stretch their money, they decided to settle in the country, rather than again face the expenses and temptations of Vienna.

"It was one of the happiest times of our lives," recalled Menotti. "We looked and looked for a quiet country house and finally landed on Lake St. Wolfgang, which at the time was not yet a terrible tourist trap, but a most charming village."

Menotti and Barber, full of dreams for important musical careers, sought a place where they could both compose. Arriving at St. Wolfgang on a rainy and foggy day, they were told of a cottage that might be available in the mountains, for $100 for the entire summer. In the rain and fog, they climbed a steep footpath, until they reached what looked like a typical Austrian chalet. They were admitted by a woman, who agreed to let them rooms and volunteered to be their cook. She lived there with her husband and daughter, her husband being the gamekeeper for a nearby estate. It was agreed that two pianos could be sent for: one would be put in the house, the other in a woodshed. These arrangements made, the two composers, tired out from their long walk in the rain, instantly went to bed. "When we woke up the next morning," said Menotti, "we found ourselves in a sunlit room. The day was incredibly clear and the view was magnificent. The whole lake was visible, and one could see for miles and miles. We were so happy! Sam took the woodshed, and it was there he wrote his *Adagio for Strings.* And it was in that house that I started the actual composition of *Amelia al Ballo.*

"When I was writing *Amelia,* opera was very unfashionable. The serious composers of the day wouldn't even mention the word 'opera.' And of course, my teacher, Scalero, was always very scornful of opera. As a matter of fact, after my work with Scalero at the Curtis, I could only imagine myself writing big orchestral pieces—symphonies, concertos. But when I saw that dressing table in Vienna, my imagination was inflamed. I think I started composing operas in spite of myself. I remember saying to myself, 'Well, I'll just write this one opera, and then I'll start composing all my symphonies, masses, and motets.' I guess *Amelia* was the beginning of my end!"

Near the composers' little cottage was the estate belonging to a Dutch baron and his English wife. Menotti and Barber were often invited to come to their villa for a game of tennis. They seldom accepted and made it clear that they would prefer to be left in peace, as they were both working. The cottage had very primitive bathroom facilities, and the two friends had to bathe in the lake. As the summer ended and the weather turned cooler, taking baths became a problem. One day they received a note from the baroness: "My dear composers, I realize that you disdain company, but I cannot help being worried by your problem with hygiene. Will you accept coming to my house twice a week for bath and dinner?"

"We used to go there on Tuesdays and Fridays," recalled Menotti. "The baron and baroness were most charming and hospitable. But there was also something puzzling about them. After each dinner the baroness would rise from the table and say, 'Excuse me, but I must go to chapel.' She would leave the room and not return until much later. Finally I could not resist asking the baron about his wife's mysterious visits to an invisible chapel. He said, 'It isn't really a chapel. It's a room in which my wife holds seances. You see, we had a daughter named Doodly—that was her nickname. She died when she was fourteen of an infected tooth. My wife never got over her death. Of course I don't believe in such things, but my wife met a medium in London who introduced her to the powers of seances. My wife retires into that room every evening because she thinks she sees our daughter and is able to speak to her.'

"Of course, I became instantly fascinated and asked the baroness whether she would allow me to come to one of her seances. The baroness said I could come at any time. A few days later, when we again had dinner at their house, the baroness asked me to come with her into the so-called chapel. We sat in the dark around a table. Suddenly she went into a trance and began speaking to her daughter. She kept saying, 'Doodly, Doodly, can you hear me?' It was a tremendously moving experience for me, so much so that I found myself with tears streaming down my cheeks. There was no doubt that the baroness was actually seeing her daughter. I, on the other hand, saw nothing at all. It gave me pause, because she *believed* and could see, while I didn't believe and therefore couldn't see anything. It made me wonder whether belief was a creative power and whether skepticism could destroy creative powers. Anyway, this episode was the beginning of *The Medium*."

Like most composers of imagination, Menotti was affected by events and encounters that would ultimately find their way into his works. The meeting with the strange baroness who held seances, as with the old couple in the sea resort near Genoa who did likewise, filled Menotti with ideas, both musical and theatrical.

There were other such meaningful experiences. While he was still a young child in Cadegliano, writing his little songs to the poetry of Pascoli and D'Annunzio, he had traveled with his mother to the nearby town of Gardone to meet the great Gabriele D'Annunzio. The poet had invited the boy to play his songs for him. When they arrived at the hotel in Gardone where D'Annunzio was living they learned that he was ill and would not be able to receive them immediately. The fact was, D'Annunzio's stormy love life had caused one of his mistresses to push the poet off his balcony, and he was recovering from the fall. It was the middle of winter. The hotel, a large and gloomy one, was practically empty. Hoping for an interview, mother and son decided to wait until the poet would be able to see them.

Menotti and his mother took their meals in the half empty hotel dining room. At a nearby table sat a couple—apparently a father and his daughter. He was a distinguished-looking man, and the young woman, some thirty years old, was most attractive. Menotti observed that the woman's hair had a white streak in it. She would talk to her father in quiet tones. In the middle of her conversation, however, she would suddenly run her hand through her hair and in a loud voice exclaim, "No!" She would almost scream it and at the same time make the odd gesture. This was a recurrent interruption in the woman's conversation. At night, when Gian Carlo was in bed, he could not fall asleep, for throughout the night he heard the woman screaming the word "no," which would echo through the empty corridors of the hotel.

Menotti and his mother never did get to see D'Annunzio, but the memory of the woman in the dining hall remained with the boy. Years and years later, she would become the character of Anna Gomez in *The Consul*.

Menotti remembered another incident, which indirectly colored a character in his opera *Maria Golovin*. "I had an aunt who lived in a huge and depressing Victorian villa in Cadegliano. One summer she rented it to a countess who arrived there with her son and a tutor. The child was a very affectionate boy with reddish hair. He looked so frightened all the time. On certain days, one of my brothers and I were allowed to come and play with him. Sometimes we would be invited for lunch. I remember sitting at the table and noticing that the contessa had brought with her a small whip, which she laid on the table. Each time her little son would deviate from good table manners, she would pick up the whip and strike his hands. The boy's name was Trottolò, and he later became the little boy in *Maria Golovin*."

Menotti recalled that, after the first performance of *Maria Golovin* at La Scala, he met Count Lulling (the proud owner of the famous Palladian Villa Maser), who questioned him closely about the character of the little boy. Why, of all names, had he chosen Trottolò? Menotti told him the story and Count Lulling stood amazed: "But *I* am that little boy—*I* am that Trottolò—but I never thought that you were *that* Gian Carlo!"

Thus it was that Gian Carlo Menotti, the child, the teenager, the young man, fixed in his mind those moments and events that would in future years yield the symbol-fraught stories that provide dramatic and theatrical impetus to his operas. At this moment in his life he could not guess or suspect that he would also produce music which would eventually become a unique and original signature— a style of music that would influence an entire generation of young American composers, who would venture into the writing of operas à la Menotti.

THE
GORGON

Behold the Gorgon, stately and proud,
His eyes transfixed but not unaware
Of the envious stare
Of the common crowd.
Behold the Gorgon, tall, big and loud.
He does not see the smiling enemy.
He does not pause to acknowledge
The racket of the critical cricket
Nor to confute the know-how
Of the sententious cow.

(*The Unicorn, the Gorgon and the Manticore*)

CHAPTER
5

"The rose holds the summer in her winter sleep,
the sea gathers moonlight where ships cannot plough . . ."

(*The Consul*)

In the spring of 1937, Menotti had nearly completed *Amelia al Ballo*. He returned to America and, at the invitation of Mary Louise Bok, stayed at her estate in Rockport, Maine. Mrs. Bok had received reports from a friend in Vienna that Menotti's opera was altogether charming. With anticipation and enthusiasm she asked to hear some of it. Menotti called on his former student at Curtis, the singer Irra Petina, who came to Maine, and the two sang some of the arias and duets from *Amelia*. Mrs. Bok was enchanted by what she heard. She insisted that Menotti stay put at Rockport so that he might finish his opera.

That spring, the Curtis Institute was presenting a benefit performance. The school had decided to mount two operatic works, which would be conducted by Fritz Reiner, then teaching at the Curtis. It was Reiner's idea to present Darius Milhaud's 1926 one-act opera, *Le Pauvre Matelot*. Mrs. Bok had been approached to finance the presentation. She agreed to do so, on the condition that the Milhaud work be given together with Menotti's *Amelia al Ballo*. Reiner, who would have to conduct it, was far from pleased. He deemed it unwise to present a student's first operatic effort together with a work by so respected a composer as Milhaud. He insisted that another celebrated composer's work be chosen for the event. But Mrs. Bok was adamant, and Reiner unwillingly capitulated. As he began working on Menotti's score, he seemed to warm up to it and, as it turned out, gave it an exquisite performance.

Menotti's *Amelia al Ballo* (or *Amelia Goes to the Ball*, as it was called in English) thus received its first performance at the Academy of Music under Fritz Reiner on April 1, 1937. Its libretto had been written by Menotti in Italian and was translated into English by George Mead. It is an hour-long work, composed in the Italian opera buffa style. Its theme deals with a spoiled and coquettish married woman, her adoring lover and her enraged husband. The story centers on Amelia's insistence on being taken to a fashionable ball, despite the droll and melodramatic convolutions of the plot, which continually prevent her from going. It is her single-mindedness— her faith—which ultimately prevails. In arias, duets, trios, the music flows in bubbling and lilting continuity, exposing Menotti's skill in orchestration, his wit, and love of buffoonery.

The Curtis production was staged by the Austrian director Ernst Laert. The settings were by Donald Oenslager. For the momentous occasion, Samuel Barber returned from Europe. There were three benefit performances: one given in Philadelphia, the second in Baltimore, the third in New York. To Reiner's pique, the Milhaud opera turned out to be a fiasco, while *Amelia* proved a great success.

"*Amelia* was dedicated to Mrs. Bok, towards whom I have so much to be grateful for," said Menotti. "I have a very great fondness for it. Not only was it my first opera, and my first success, but it was also the only opera of mine that was ever heard by my mother. At the time, she was living in South America, and already quite ill. Again it was Mrs. Bok who proved a great friend, because it was she who thought that my mother should be brought to the United States for the New York performance of *Amelia.* Mrs. Bok sent my mother a ticket to come over by boat, and so my mother arrived, and I'll never forget her appearance on the evening of the performance. She wore a lovely black velvet dress and looked very beautiful and regal. After the performance everyone was terribly excited over *Amelia* . . . everyone except my mother, who kept saying, 'But I always *knew* that my little boy would have such a success.' People were amazed that she could be so serene about it all. Mother returned to South America, and a few years later died."

Menotti was more than satisfied with the reception of his work. After the great success of *Amelia,* Menotti and Barber, who were now installed in an apartment in New York City, once again decided to travel to Cadegliano. The visit proved memorable.

"We stayed in my family's villa," said Menotti. "Sam was enchanted by Cadegliano. We visited all my relatives. We took long walks, and it was a very sentimental time for me, being back with my family. It was 1938 and Italy was under the regime of Mussolini. Things had changed—but not in Cadegliano. At any rate, I remember how one morning the village postmistress arrived on bicycle to deliver the mail. She was a funny little woman who knew everybody's private life because it was her habit to steam open every letter that arrived in Cadegliano. She was finally fired from her job. While the village tolerated her reading everybody's mail, it drew the line when it was discovered that she also altered the contents of the letters, telegrams, and postcards. At any rate, that morning she was nearing our house on her bicycle and shouting at the top of her voice, 'Signorino Gian Carlo! Signorino Gian Carlo! Il Metropolitáno! Il Metropolitano!' Well, she was waving a cable from the Metropolitan Opera of New York, telling me that they would be staging *Amelia Goes to the Ball.*"

While Menotti had achieved a certain renown after the Curtis production of *Amelia,* it had never occurred to him that his little opera would reach so hallowed a stage as the Metropolitan. But on March 3, 1938, the curtain rose promptly at 8:00 P.M. Conductor Ettore Panizza lifted his baton, and the delightful overture to *Amelia Goes to the Ball* filled the air. The cast included Muriel Dickson as Amelia, John Brownlee as the husband, and Mario Chamlee as the lover. When it was over the audience acclaimed the new work, and the twenty-seven-year-old composer came before the curtain with the principal artists and took several bows.

The reviews for the Metropolitan production of *Amelia Goes to the Ball* were not far short of ecstatic. Olin Downes of the *New York Times* wrote:

"The Metropolitan Opera Company produced a work in the lighter vein last night by a young composer who has made an extremely brilliant and amusing start as a musician of the lyric theater. . . . [Gian Carlo Menotti] has written the text of *Amelia Goes to the Ball,* a one-act opera buffa, as well as the music, and he shows instinctive talent not only for composition, but for the theater.

"There is something here, as it must tearfully be admitted, that has not materialized so far from an American-born composer. This is dramatic music, and it is vocal music. The flexibility and spontaneity of the score is inborn. The recitative, which is sometimes spoken and sometimes sung, does not make the English language sound stupid or futile in the mouths of the singers. Mr. Menotti has done striking things with the form.

"The form includes set pieces, solos, duos, trios, yet nothing hackneyed in treatment, and whatever the weak places may be, there is nothing stiff or affected. The set pieces, when they are intentionally introduced, are parts of a deliberate artistic design, and there is witticism and mockery in the way they are handled. For it's all in jest and capital fooling.

"The music, since it is genuine, is fundamentally Italian in texture and spirit. The manner is the composer's birthright. It is natural and instinctive for him to write that way, clearly, dexterously, melodically and with laughter. . . . What is fascinating is the dramatic continuousness of the musical fabric, the swift tonal punctuation of all that goes on on the stage, the adroit characterization, the capacity to combine all the musical elements in ensemble movements which are so gay, and which come so directly from that architectural triumph of Italian light opera—the concerted finale. In one place, for his crowd scene, the composer has the nerve to write fugally, and to succeed surprisingly well in the undertaking. . . .

"The opera, from the standpoint of a great opera house, has defects of structure and inexperience. It is too small a work for the large stage. The score is uneven in the quality of its invention. Last night a small stage-within-a-stage was erected . . . this was a good solution to a difficult problem. It also allowed for novelty and extravagance in action.

". . . The opera, which previously had been given a charity performance in this city, gave great pleasure. After the curtain, the composer was repeatedly called before it. He had reason for self-congratulation."

Other reviewers praising Menotti's hour-long opera included Pitts Sanborn of the *New York World-Telegram*, who found the score in the great comic line of *Le Nozze di Figaro, Il Matrimonio Segreto, Il Barbiere di Siviglia, Don Pasquale,* and *Falstaff.* "As in the case of these masterpieces," wrote Sanborn, "the orchestra maintains a constant and relishing commentary on the action." Mostly, however, Sanborn, as well as other reviewers, considered *Amelia* primarily influenced by Wolf-Ferrari.

Amelia Goes to the Ball was the first of a double bill at the Metropolitan that also included Richard Strauss's *Elektra,* conducted by Erich Leinsdorf. It seemed an odd companion piece, which Menotti found amusingly inappropriate. The Metropolitan Opera, never noted for championing American opera, showed unusual courage in presenting a work that was simply a brilliant student effort. At the time, the Met had produced eighteen United States operas. But only Deems Taylor's *The King's Henchman* (1927) and *Peter Ibbetson* (1931), and Louis Gruenberg's *Emperor Jones* (1933) were mild successes. The last pre-Menotti U.S. opera was Walter Damrosch's *The Man Without a Country,* which received but one performance on May 12, 1937.

Amelia Goes to the Ball is Menotti's only work besides *The Last Savage* written in Italian. The orchestration is extremely rich contrapuntally. The fugue, at the entrance of the chorus, is particularly masterful. There is no question that *Amelia* is full of influences. One hears Richard Strauss and Donizetti. And there was good reason for critics to have discerned strong echoes of Ermano Wolf-Ferrari. As it happened, Menotti met that composer at the very time *Amelia* was being written.

"Wolf-Ferrari lived not very far from St. Wolfgang, where Sam and I were staying," said Menotti. "I resolved to visit him. Actually he was very reluctant to see me, saying that he didn't like contemporary music and that he was practically certain not to like *my* music. To be honest about it, I didn't much admire his music either. I think he's a sort of fake Mozart. But I did admire his orchestration. I think he would have been a very good composer if he had a true melodic gift. His thematic material I thought was very second rate. Still, I went to visit him and he was very nice. He gave me lunch but begged me not to play my music for him. Finally I insisted on doing so and played him bits from *Amelia.* Well, he changed his mind and said I was on the right track. At the end of the afternoon he told me, 'I'll give you a little parting secret: if you write an opera, especially an opera buffa, remember that the orchestra and the voice must be knitted together like the cogs in tow wheels. The accents of either must never come at the same time, so that the words will be understood. In other words, the accents must never meet, otherwise they destroy each other.' It was a small detail, but I've always remembered it, because it is very true."

Soon after the Metropolitan production of *Amelia Goes to the Ball,* Menotti received an invitation from the Italian minister of culture, Dino Alfieri, to come to Rome and discuss the opera's Italian premiere, which would be given at a festival in San Remo, at that time an important musical center. Menotti flew to Italy and was warmly welcomed by the minister. Menotti recalled the meeting:

"I saw Alfieri, who couldn't have been more cordial and enthusiastic. He told me that he wanted to launch me in Italy. As an Italian with a great American success, I would now be hailed in my homeland. I kept thanking him profusely. Toward the end of our meeting, he said, 'There's only one thing: you must join the Fascist party.' This I absolutely refused to do, as I had no interest whatever in Mussolini or his politics. As a result, orders were given to the press to 'kill' my opera when it was given in San Remo. I remember that *Amelia* was premiered during April, and one of the headlines of an Italian paper read 'April Fool!' and the reviews were simply terrible. After that my music became taboo in Italy—at least throughout the Fascist regime."

The success in America of *Amelia Goes to the Ball* had one slight cloud. Happy over Menotti's triumph, Samuel Barber nevertheless became sensitive to the fact that their friendship seemed somewhat threatened by Menotti's sudden acclaim. Said Menotti, "Although he wanted me to write music, and to be successful, Sam considered my very music an enemy. There was never any question that we were still the closest of friends, but throughout those early years the friendship could get very stormy. Even though we were like brothers—like blood brothers—I would often get frantic with Sam and would wish that things could be smoother between us."

Samuel Barber had been the single greatest influence on Menotti's early life in America. It was Barber who had introduced the young Menotti to the ways and mores of America, and it was with Barber that Menotti shared his first extrafamilial life. Barber's curious Anglo-Saxon sensibilities—an absolute need for the measured and the constrained—balanced Menotti's unabashedly Mediterranean instincts; Barber's sense of balance and his acerbic wit tempered Menotti's love for the fantastic, bizarre, and humorous.

Oddly enough, this influence did not carry over into the composer's music—at least in any pronounced way. Their personalities in many ways complemented each other, but each remained his own man as far as composition was concerned. If there was a musical similarity between them, it made itself felt only through the careful workmanship that attended each composer's music. In matters of style the two could not be more different.

Menotti always wore his heart on his sleeve; his music is frankly emotional. Its melodies are admirably accessible and have the power to move one deeply. It is music at once from the heart and from the mind. It is never pretentious, and almost always skirts the banal.

The music of Samuel Barber, on the other hand, is more astringent. Like the man, the music is diffident, although beneath the diffidence there exists a vast storehouse of strong emotion. A brilliant orchestrator and a fertile melodist, Barber conveys feeling through understatement and subtlety. Like the man, however, the music can become too witty, or plunge into glowing romanticism. But unlike Menotti, Barber tends to be a lean and judicious composer. There is a noble symmetry, which often eschews the temptation of easy accessibility. The contrast between the two could not help but cause some resentment on Barber's part, as he, with a charming sense of humor, readily admits. He had won prestigious prizes; his music had been performed in Europe; but his work had not been popularly accepted in this country in 1938—while Menotti's *Amelia* had been quickly embraced by the American public. And *Amelia* was only the beginning of the problem.

CHAPTER

6

"Light up and fly on winged bicycle
Like a Victorian Icarus . . .
Victor . . . vincit . . . Da Vinci . . .
Fall . . . fall . . . and scatter
In spiralling dandelions
Down, down where dark is cool . . ."

(The Most Important Man)

Among the critics who unstintingly praised *Amelia Goes to the Ball,* Samuel Chotzinoff, who at the time was writing for the *New York Post,* was to prove a valued friend and an invaluable influence on Menotti's career in years to come. The Russian-born Chotzinoff eventually became music consultant to the NBC Radio Network. In this capacity, he approached Menotti in 1939, asking him to write an opera specifically for radio—the first such commission ever given. Chotzinoff suggested that the opera bear an American theme—something that would make it widely accessible to a vast radio audience. Menotti accepted the commission with alacrity, although he was somewhat apprehensive about plunging into Americana. Indeed, his English was not yet altogether fluent. With characteristic aplomb and enthusiasm, however, he began an opera that he called *The Old Maid and the Thief.*

The closest Menotti had come to so-called Americana was his contact with Samuel Barber's family. *"The Old Maid and the Thief,"* said Menotti, "was inspired by Sam's birthplace, West Chester, Pennsylvania. I was frequently invited to go there. When Thanksgiving would come around, Sam used to invite me to be with his family. I had no idea what Thanksgiving meant. Anyway, I would go there, and it was a revelation. It was a Presbyterian family with some Quaker ancestors. It was a somewhat straight-laced and morally conventional family, but a family full of charm. Sam's father was a very respected doctor. His mother was a rather naïve and sweet woman. Sam's sister, Sara, was a very lively and intelligent girl and full of talent. The whole family was immediately very loving toward me.

"My own family was in total contrast to the Barbers. I mean, when lunch was announced at our house in Cadegliano, my mother wouldn't think for a moment of stopping in the middle of a Beethoven piano sonata—nor would we children leave our games unfinished. We all dribbled into the dining room at leisure, and there was an awful lot of gong banging and maids running up and down stairs, or calling into the garden, before the first course could be served. In West Chester, things were very different. A chime would announce lunch or dinner. Everybody would rise and gather around the dining table. Then everybody would hold hands. Grace would be said, something practically unheard of in Italy.

"I was very impressed and quite moved by all this formality. Remember, we in Italy thought of America only in terms of skyscrapers and Hollywood, certainly not of solid old patriarchal families sitting around the dinner table thanking God for their food. Anyway, Sam had a very charming aunt called Allie whom we all adored. She loved to gossip about the people in West Chester. I learned that behind the façade of those charming old houses, all sorts of terrible things were going on. There were stories about alcoholism, incest—terrible things. Upon hearing all these stories, I was inspired to write *The Old Maid and the Thief*."

The NBC premiere of Menotti's second opera took place on April 22, 1939, in Studio 8H at the NBC broadcasting center at Radio City. The orchestra was under the direction of Alberto Erede. In its cast were Margaret Daum, Robert Weed, Mary Ropple, and Dorothy Sarnoff. The reviews were predominantly favorable, and most critics felt that a milestone had been achieved in bringing American opera to the medium of radio. The press considered the plot a charming trifle, dealing as it does with a pleasant and honest hobo who so beguiles an old maid and her pretty maidservant that to detain their attractive lodger, they rob the neighbors and pillage a liquor store. The old maid, a member of the town's temperance league, learns that a notorious criminal has just escaped from the nearby jail. While this frightens her somewhat, she reflects that "it is better to be killed by a man than to live without one."

The police, investigating the liquor store robbery, make a search

of the house, terrifying the hobo, who had been innocent of any
crime at all. In his fear, he flees the house in the old maid's car,
taking along the pretty servant as well as the silverware. The moral
of this tale: "A woman can do what the devil himself can't do: make
a thief of an honest man."

The *New Yorker* magazine wrote, "*The Old Maid and the Thief*
is somewhat too long, for it's held up now and then by formal airs
and things that aren't in themselves strong enough to compensate
for the lag. The text, which is generally fetching, suffers from occa-
sional outbreaks of off-accent musical setting, about which Librett-
tist Menotti might speak to Composer Menotti." *Newsweek* commented that within the span of an hour Menotti convinced
thousands of listeners all over the country that English is really a
great language to sing in, and that he also convinced his audience
that microphones and loudspeakers can do a brilliant job of dispensing with the need for costumes, footlights, and greasepaint. It
went on to say that the work was smartly produced and amusing.

In *The Old Maid* Menotti tried to keep his harmonic texture
much simpler than he had in *Amelia*. At the time he wrote it, he
had come under the influence of Schubert, noting how this composer obtained melodic originality through complete harmonic
simplicity. Menotti was particularly drawn to Schubert songs and
found them containing a compressed musical language that was
both economical and highly moving. It was this economy and
simplicity that Menotti strove for in *The Old Maid*. The score bears
none of the influences that were so apparent in *Amelia*. Neither
Strauss, Wolf-Ferrari, nor Puccini (to whom Menotti would be
constantly compared) was in evidence. The score is lean and unencumbered by ornate musical textures. As in *Amelia Goes to the
Ball*, the question of faith and belief is touched on. Because everyone *believes* the hobo-tenant to be a thief, he becomes one.

The Old Maid and the Thief, which Menotti subtitled "a grotesque
opera in fourteen scenes," easily adapted itself to stage production,
and its popularity continues to this day. On the occasion of the
opera's recording, Menotti wrote a touching program note: "In his
middle age an artist is apt to look back at his youthful works with
much embarrassment. Later in life, more often than not, the embarrassment turns into sentimental affection. On listening to *The Old
Maid and the Thief*, I no longer smile at what for a while seemed
utter naïveté, but rather admire the courage of the young man who
wrote it. . . . As for the music, what can I say? If, as I believe, the

true artist is he who is able to reveal his inner self with both precision and spontaneity, I cannot but envy the young man who wrote
The Old Maid and the Thief. It is now with gnawing self-doubt that
I try to capture my real face beneath the layers of masks that little
by little life imposes on me. What seemed so easy then has become
unbearably difficult. If *The Old Maid* has any merits the main one
is that it faithfully reveals the young man I was. But of course, not
all young men are charming or amusing. Besides, in art, youth in
itself has little value unless it is able to capture, as Bizet did in his
Symphony in C, the very essence of youth. Be it far from me to
claim the same for *The Old Maid*, but as long as its youthfulness
can still make people smile, I am glad that the ever-ready under-
takers have not yet succeeded in burying her."

The Old Maid and the Thief remains one of Menotti's most popular works and has been performed often, both in America and
abroad. Its success brought the twenty-eight-year-old composer re-
newed celebrity. Scores of articles and publications the world over
began to appear about the new young genius of opera. As would
happen throughout Menotti's life, detractors reared their heads.
The musical intelligentsia, while conceding that the composer was
breaking new ground for American opera, were disdainful of his
simplistic and traditional manner of composition. In a period when
the musical avant-garde celebrated dissonance, the simple, joyful
melodies of Menotti were scorned and secretly ridiculed. His increasing success was also frowned upon, for "serious" composers
were a breed apart, misunderstood by the public, and untainted by
acclaim and its concomitant social and financial rewards. Menotti,
gregarious, handsome, and increasingly sophisticated, was wined
and dined. He was now living in a penthouse in New York with
Barber, who had returned from Europe that year, having been
warned in Paris that because of the political situation in Europe, all
Americans should leave immediately.

Menotti loved attending parties, and his reputation for being
"charming" took strong hold. He was not only charming, but an
engaging and informed conversationalist, a man of explosive good
spirits with a capacity for being both witty and wicked—someone
any host or hostess would be delighted to entertain. He began to
meet the famous of the day and thoroughly enjoyed their company.

The superficial rewards of America, while enticing and enthusi-
astically embraced, did not deter Menotti from the main purpose
of his life—to continue composing and producing works of sub-

stance and meaning. Menotti was well aware that both *Amelia Goes to the Ball* and *The Old Maid and the Thief* were essentially light works possessed of quality and inspiration, but they did not answer the composer's need to become involved with a more serious and authoritative work.

Because of the success of *Amelia*, and now *The Old Maid*, the Metropolitan Opera asked Menotti for a new one-act opera. The composer was elated and considered this the perfect opportunity for embarking on what he hoped would be a major and substantial work. He was ready to try his hand at tragedy. "You see," said Menotti, "although my admirers kept saying I was a new Rossini, I was haunted by feelings of guilt, for not yet had I written a single one of those symphonies, concerti, motets and masses my teacher, Scalero, had trained me to write. Hopelessly trapped as I was by the theater, I thought I would at least try my hand at a heavy and tragic opera. What I wrote was a big bore."

On February 20, 1942, Gian Carlo Menotti's third opera, *The Island God*, was performed at the Metropolitan. It was a resounding flop, unanimously damned. The subject of *The Island God* was based on a problem that has always haunted Menotti: the relation between faith and reality. The action takes place on a small island in the Mediterranean. Two modern exiles, who have lost all their faith in things both human and divine, are shipwrecked on this island while escaping from their invaded country. They find nothing there but the ruins of an old Greek temple, and in their despair they invoke its god. Thus the Greek god is brought back to life by their faith, appearing before them, encouraging them to rebuild the temple and become his new apostles. But he also warns them that he lives upon human sorrow. In the second scene, sometime later, a fisherman appears on the island. He represents the sensual and immediate pleasures of life as opposed to the demands of spiritual values. Through his influence the followers sin against the god and finally rebel against him. The sacrilege must be punished by death, yet the god does not wish to destroy his votaries, for he realizes that he would in this way destroy himself. When those who have restored him through their belief realize that the god is more afraid of them than they are of him, they allow themselves to be destroyed, knowing that he will be destroyed with them.

This somewhat cumbersome though interesting plot engaged Menotti's imagination but left audiences stunned and puzzled. They were not used to a "serious" Menotti. The composer, though crushed by the opera's failure, agreed that it was a mistake:

"In a sense it was a salutary lesson for me. Actually it's the only work I didn't write for myself, but for other people. I wrote it for the critics. Everybody kept saying, 'Oh, Menotti is just good for opera buffas, but he can't do anything serious.' Of course, it was a stupid accusation, because I think that opera buffa is just as profound as opera seria. The profoundity of a work is not measured by whether it is funny or not—only by whether it is perfect or not. For me, Rossini's *The Barber of Seville* is just as profound as Verdi's *Rigoletto* or Strauss's *Elektra*. Musical values can only be measured within the boundaries of music's own secret logic, and not by its mood or by its subject matter. I agree with Stravinsky that it is essentially an abstract art.

"Anyway, I was still quite young, and I said to myself, 'I'm going to show people how serious I can be. I'll write a big, heavy opera for a big, heavy orchestra.' I made lots of noise with it. And I must admit the music was very uninventive. It's made up of very bad Italian music. I recently looked it over and found no saving graces. While I think the idea of the libretto is a good one, musically it's uninspired. The lesson I learned from it was that I should always be myself, that I should not try to impress anyone. And so I withdrew the opera. It's never been published, and I've tried to destroy every trace of it. It is the only one of my children that I've willfully murdered."

With the demise of *The Island God*, Menotti's previously enthusiastic public began talking about him as something of a flash in the pan. Suddenly Menotti was dropped from the social whirl. The invitations for dinner stopped, and no one sought interviews or the pleasure of his company. A spate of problems assailed the crestfallen composer. In 1942 Menotti was still receiving financial aid from his family in Italy, but Mussolini declared war on Ethiopia and all funds from Italy were stopped. Despite the success of *Amelia* and *The Old Maid*, Menotti was not financially solvent. "Mrs. Bok helped me a little," said Menotti, "but I was having a terrible time of it. I remember begging people to give me a job, including Samuel Chotzinoff, who had commissioned *The Old Maid*. To my shock, he never answered my phone calls. Suddenly I was dropped by everybody. I tried to get a job at an Italian radio station, and that didn't work out. I didn't know how I was going to earn a living. Fortunately I had Sam, who helped me. He lent me money and was very generous. I had also met a family called the Marescas, who gave me money and helped me along. It was during this period that I composed my Piano Concerto."

The Piano Concerto was Menotti's first important nondramatic work. It was not commissioned, and he did not write it with any particular pianist in mind. The structure of this buoyant concerto consists of the conventional three movements. The character of its style harks back to Scarlatti. It is a light and transparent work, with grateful and expert passages for the piano. Its second movement recalls the operatic Menotti, with its lyrically sustained flow of melody and haunting harmonic development. The closing movement seems somewhat facile and empty, but bears the brilliance appropriate to a dazzling concerto finale. The Piano Concerto was ultimately premiered by the Boston Symphony Orchestra. The soloist was Rudolf Firkusny. It enjoyed a modicum of success but is not frequently heard these days.

CHAPTER
7

"Those of us who find our love on earth,
must celebrate our fleeting triumph.
Who welcomes love in silence
or hides like a crime
shall soon run to the wastelands
to escape its blinding vengeance."

(*The Saint of Bleecker Street*)

Gian Carlo Menotti's personal relationships have veered from lasting to passing. As a bachelor and as a man disposed to gregariousness, he has acquired an endless stream of acquaintances. People have moved in and out of his life with unending regularity. Menotti has the gift of extracting from people the most they have to offer. His famous charm has seduced many individuals who all too willingly included themselves in the orbit of so enchanting a man; it has often been maintained that Menotti could charm the birds off the trees.

Because his interests do not fix exclusively on music and because his mind is as inquisitive as it is open, any number of writers, poets, people in the theater, philosophers, engage his interest. Whomever he meets, in whatever field, becomes the subject of a stream of questions. While quickly losing interest in pedants or bores, he takes endless delight in learning whatever he can from people of intelligence and flair, and the circle of his acquaintances has included acknowledged masters in a wide range of fields.

Menotti, however, has remained a man alone, and only a handful of men and women—besides Samuel Barber—have succeeded in touching his life in any meaningful way. Menotti's sudden success and thriving social life did not so much upset Barber as perhaps threaten him, and although they have remained lifelong friends, the friendship was not without turmoil.

'The fact is," said Menotti, "that Sam was always the first to defend me, if anyone ever criticized my *music*. But little by little, he began to hate the people who loved me. He felt our friendship was threatened. He felt ours should be an immortal friendship. It is that, but somehow it didn't turn out the way he imagined it. To this day, Sam considers every friend of mine a threat.

"In some way, I feel I hurt him a great deal. I just couldn't live up to what he wanted me to be. Through the years, some people felt that Sam was becoming caustic and bitter. This couldn't be further from the truth. Sam is a very pure and noble person. It is perhaps my fault that he has become aloof and diffident these days. I destroyed many of his illusions about me. You see, Sam is very much of a puritan, and he has no interest in petty things, while I have the soul of a concierge. The sort of world that would unavoidably surround us didn't interest him at all and actually made him unhappy. I can cope with it, and am often amused by it, but Sam gets no pleasure out of that kind of frivolity. I have friends who could never be Sam's friends. I could always get along with so many more people than he could."

In the early forties, Menotti and Samuel Barber rented a small apartment in a house on 79th Street, near Fifth Avenue. They lived on the top floor and dubbed their home "The Water Tank," as an old empty water tank had to be removed from the main room, which was to become their living room. Because the building would soon be demolished, their rent was very low, and they remained at 79th Street for nearly three years before moving to another apartment on East 95th Street. There they composed and entertained. It was around this time—during the late fall of 1941—that Menotti and Barber met a young man, Robert "Kinch" Horan, a talented poet who would play an important part in Menotti's life and intellectual development for the next ten years.

"Kinch" Horan arrived in the two composers' lives unexpectedly. Menotti recalled the unusual circumstances of their meeting:

"Sam and I had gone to the Metropolitan Opera with two lady friends. After the performance, we took them back to the hotel where they were staying. We then began to walk home toward 95th Street.

"We walked along Fifth Avenue, and we noticed a young boy standing in front of the window of Saks. He looked extremely pale and seemed to be ill. We walked past him, and I remember saying to Sam, 'That boy acts so strangely. He must be sick.' So Sam said, 'Well, let's ask him if he's all right.' I went up to him and asked whether there was anything we could do for him. He said he had hitchhiked from California. Later, we learned from him that he had been sleeping at Grand Central Station for three days and didn't have a penny.

"Sam and I took him to our apartment and gave him something to eat. He ate and ate and drank and drank. We then asked him if he wanted to sleep over. He said he'd feel much too guilty staying over, because he was with a girl he had traveled with from California, and she was waiting for him at Grand Central Station. The girl, as it turned out, was Pauline Kael. Kinch had been in love with Pauline and was still tremendously attached to her, and Pauline seemed also to have been in love with Kinch. At any rate, Kinch arranged for Pauline to stay with a friend, and he stayed with us— for many years. Pauline, who has become a famous film critic, came often to visit us, and I remember having violent discussions about politics and aesthetics with her. In a way, with her brilliant mind, she seemed to be a kind of Svengali over Kinch, and I was unconsciously battling with her for the greater influence over his mind. I think, however, that by and large he influenced me more than I influenced him.

"Those early years with Kinch were wonderful. It was he who introduced me to the works of James Joyce. At the time I was entirely taken up by Proust. So we exchanged authors, so to speak. He also introduced me to the poetry of Dylan Thomas, who was not yet very well known. He also influenced my taste in abstract painting and modern dance. I made with him a more detailed exploration into contemporary art. I had been, of course, always conscious of it and had never hid from it. But he encouraged me to encounter it with an open mind and even hoped that it might influence my own work. He pushed me into going to concerts of John Cage and Varese, and exhibits of Calder and Kandinsky. He was so fascinated by all that was new.

"His influence on my literary style was also very great—particularly on my librettos. The point is, he exposed me to certain currents in art which I would probably have explored—but most likely not until much later, as I was much too fascinated by surrealism at the time.

"Kinch was a very strange boy and an extraordinary person. Perhaps of all the people I met in my life, he was the *most* extraordinary. He had a great intelligence and was 'mad'—like, I am convinced, all the Irish."

Menotti, Barber, and Kinch Horan set up a kind of household. Also at about this time, the two composers began to think about finding a place in the country where they could work in peace and solitiude, away from the distracting pace of New York. They mentioned this idea to their good friend and patroness, Mary Louise Bok—by now, Mrs. Efrem Zimbalist. With her customary generosity, Mrs. Zimbalist offered to underwrite the purchase of a country house. She told the young composers, "Why don't you just go and buy whichever house you want." She sent a large check forthwith. In return, Barber and Menotti signed a deed for the sum of one dollar to Mrs. Zimbalist. With this backing, the two began their search, aided by Kinch Horan. What they found was "Capricorn," the house in Mt. Kisco, New York, that would be synonymous with the names Gian Carlo Menotti and Samuel Barber for the next thirty years.

In a vivid and most amusing article, Kinch Horan wrote what must be considered the definitive description of this fabled country house:

"We were looking for a house that would hold three people at an amicable distance, the composers demanding a studio apiece, each large enough for a grand piano, and far enough away from each other, so that they would not be hearing double when both were at work. In the middle of the maelstrom, I required a studio to write in . . . preferably with windows that were not overlooking a steel foundry or someone else's kitchen. To make it worse, we preferred it quiet, somewhat isolated in beautiful country, but near New York, not too difficult to clean or maintain, and not ornamented with many antiques and breakable objects. It seems to me one of those rare gratuities of fate that we found, on a beautiful uninhabited hill outside Mount Kisco, this particular house.

"It was, I believe, the first house to be designed by Lescaze in America, and perhaps resembles, from the outside, a modern but not *moderne* chalet set into the side of the mountain and overlooking Croton Lake and the far hills. . . . I should point out that the plumbing and the oil furnace function with minimum eccentricity, subject, of course, to lightning and our own inattention; the roof does not leak, the windows rattle only in March, the floors are not uneven, and the space is used with a fair balance of economy and proportion.

"The outside of the house—alternating widely spaced and irregular planks of wood, with foundation and chimneys of brick and with natural stone used for terrace and steps—accents . . . the structure of the house and its wing formation. There is a small raised stone terrace at the front of the house, bordered with flowers or weeds, depending on our industry and the mysteries of the weather. . . .

"Inside, it is a private house and a triple workshop simultaneously. All built on one floor in wings from a central, two-storied living room, it makes three-or-four-story heart failure obsolete. . . . The living room is just that. It is a general refuge when work is going badly, serving intermittently as a dining room and a library. In the summer, the half of the room nearest the windows is in general use. In the winter, we migrate to the fireplace side. . . . A tiny window, high in the wall, next to the fireplace, seems at first irrational. But I have often noticed how it admits winter sunlight and elm beetles.

"Several hundred feet down the hill from the house is a separate cottage or guest house, with a small living room, bedroom, kitchenette and bath, and, although insufficiently heated for winter, is very livable for half or two-thirds of the year. . . . The cottage provides guests and hosts with that privacy that both secretly desire, making it possible to have 'company' and carry on normal working conditions at the same time.

"With each wing widely separated from all others, providing quiet for concentration and privacy, each studio of a different character and reflecting a different necessity and taste, it made it possible for three people to abandon crowded, noisy and depressing apartments in New York for this amplitude of space."

Menotti, Barber, and Horan moved into Capricorn in the summer of 1943. It being the war years, Barber was inducted into the Army but, due to defective vision, was placed in the Special Services Division and became a clerk in New York City. He was frequently called upon to ride in a truck and (being a composer!) pick up pianos and other musical instruments that were being donated to the armed forces. Being stationed in New York, Barber could thus make frequent visits to Capricorn. Eventually transferred to the Army Air Force, he was made corporal and was also commissioned to write a symphony, which would be dedicated to the Army Air

Forces. The work was completed in 1944 and performed that year by the Boston Symphony, under Serge Koussevitsky. In 1945 Samuel Barber returned to civilian life.

For his part, Menotti duly registered as an "enemy alien," but was saved from internment through the intervention of his friend Francis Biddle, then Attorney General. It was during this period that Menotti worked on his Piano Concerto. Kinch Horan, in the meantime, continued living at Capricorn writing poetry and also commuting to New York, where he took dance classes with Martha Graham.

Almost from the first, Capricorn became the scene of a series of weekend social gatherings. Celebrities would appear with regularity. Glittering names of the music, theater, film, dance, and literary worlds would gather at Capricorn and be entertained with style and generosity by their young, imaginative, articulate, and highly gifted hosts.

"It was like a family of Gian Carlo, Sam, and Kinch," recalled choreographer John Butler. "And Capricorn was marvelous in those early years. There were always exciting people in the house. Gian Carlo was always inventing games—very wicked games, yes. But I noticed an innate jealousy in Sam of anyone who was terribly close to Gian Carlo. I think there was a tendency to categorize: 'This is Gian Carlo's friend, this is Sam's friend,' up at Mt. Kisco."

Designer Oliver Smith recalled several weekends at Capricorn:

"I met Gian Carlo through Jane and Paul Bowles. They kept telling me about the very enchanting weekends they spent with Sam and Gian Carlo up at Mt. Kisco. I kept listening to this, and after about eight months of it, I couldn't stand it anymore. I said, 'For God's sake, why don't you get me in on this? I'd love to enjoy the fun of it and get out of New York on weekends occasionally.'

"Well, they arranged it. My first impression of Gian Carlo was that he looked like a very aristocratic sort of wolfhound—very lean, extremely alert, very tense, like a highbred. Sam I thought of as a sort of gray pussycat—that liked to play with wolfhounds. Of course, in the beginning I was rather shy and just content to sit there like a bump on a log, listening to all of them talk. They were all very loquacious and very articulate people. Their conversations were enormously amusing.

"Gian Carlo was extremely fond of Jane Bowles. Her sense of fantasy appealed to him. She would keep remarkable conversations bubbling. Soon we all became a little family—a family within a family. I was fairly poor at the time, and of course, Gian Carlo and Sam were supported by the Curtis-Bok Foundation and seemed to be very affluent, and they were very generous. They kept open house and entertained all of us.

"Often Tallulah Bankhead would come over. I remember one time we were trying to get her to play in Sartre's *No Exit*, which had been translated by Paul Bowles. We wanted her to play the role of Estelle. And she said, 'A lesbian part? How dare you? I don't know anything about such things.' She thought the play was stupid. Anyway, Gian Carlo, Jane and Paul Bowles, and I were going to talk her into doing it.

"She had brought her sister Eugenia along. Sam couldn't bear her. He said, 'I can't stand that woman.' Tallulah announced they could only stay half an hour, at which point Sam locked himself in the bathroom to wait out their visit. What happened, of course, is that they stayed for eight or nine hours. Sam continued to stay in the bathroom. We had to get food to him through the outside window. Tallulah spent her time chasing Jane Bowles throughout the house. We couldn't ever get her to discuss *No Exit*. Finally, at the end of eight hours, she rolled off, absolutely tanked, with Eugenia in this huge old Studebaker. Just before they left, Eugenia came up to me and said, 'For ten percent of the gross, I'll get Tallulah to do *No Exit*.' At this point, Tallulah and Eugenia got into a terrific row. They were already in the car, and we saw them scratching and pulling at each other's hair. After a while of this, they drove off into the snowy night. After they had finally left, Sam had to be coaxed out of the bathroom where he had entrenched himself, and it took us the rest of the evening to rescue him from a mood of complete prostration."

Oliver Smith recalled a birthday party at Capricorn:

"I can't remember whose birthday it was—it may have been Horowitz's. It was a tremendous party. We were all brought out to Capricorn in Cadillac limousines—that was part of Gian Carlo's style. At this party were the pianists Arthur Gold and Robert Fizdale, Paul and Jane Bowles, Virgil Thomson, Horowitz, and myself. There were others. It was a wonderful evening. Horowitz played beautifully. Sam sang lieder. There'd be games going on. People played bridge, charades, or whatever. There was conversation and constant eating. As it happened, a tremendous snow storm began. We decided we couldn't possibly leave. And suddenly it was just like boarding school! We were all sleeping over—three in a bed,

four on the living room floor, and on all the couches. I think only
Virgil Thomson managed to leave because he was very pulled
together and could get to the North Pole for an appointment. I
think Horowitz also left. But the rest of us just stayed, and we
stayed for four days. We ate everything out of the house. There
wasn't a scrap of spaghetti, macaroni—nothing. Finally, after four
days, Kinch got a little edgy and Gian Carlo said, 'Well, you've all
got to go because there isn't any more food.' It was the best country
party I've ever been to."

In 1944 Menotti met the Marquis de Cuevas, who had just
formed a ballet company named Ballet International. De Cuevas,
a man of high culture and imagination, was Chilean by birth and of
Spanish-Danish parentage. His full name was the Eighth Marquis
de Piedra Blanca de Guana de Cuevas. This flamboyant nobleman
had married the granddaughter of John D. Rockefeller, and with his
wife's enormous wealth attempted to establish himself as a lion of
the arts. He began his career auspiciously enough by mounting an
exhibition of world-famous masterpieces at the New York World's
Fair of 1939. Becoming enamored and fascinated by dance and the
world of ballet, he next wished to create a major ballet company
that, along with the classics, would present new works commissioned by the Marquis and danced by internationally renowned
artists.

Oliver Smith had already met de Cuevas. "De Cuevas was a very
complicated, fascinating character. He was rather Proustian, and had
a Diaghilev complex. He loved to spend the Rockefeller money, and
he wanted to create this ballet company. He was very interested in
meeting composers and painters and writers. He asked everybody
for ideas, and he would pick the brains of people like Dali, Balanchine, and Massine. He also came to me for ideas, and it was I who
suggested that he engage Gian Carlo Menotti to write a score for
him. At any rate, when Gian Carlo received the commission, I
enterprisingly got myself the job as designer. I don't think Gian
Carlo particularly knocked himself out for me. He was crazy about
his friend Milena, who did the costumes for *Sebastian*—and very
brilliantly. As for my own sets, I think they were not my best things,
but were adequate enough."

When the marquis and Menotti met, discussion instantly turned
to a score for a new ballet, and Menotti was much taken with
de Cuevas' exotic personality. "I was very excited at the idea of

writing a ballet," said Menotti, "particularly because I had always wanted to work with my friend Milena, who I was certain would produce the most beautiful costume designs. I was also eager to obtain a commission as I was very low on funds. And so for the very meager sum of fifteen hundred dollars, I accepted to write *Sebastian*. Unfortunately I had made a totally mad mistake in giving the marquis the exclusive rights to the ballet for a period of ten years! It was a clause I later had reason to regret bitterly, because the marquis would never release the rights to *Sebastian*, even after he ceased to perform the ballet. At any rate, the atmosphere of the Ballet International was very strange indeed. At the time, Alexander Iolas was the company's director and between the marquis' megalomania and Iolas' 'nepotism,' there was constant havoc. People were fired daily, and without much explanation, while others were hired without apparent reason or necessity. It was a shame, because de Cuevas' love for the arts was genuine and Iolas had imagination and a keen eye.

"Despite my somewhat desperate arrangements—I simply needed to make money—I was excited with the idea of writing a ballet. The marquis chose the dancer Edward Caton to choreograph *Sebastian*. It was his very first choreographic effort, and I had quite a strange time with him. Caton was undoubtedly a man of great talent, but it was almost impossible to work with him. Caton himself suggested coming to Mt. Kisco to discuss the project. We made an appointment. I prepared lunch for him. At the last moment he called to say he couldn't make it. This went on for four consecutive days. Each time lunch would be prepared, and each time he would call with some dramatic excuse—sudden sicknesses, hospitals, deaths in the family. Finally, in despair, I called the marquis, who explained that Edward Caton seemed to have a train phobia. He was unable to board a train alone. The only way Caton could manage to come to Mt. Kisco would be if I came into the city and accompanied him back to the country. This I volunteered to do. I came to New York, picked up Caton, and we went to Grand Central Station. As we approached the train platform, he became visibly more and more nervous, and as we were about to step onto the train, he suddenly screamed, 'O, my God, I forgot my doctor's appointment!' and he ran away."

Menotti quickly abandoned the idea of working with Caton at Mt. Kisco. He took lodgings in New York and the collaboration began promisingly enough. Caton seemed captivated by the subject

Menotti proposed and seemed delighted at the prospect of working with Milena and Oliver Smith. As soon as rehearsals began, however, problems set in.

"There were all sorts of hysterics," recalled Menotti. "As time went on, I began to realize that brilliant as his choreography was, it remained fragmentary. He seemed incapable of conceiving the ballet as a whole. Long chunks of music remained unchoreographed. I kept warning de Cuevas that if Caton continued to work in so disjointed a fashion, *Sebastian* would never be ready for its premiere.

"Finally I cornered Caton and told him that he simply would have to finish the ballet. It seemed to be going nowhere. Well, Caton told me he could not finish *Sebastian*. The dancers, including Francisco Moncion and Viola Essen, had learned their roles as far as they could. But things were at a standstill. Finally, on the day before the premiere, which I remember was October 31, 1944, I called in Kinch Horan, who was then a new member of the Martha Graham Company. He came to the rescue. Horan had no choreographic experience whatever, but he did the best he could, filling in the missing links and somehow putting the ballet together. Of course it looked it. It could have been a brilliant work, but it remained an unfinished work. Caton never came to see it and avoided meeting me."

The scenario of *Sebastian*, clearly inspired by Menotti's love of fairy tales, added immeasurably to its subsequent success. The ballet, in one act and three scenes, is set in seventeenth-century Venice. A prince falls in love with a beautiful and notorious courtesan, but his two sisters, Fiora and Maddelena, are both possessive and determined to break their brother's liaison. They steal the courtesan's veil, knowing that its possession will enable them to exercise their black magic over her. The sisters construct a wax image of the courtesan and cover it with her veil. They plan to kill her by piercing the image with arrows. But the Moorish slave, Sebastian, who loved the courtesan, substitutes himself for the wax figure and receives the deadly arrows. By his self-sacrifice he breaks the evil power, reuniting the prince and his beloved.

The title role was brilliantly created and danced by Moncion, and Viola Essen's courtesan was equally powerful. John Martin, writing in the *New York Times*, found Caton's choreography only creditable, but considered Menotti's score superlative. "The music is by all odds the best part of the work, and in its excursions into unblushing melodrama, it is brilliantly effective."

The history of *Sebastian* is a long one. It received many performances subsequent to its premiere in 1944, and it is in the repertoire of major ballet companies, which perform it to this day. In 1946 *Sebastian* was given by the so-called Original Ballet Russe at the Metropolitan Opera. Moncion again danced the title role, while the courtesan was danced by Rosella Hightower and the prince by George Skibine. In 1947 *Sebastian* was given by the Grand Ballet de Monte Carlo. This time George Skibine danced the title role. These productions retained the original Caton choreography, costumes, and scenery. In time, other companies took on *Sebastian*, assigning new choreographers to work with Menotti's melodious score. One of these was Agnes de Mille, who choreographed *Sebastian* for the American Ballet Theater Workshop on May 27, 1957. The leading dancers were John Kriza and Lupe Serrano. The work did not seem to have been a success, as it received but a single performance. The next choreographer to collaborate with Menotti was John Butler. He mounted an entirely new version of *Sebastian* for the Nederlands Dans Theater on October 22, 1963. Butler then refined his adaptation for the Harkness Ballet, and *Sebastian* was given its first performance with that company at the Casino Municipal in Cannes, on March 4, 1966. The company brought Butler's *Sebastian* to New York during the same year, with Lawrence Rhodes in the title role and Brunilda Ruiz as the courtesan. This time, the decor and costumes were by Jacques Noel. The Harkness Ballet kept *Sebastian* as one of its major staples, and the work never failed to elicit high praise. In 1974, when Rebekah Harkness opened her $5,000,000 Harkness Theater near Lincoln Center in New York City, its opening night production was Menotti's *Sebastian*, this time choreographed by Vincente Nebrada. Overproduced in every way, with whorls upon whorls of dry-ice smoke inundating the stage, this *Sebastian* proved as cumbersome as it was heavy-handed. Only the succinct magic of Menotti's music wielded its usual power.

Menotti's interest in the ballet was surely developed through his association with Kinch Horan. It was through Horan that Menotti met Martha Graham, who later created ballets based on works by both Menotti and Barber.

"Sam and I both adored Kinch," said Menotti. "In a funny way we formed a very strange trio. We quite happily worked together. Those were the happiest years at Capricorn. The weekends were alive with artists, with people, with ideas. (By the way, it was Kinch who invented his own nickname. It comes out of James Joyce. Kinch was mad about Joyce.) He had a very personal and unexpected sense of humor and an unusually rich vocabulary. When he was twenty-six, he published his first book of poems, which was called *A Beginning*. It had a preface by W. H. Auden, and it got marvelous reviews by, among others, Jacques Barzun. Kinch was compared to Rimbaud, but as with Rimbaud, this early success was the beginning of the end.

Robert Horan has recently recalled that his early success with his first book of poems was in no way responsible nor significantly connected with his problems with alcohol. As he put it, "The writing was not the triggering factor. I could never do *anything* without drinking. As many writers could attest, very little writing of any quality is done under the steady and excessive influence of alcohol. The tensions and anxieties surrounding the premieres of Menotti's stage works as well as the many performances of Sam's music were much more acute for me than the publication of my own poems, which by comparison was a quiet event. Additionally, the emotional strain of the three-way relationship and the fascinating but rather high-powered personalities in their social world, made life perhaps not quite so serene as it seemed for a highly nervous and very young man."

Robert Horan, in addition to his talent as a poet, seemed possessed of psychic powers. Menotti said that living with him was a continuous adventure, but that Horan's extraordinary sensitivity made his life a terrible trial. During the years the three men shared, Horan developed alarming physical symptoms which may have been allergic reactions to medicine he was taking. Eventually the strain of Horan's behavior became too much for Menotti and Barber.

"His sudden changes of mood began to be a strain on the Capricorn household," said Menotti. "It soon became obvious that the apparent success of our triumvirate was illusory. We became fretful and jealous of each other's work and outside friendships. Terrible quarrels took place. Finally, all those wonderful years at Capricorn ended. From paradise, things became utter hell. Kinch would disappear in the middle of the night. We would get phone calls from him saying he was stranded in the Bowery. We would have to drive into the city and pick him up. Things became so impossible that we decided something had to be done. Kinch had said he wanted to take a trip to Europe, so Sam and I raised some money to send him.

We felt it would be best for him to be on his own, away from the turmoil of such a complicated household."

Horan traveled by freighter to Cairo, then headed for Italy. Letters came back detailing his travails, but he constantly assured his friends that he was writing and in good health. Menotti believes that the illnesses and strange symptoms were all caused by episodes of excessive drinking. When the composer was in Rome for the filming of *The Medium,* the two had occasion to meet, but it was clear that their relationship, though not their friendship, was coming to a close. It was the end of a magical era in Menotti's and Barber's personal lives. Still, their individual successes buoyed them up despite their problems with Horan.

During this period Barber wrote such works as his Symphony No. 2, the Concerto for Violoncello and Orchestra, the ballet *Medea* (commissioned by the Alice M. Ditson Fund of Columbia University for Martha Graham, and later titled *Cave of the Heart*), *Knoxville: Summer of 1915* (commissioned by the soprano Eleanor Steber), and the Piano Sonata (which would be given its premiere by Vladimir Horowitz). Menotti, in the meantime, had written the opera that would catapult him into fame far surpassing that which he had known earlier with *Amelia.* This work, completed in 1946, he titled *The Medium.*

CHAPTER

8

"If there is nothing to be afraid of, why am I afraid of this nothingness?"

(*The Medium*)

It all began inauspiciously enough. Menotti received a letter from Columbia University asking him if he would write a little work for their Brander Matthews Theater. He wrote back saying that he would do so on the condition that he might be allowed to stage it himself. Menotti blamed part of the failure of *The Island God* on its poor staging and resolved never again to entrust the premieres of any further works to anyone but himself. Columbia agreed to the conditions. He asked his friend Oliver Smith to design the sets and Fabio Rieti, son of the composer Vittorio Rieti, to do the costumes. It should here be noted that Menotti's *Amelia Goes to the Ball, The Old Maid and the Thief,* the Piano Concerto, and *Sebastian* had by this time been published by Ricordi. (Menotti had first approached Barber's publisher, G. Schirmer, but they did not take him on.) When Menotti told his publisher that his next work would be an opera called *The Medium* and that it would be given its world premiere at the Brander Matthews Theater, they were appalled. Ricordi felt that after having been performed at the Metropolitan Opera, it was too great a comedown to write a work for Columbia University. What is more, they felt disinclined to publish a small chamber opera. Menotti had no intention of changing his plans, and his contract with Ricordi was cancelled. There would be further complexities with publishing houses. When *The Medium* was completed and successfully performed, G. Schirmer's, then under the direction of the composer William Schuman, took him on—even though Schirmer's had initially turned *The Medium* down. Later,

Menotti would break his contract with Schirmer's and return to Ricordi; later still, he would have a fight with Ricordi, and return to Schirmer's—his present publisher.

The Medium received its first performance on May 8, 1946. What the audience saw was an altogether gripping melodrama. The story of Madame Flora (Baba) who, like the Sorcerer's Apprentice, can no longer control the unknown forces she has set in motion, and the sinister atmosphere of her metaphysical battles with the mute Toby, from whom she tries to obtain the impossible answer she needs to quench her fears, make for exciting theater. The final scene, when Baba tries to destroy her obsessive doubts by killing Toby through the puppet theater curtain, can be hair-raising.

The production was conducted by Otto Luening. The role of Mme. Flora was sung by Claramae Turner, Monica was Evelyn Keller, and the mute boy was danced and mimed by Leo Coleman —a pupil in the Katharine Dunham school. On the next day, Olin Downes wrote in the *New York Times:* "Gian-Carlo Menotti's two-act chamber opera, *The Medium* . . . begins so badly that it seems hopeless. But by the end of the second act it has gripped the audience by means of its realistic musical theater.

"It is so ineffective in the first act because Mr. Menotti has written his own libretto. This, at least, is the only possible conclusion in the light of the evidence." Downes, while damning *The Medium* in his first paragraphs, nevertheless concludes on a bright note: "So there was a success instead of failure—a success of good theater and fluent theatrical composition. But someday we ought to get a real opera from Mr. Menotti."

Upon the conclusion of *The Medium*'s run at the Brander Matthews Theater, Menotti read in the papers that Ballet Society would be presenting a series of one-act operas during its next season. They announced Benjamin Britten's *The Rape of Lucricia* and Ravel's *L'Enfant et les Sortileges*. Menotti had met Lincoln Kirstein, who had, in fact, organized Ballet Society for George Balanchine, its artistic director. At the time, the company gave its performances at the Hecksher Theater in New York City. Menotti called Kirstein and asked him to lunch. He knew that Kirstein had seen *The Medium*, and that he had liked it. During lunch, Menotti asked him whether it might be possible to include *The Medium* in Ballet Society's forthcoming season. Kirstein promptly agreed to put it on but felt it would not make a complete evening. He asked Menotti to write a short work that might serve as a curtain raiser. To this

Menotti agreed and a few months later completed his short opera *The Telephone*. Thus it was that *The Medium* and *The Telephone* received their Ballet Society premiere on February 18, 1947. This time the critics were unanimous in their praise for both operas. The cast for *The Medium* remained the same as it had been at the Brander Matthews Theater, while the roles of Lucy and Ben in *The Telephone* were sung by Marylin Cotlow and Paul Kwartin.

The Telephone, subtitled *L'Amour à Trois*, is one of Menotti's more frivolous—yet delightfully wise—works. It stands together with *Amelia Goes to the Ball* and *The Old Maid and the Thief* as a typical example of Menotti style in opera buffa. There is a brief overture in the classic style, full of ironic and incisive melodic phrases. The curtain rises on Ben's ill-fated attempts to declare his love to Lucy—attempts invariably frustrated by a jealous rival: the telephone. Only through the telephone itself (hence the subtitle) does Ben finally reach Lucy's heart.

Writing in the *Herald Tribune*, Virgil Thomson reviewed the Ballet Society's new double bill. After outlining the plot of *The Medium*, Thomson says, "No such reduction of the plot can give an idea of how absorbing this work is from beginning to end. I have heard it three times, and it never fails to hold me in thrall. Mr. Menotti's libretto, which he wrote himself, and his music, form a unit in the most satisfactory way imaginable. The whole is deeply touching and terrifying. . . . The play rings every heartstring. I cannot conceive the whole work otherwise than as destined for a long and successful career. *The Telephone* . . . is gay and funny and completely humane. Both operas, indeed, are infused with a straightforward humanity that, for all their being cast in the mold of classic theatrical genres, is a welcome note of sincerity in contemporary operatic composition. Their librettos are skillfully made, and their music is skillfully composed. But that is not the main point. Their unusual efficacy as operas comes from their frankly Italianate treatment of ordinary human beings as thoroughly interesting in every way. . . . *Evviva* Menotti!"

In 1946 a tall, handsome, athletic-looking young man named Chandler Cowles had just gotten out of the navy. He came to New York to start a career in the theater. He looked up a college friend, Efrem Zimbalist, Jr., whom he had known at Yale. Zimbalist was also seeking a career in the theater. Chandler Cowles soon found himself in the successful Broadway revue, *Call Me Mister*. During the run of the show, Zimbalist came to his friend and told him he had something he wanted to discuss. "I have a friend who has written a little musical," he told him. "He wants to put it on in New York, but he doesn't know how to go about it." "Who is this man?" asked Cowles. Zimbalist dodged the question. He would only say that he was an Italian, and that the "musical" was called *The Medium*.

"I thought Efrem was crazy," recalled Cowles. "But I said that I knew a few people in the theater, and if I could get a copy of the script, I would send it around to them. Of course, the man who wrote the "musical" turned out to be somebody called Gian Carlo Menotti. And of course, the musical turned out to be an opera, which was a bad word in those days. Anyway, Efrem gave me the piano score with the words in it. I put it on my bed table. It remained there for three weeks. One night I came home very late and had nothing to look at. I picked up *The Medium* and started to read it. What caught my eye was the libretto. The first thing I read was the aria 'Mommy, mommy, dear, you must not cry for me.' That started me off. I read the whole libretto and was knocked out by it.

"I called Efrem the next day and said, 'This is extraordinary! Who is this man Menotti?' Efrem said that Menotti was a composer who was teaching composition at the Curtis Institute and wanted to put this thing on Broadway." Chandler Cowles made some halfhearted attempts to interest producers. None of them showed the slightest interest in *The Medium* or *The Telephone*. Finally he went to Zimbalist and said, "Let's you and I produce it. Let's take over the Ballet Society production." Zimbalist agreed and arranged for Cowles to meet Menotti.

"I'll never forget our first meeting," said Chandler Cowles. "It took place at Sardi's Restaurant after a performance of *Call Me Mister*. Gian Carlo came with Sam Barber. I had, of course, heard of Sam Barber and was impressed and happy to meet him. And with Sam was this man who turned out to be young and amusing and intelligent and funny and charming. I had thought Menotti would be some old professor with pince-nez and very academic. Gian Carlo was very excited about the prospect of our producing *The Medium* on Broadway. He went around calling me his 'prodooocer.' And so we took over the production from the Ballet Society and put it on Broadway. We rented the Barrymore Theater and spent thirty thousand dollars. I put up ten thousand myself. Between Efrem and me, we raised the other twenty thousand."

Menotti had hoped to retain his original cast of *The Medium,* but Claramae Turner, the original Baba, decided not to risk the transfer. "We looked for a replacement," said Menotti, "and couldn't come up with anyone. One day a friend of mine, Lanfranco Rasponi, called me up and said, 'There is an absolutely marvelous woman whom you must hear. Her name is Marie Powers.' I invited Marie Powers to come to Capricorn. She arrived looking very grand and announced that she was not "Marie Powers" but Contessa Crescentini. She gave herself many airs. She kept saying, 'Well, I must look at the score. I must think about it. It sounds quite interesting, but I must think of my career because I have sung in many important theaters of the world. Just let me keep the score for some weeks and I'll let you know.'

"Well, we all just sat there looking at this *grande dame.* All of a sudden, she changed her tune entirely. She sort of sprawled herself on the couch and said, 'Oh, for God's sake, let's cut this out. I've got exactly forty cents in my pocket and I may as well say yes. Of course I'll do it.' We became instant friends—though not for very long."

Marie Powers was hired to sing the role of Baba. Menotti also wanted to retain the services of Leo Coleman, who had enacted the role of the mute boy, Toby. "We couldn't find him anywhere. We went to the Katharine Dunham school to look for him, and were told he was no longer there. But they gave us an address in Harlem. Well, we finally found him, practically starving. We bought him food and milk and told him he had a Broadway contract. He could hardly believe it."

The Medium and *The Telephone* opened at the Ethel Barrymore Theater in 1947 to extraordinary reviews. Menotti, who remembered the poor *New York Times* review by Olin Downes when *The Medium* was done at the Brander Matthews Theater, decided to announce in the press that the opera would be given in a completely new version. "It was very funny, because I didn't change a thing," said Menotti. "It was exactly the version we did at Columbia. The only change was some additional music for the end of the first act. When Olin Downes reviewed the Broadway production, he said, 'Now that Menotti has cut it, it makes the work tighter.'"

In point of fact, Olin Downes had written: "*The Medium's* first act has been tightened up and given more concentration. . . . Whether Mr. Menotti is utilizing ideas of his own or idioms which he has absorbed from Puccini, Ravel, Rimsky-Korsakov, and other composers, we have here the quality of opera. It is dramatic music, emphatic in action as well as feeling, and in essence song, which is what opera must be. No other American composer has shown the inborn talent that Mr. Menotti, Italian by descent, unquestionably possesses for the lyric theater." Other rave reviews ensued, and Gian Carlo Menotti was launched as a major figure on the American musical scene.

Despite the enthusiastic reception by the press of Menotti's operatic double bill, theater-going audiences did not at first flock to the Barrymore. Before *The Medium* opened, Menotti walked into the Edison Hotel and asked for a room overlooking 47th Street. There he sat vigil, watching the box office at the Barrymore to see how many people stopped to buy tickets. He learned that the total advance sale came to forty-seven dollars. No Broadway house had ever before presented anything as musically serious as an opera. No matter how theatrical and dramatic, *The Medium* was something entirely new on the New York stage. Chandler Cowles remembered the first perilous weeks of Menotti's strange presentation.

"Well, nobody came. The notices were marvelous and the houses were empty. The production had no stars and nobody had ever heard of any of us. Also, we were playing against a big Ethel Merman hit at the Imperial Theater—I think it was *Call Me Madam*. And so we strung along for five weeks, pouring more and more money into this thing, just to keep it going. We all thought we'd land in jail because we had a $5,000 a week 'nut,' and very often our ticket sales would come to $700. If we had been intelligent, we would have closed. But we had the enthusiasm of youth, and we just refused to close it. Then an extraordinary thing happened. Menotti decided to write a letter to Arturo Toscanini, inviting him to come to see the show."

Menotti recalled the event. "Knowing of Toscanini's propensity for doing the opposite of what was expected of him, I wrote him saying that I knew he would never come, but that as a fellow Italian, I felt it my duty to invite him to see *The Medium* and *The Telephone*. To my great surprise the ruse worked and he answered and said, 'Dear Menotti, why do you say I will not come to see your operas? Of course I'll come. Reserve a box for me.' Naturally, we told our press agent about this and he let it out to the press. As Toscanini was hardly ever seen in the midst of a New York audience, his presence at the Barrymore caused a sensation, and was commented upon by almost every newspaper columnist. Astonishingly enough, Toscanini returned on the following night, and a few days later he called me and said he wanted to see *The Medium* again. We spread the word that Toscanini was coming for a third time. Of course by then we had sold-out houses. *Life* magazine came, and Gjon Mili photographed the production. We ran on Broadway for eight months."

It was a triumphant period for Menotti, and *The Medium*'s success brought stardom to the quixotic and eccentric Marie Powers. Olin Downes had called her "a wholly exceptional singer with all sorts of colors as well as dramatic brilliance. She is a great actress." The contralto had grown up in Mt. Carmel, Pennsylvania, and had majored in music at Cornell University. She hoped for an operatic career, and was taken abroad by her family to study at the Royal Conservatory in Florence. Singing primarily in Europe, she returned to the United States in 1940 and for the next six years toured with the San Carlo Opera Company. In 1947 she scored her greatest triumph as Mme. Flora and would appear in countless revivals of *The Medium*.

Menotti considered the contralto as something less than amiable. "Of course, she was the perfect Baba. But as time went on, she became a terrible prima donna. Also she was quite bizarre. She took fencing lessons on her day off and used to roller skate to every performance. She lived at the Hotel Wellington, and every night she'd put on her roller skates and roll down Broadway to the theater. She was a mad, mad woman. Unfortunately she developed a sado-masochistic obsession about me and loved to make me angry. The sad thing about Marie was that as soon as she became famous, her performances became very campy and very hammy. Although she was an artist, she could become a very undisciplined actress. It was through Marie that I came to realize that I was a good stage director, because I really taught her how to act—almost gesture by gesture. I had to watch over her all the time. If I hadn't controlled her, she would have turned *The Medium* into a farce.

"Anyway, she became more and more difficult. One day she called a meeting. She asked Zimbalist, Cowles, and me to meet with her lawyer. When we all got together, the lawyer made a very long speech to the effect that Marie Powers was responsible for the great success of *The Medium;* consequently she was now entitled to receive top billing over mine. And what is more, she wanted her name three times as big as mine on the marquee. I immediately agreed to her demand, for I couldn't care less about billing. I was, however, offended by her supercilious and unfriendly attitude. How much nicer it would have been if she had come to me personally. At any rate, this is just to point out that Marie Powers proved incredibly vain and terribly difficult."

When *The Medium* and *The Telephone* closed on Broadway, its two young producers decided to take the works to Paris and to London, where again the production met with extraordinary success. This resulted in innumerable stagings throughout Europe, and Menotti's name now became internationally known. Chandler Cowles recalled the Menotti of those years:

"Gian Carlo was a great influence on me—enormous. He taught me about the integrity of the arts. In those days he was exactly as he is now, except that he seemed more innocent. But he was always an artist. You see, I believe all great artists are basically magicians, and Gian Carlo is a magician. He had this enormous idealism about his art, about the art of the theater, and about life in general. As a person, Gian Carlo could cast spells on people. He cast spells on all of us. He had a very strong psychological hold on us. We all adored him and still do.

"Gian Carlo is a combination of a saint and a devil. He is capable of the most extraordinary kindness and sensitivity. At other times he can be full of intrigue. This has caused chaos in his life. Of course, I didn't understand his life at all. I was very innocent about all that. I was brought up a New England puritan—and I was married. But it was the childlike thing in Gian Carlo that got to me. He was a magician, a real Merlin to us! He would dominate us and we didn't even know it. Then he would take over our lives. Gian Carlo's compulsion is that he is the mother of us all. He tells people how they are to live, who they are to live with, what they are to do. He has a very strong maternal instinct. This is very touching. He will do anything for his friends. He will give everything away for them. I didn't understand that part of his nature at all. We were very close friends for a long time, but I didn't understand that part of him at all."

Samuel Barber echoed these sentiments somewhat: "Gian Carlo immediately had the humor of Alice in Wonderland. From that developed his sense for the 'buffo,' which was not really very Italian after all. In a way he had an Anglo-Saxon humor. He was a passionate reader. He read all the Russians—in French. And he spoke French very well by the time *The Medium* rolled around. He was always compassionate, and there would always be a couple of underdogs hanging around whom he would help in some way. He rather liked that role. He liked living well. When he began to have money, I noticed that. He likes a rather luxurious life—if it's possible. If it isn't, he doesn't complain."

Reflecting upon the Menotti of that period, Barber said further: "Gian Carlo is much more intelligent than people give him credit for. That was one of the reasons I liked him to begin with. I also liked him because he was outside of the mainstream of new music. Most of the new music of the time bored me utterly. Gian Carlo was striking out on his own. He found his own idiom. Nobody was writing operas when he did. He's worked much harder than people think. He's a much better musician than people realize. And he's an excellent critic. He's the best critic I know, of music in general, and he has an independent mind. In the early years he would come to me for advice, and my advice was generally negative. For example, I told him that *The Medium* had the most idiotic story imaginable, and that it would never have a success. So you see. . . . The point is, Gian Carlo saw the whole stage, and I didn't.

"From the first, I was jealous of Gian Carlo. I was jealous of his success. Of course, I'm jealous of everybody's success. Even the slightest thing at the bottom of the page of the *Times* upsets me. And yes, it was hard to see all those people around him. When there are no people around Gian Carlo, we have absolutely fine times together. But there are all these people . . . and they just won't go away! At any rate, when *The Medium* turned out to be a huge international success, Gian Carlo was taken up by absolutely everybody, and he knew exactly how to enjoy all that attention."

In Menotti's career as a composer, *The Medium* proved a seminal work. Of all his operas, it is probably the most original. Superficial critics have called Menotti's music background music. They said so from the first. In *The Medium* the only so-called aria is Monica's song, "Black Swan." It is actually an arietta which imitates the aura of a gypsy folk song. For the rest, *The Medium* seems made up of a long series of recitatives. This enormously skillful blending of words and music, without the presence of great melodic sweeps, succeeded in keeping audiences completely riveted to the story line. People have erroneously assumed that *The Medium* works because the libretto is so strong. The fact is, no opera can be digestible unless it has musical value. One can think of gripping plays that have been turned into operas and failed. If a strong play is not transfigured by very strong music, the music becomes a hindrance. Thus it cannot be said that the score of *The Medium* is mere background music. Without the propelling drive and texture of Menotti's score, without its acute and subtly integrated momentum, which binds music to word, word to action, action back to music, *The Medium* would not have been a success.

Critics have also pointed out that *The Medium* is a work in the Grand Guignol tradition. They have called it that because someone gets killed at the end of the opera in a sinister atmosphere. This is another fallacy, for in that case, many of Verdi's operas (*Rigoletto,* for example) might be put into the Grand Guignol category. What Menotti set out to write was a purely symbolic work. As Menotti put it, "Despite its eerie setting and gruesome conclusion, *The Medium* is actually a play of ideas. It describes the tragedy of a woman caught between two worlds, a world of reality, which she cannot wholly comprehend, and a supernatural world, in which she cannot believe. Every character in it has symbolic dimensions: Baba of Doubt, the three clients of Faith, Monica of Love and Toby of the Unknown."

Menotti's friend, Robert Horan, described *The Medium* in even more telling terms, in an article entitled "Notes on the Lyric Theatre of Menotti," which appeared in a theater program of one of the opera's later productions.

"The Medium" is essentially dominated by a philosophical idea. The fact that its theatrical appearance is so vivid, filled with eerie light and ectoplastic veils, murders and madness, is apt to blind people to its curious, relentless examination of the nature of faith. The pathetic little group of believers, who have seen the disembodied loved ones in the air over their heads, or heard their remembered laughter tinkling in the dark, are not to be cheated of this grotesque but so human solace. Their faith brought them here and sustained them against the most bold and eccentric trickery. But Mme. Flora, lost and loveless, enclosed in the closet of her alcoholic machinations, has no support. Her innocent child and the enigmatic gypsy reach each other in some mute loving contact, and find some faith of their own. But for Mme. Flora what can this cold hand in the dark, this unexpected gesture that terrifies her signify? Is it the revenge of the unlettered and meanly treated boy? An accident, a delusion, a genuine phenomenon, a penance for the guilty? And the fact is, the crucial philosophic, as well as telling dramatic fact is, that she will never know. It will drive her beyond the rational into acts of violence, because she has sold her chance for peace, or even intelligent disbelief; she is the victim of her own frauds. And so rather than the mere scaffolding of melodrama, there is the firm field of tragedy.

In looking through the score of *The Medium* one notes many markings indicating "silences." These silences Menotti worked out with tremendous care, and he decries the fact that in so many productions of *The Medium* directors do not pay sufficient attention to them. "I use silences in a very histrionic way," said Menotti. "People are afraid of silences and they never quite observe them. They *must* do so." Menotti also considers the work extremely delicate and wishes his characters to be carefully balanced in terms of characterization. They must not overdo their roles. It might be added that *The Medium* is often performed in large theaters—something Menotti feels is wrong. Since it was conceived as a chamber work and intended for small theaters, he prefers that the work be given in intimate houses. Originally written for an ensemble of only thirteen instruments, the string quartet of the original orchestration must be enlarged to a full string body when performed in large theaters.

As noted, *The Medium* and *The Telephone* became international successes after the operas were produced in Europe. On April 29, 1948, they opened in London at the Aldwych Theatre, to splendid reviews.

Menotti was now sought out by the London intelligentsia, and a new round of parties commenced. It all became something of a strain. In a letter to his friend Robert Horan, Menotti describes his London sojourn:

"Well, well, well. It's all over, thank God! So exciting and so exhausting; Tragedy after tragedy before the opening—*terrible* dress rehearsal—scared to death—everybody dreadfully nervous, and then . . . a brilliant opening—wonderful performance, and an hysterical audience. They screamed until they tore the roof down. Marie Powers had to make a little speech (it is customary here), but they went on screaming, until I made one too. (Can you imagine Giaco making a speech to a London audience with his best British accent!!)

"All of the write-ups were very kind—we didn't get a single bad review (a bad review in London is downright poisonous!), but many noncommittal: 'this is something different. But what is it?' More or less what happened in New York. Also some raves and some poohpoohs! But there is no doubt that we were a success. We are becoming the talk of London. Will we run? God only knows!

"I've been seeing very few people, all of them only superficially amusing. That is to say, they quickly turn into bores, or, as some Frenchman or other said, 'they steal your solitude without giving you any company.' Supper with Robert Morley and John Gielgud. It was fun—once. Gigi Richter took me to see some painters. Amusing —once. I am so tired of the kind of people I am meeting. Too many 'amusing' people. I'm sick of them. The only thing that is keeping me here now is the filming of *The Medium.* If that cannot be done now, I'll spend a couple of weeks with Sam here or in Paris, and then, come right home."

Menotti had gone to London alone. Barber, who had suffered through the tribulations of putting *The Medium* on Broadway, declined to come to the London or Paris premieres. "Sam was always adverse to any of my more glamorous activities," said Menotti. "He thought it was all very harmful to my music. I begged Sam to come to London, but he refused. He sent me a note saying 'All that sitting around at Claridge's, and all the unsatisfactory publicity *The Medium* has had—the worry—I could not face it all over. I think you shouldn't follow *The Medium* around, otherwise you'll become like Mrs. Patrick Campbell, who said, "I used to be a tour de force, and now I'm forced to tour!" ' "

The first French production took place on June 17, 1948, at the Theatre de la Renaissance. For the occasion, the librettos of both works were translated into French and sung by the American cast, including Marie Powers.

"We had an opening night that was really quite exciting," Menotti remembered. "Actually it all began very badly because on the night before the opening, there was a big, fancy dress ball given by the Princess de Polignac. Bébé Berard had dressed himself in a costume of a concierge. He looked exactly like Marie Powers. When Marie appeared on stage the following night, the entire audience burst into gales of laughter. They all remembered Berard's costume. Of course Marie Powers went absolutely to pieces. Fortunately, there is a long pause before she starts to sing, and so she could wait for the audience to stop laughing. Nevertheless, *The Medium* was a great success in Paris."

The French press praised Menotti's *The Medium,* with accolades coming his way from many distinguished quarters, including Jean Cocteau, who wrote:

Menotti has made out of plays, operas and out of opera, plays. He has been able to find, in his admirable "Medium," a vocal style which elevates the ordinary and every-day into lyric drama. In his work everything is a *tour de force,* execution is concealed. The audience receives in the lump, as it were (but supple as waves), an amalgam of elements which, by a strange privilege, is never dispersed: proof in itself that a new element exists. New, yet as old as the world. Only that before such discipline of stage-craft as his, one might have believed that the privileges of the antique theater were never again destined to flower.

Menotti again enjoyed extraordinary celebrity and began to meet Paris artists and intellectuals. He attended innumerable soirees and had memorable encounters with such well-known figures as Cocteau, Jean Genet, and François Mauriac. It was in Paris that he met Lila de Nobili, who remains one of his closest friends, as well as Edmonde Charles-Roux, then the editor of French *Vogue*. Both women greatly influenced his life over a certain period, and Menotti's collaboration with de Nobili, whom he still considers the best theater designer in the world, is among his fondest recollections.

In 1950 *The Medium* was made into a film. It was shot in Rome and starred Marie Powers, as well as a young newcomer, Anna-Maria Alberghetti. It was Menotti's first encounter with film direction.

"In the not-too-distant past," wrote Menotti, "when the city of Hollywood still existed and its inhabitants were vaguely interested in my work, I had a charming conversation with Jean Cocteau on the subject of filmmaking. When I told him how worried I was at the prospect of having to face a camera, he gave me this delightful, if somewhat irresponsible, advice: 'The only way to make a good film is to know nothing about technique. Go straight at it, unprepared, and ask for the impossible.' Had this been an oracle from the mouth of the Cumaean Sibyl herself, I couldn't have obeyed it more religiously.

"There we were, the whole lot of us, plumb in the middle of the Scalera Studios in Rome, in our country clothes and with our picnic baskets, carelessly trampling on forbidden grounds, disregarding all No Trespassing signs, and enjoying the fair weather while it lasted —a director who had never before done a film, and who had an invincible distaste of anything mechanical (cameras in particular); a conductor who had never recorded a note of music (least of all for a sound track); a cast of singers who had never seen a film studio (much less acted in one); and producers who had very little money to spend.

"The first few days of shooting were indeed very trying for everyone concerned. I soon found out that when I asked for the impossible, I often got it, and it looked impossible too. I became timid and awkward—like those people who, on their first flight, never move from their seats, afraid that if they were to walk about, they might upset the balance of the plane. But picnics must have guardian angels, and my producers had just enough money to hire two of them. One was Alexander Hammid, the distinguished director-cameraman of *Forgotten Village,* the other Enzo Serafin, the man who actually photographed *The Medium.*

"We soon formed a telepathic trio. I announced what I wanted, Sasha [Alexander Hammid] explained to everybody what I really should have said, and Serafin, a quick syllogist, finally did whatever he thought best. It would be highly inaccurate to say that I enjoyed making my first film. I missed all along the spontaneity of the stage and its immediacy of expression. I felt all the time the defeating personality of the camera, whose elaborate steel mask one must always wear, through whose glassy eyes one must look at the world— that devourer of time, that merciless Medusa which petrifies all freshness before it. Of one thing I soon became convinced: the director must be his own cameraman if his film is to be a real work of art, because to give personality to a film the poet-director's mind must live in the black-room behind the lens, he must lend his human soul to the artificial limbs of the camera. That is the reason why so many films, exciting and convincing though they may be, never reach the level of a work of art. Too often they are nothing but photographed plays, while the camera is a hack reporter rather than a visionary recreator. I even go so far as to believe that one shouldn't plan shots in advance, for in that way one cheats the camera of its creative power, as no one can really tell what its eye may unexpectedly discover. An accidental light, a seemingly unimportant detail, may suddenly be transfigured into all-important elements by the candor of the lens.

"A great deal of the film of *The Medium,* as a matter of fact most of it, was improvised. My colleagues can bear witness that I never looked at my carefully prepared script, and that very soon everybody else stopped looking at it. To the orthodox, this may sound an extremely dangerous method of working, wasteful of time and money, but actually the improvised shots took less time than the carefully planned ones and were by far the most satisfactory. Yet in spite of my brilliant co-operators, I often felt frustrated at having to depend so much on other people's skill. On looking at the rushes, I often felt like a young orchestrator who is surprised at the actual sound of what he has written.

"Apart from my inexperience, I was hampered by another obstacle which few directors have to face—a prerecorded sound track, an inflexible framework which forces both action and timing into its pattern. In my moments of frustration, I was often reminded of a story I heard many years ago from Sam Barber. A man was climbing mountains in Switzerland and met, on one of his excursions, an enchanting woman with whom he fell madly in love. He felt certain that she was to be the woman of his life, and having a camera with him, he took twelve photographs of her. On the way back, the girl slipped and fell into a crevasse, never to be seen or heard of again. He did not even know her name. All that he had left of her were those twelve photographs on the little roll of film. When he arrived back home, he locked himself in the darkroom and, trembling with excitement, developed the spool. He discovered that all of them were overexposed; so he strangled himself, twisting the shiny black film around his neck.

"I am often asked whether I liked the filming of *The Medium*. I feel that that is like asking a surgeon whether or not he liked a certain operation. All I can say is that the patient is still alive, and even looks a little better than before."

Menotti spoke of his tribulations with Marie Powers during the filming of *The Medium*:

"By that time, Marie had become such a paranoid bitch that it became impossible to work with her. One of the reasons was that *The Medium* was going to have another premiere, this time in Genoa. The famous Italian contralto Pederzini was asked to star as Mme. Flora. Of course, when Marie learned that someone else was going to do her part, she was furious and did everything to delay the completion of the film. She did this so that I would be unable to leave Rome and attend to the direction of the Genoa premiere.

"I remember, we were shooting our last sequence, a difficult close-up involving Marie and Leo Coleman, who played Toby. For the shot, Coleman had to keep his eyes open for a very long time, while Marie knelt over him to sing the words 'Is it you? Is it you?' I wanted a shadow to fall over his eyes, but each time Coleman would blink his eyes instead of keeping them open. Finally I found out that the reason he blinked so often was because Marie kept blowing in his eyes. She stopped her antics only when, after endless retakes, I threatened to leave for Genoa anyway and let someone else finish the film. That very night I received a hysterical call from Leo Coleman. He said he thought he was going blind. He had kept his eyes open so long under the bright lights that for a whole day he was completely blind. Of course, we were all terrified. Luckily he got over it. Poor Marie—peace to her soul—was a terrific performer but a pitiless colleague."

The film version of *The Medium* opened to mixed notices. Bosley Crowther, writing in the *New York Times,* said, "For all its musical mannerism, and its pictorial potency, *The Medium* is doubtfully valid as a dramatic presentation on the screen. Essentially, it is written in music, and through an orchestra and voices, it is conveyed. The illustrative capacity of the film medium is only supplementary thereto." *Time* magazine found the film skillful and imaginative but felt that a large gap still remained between its power as an opera and its translation into film. Olin Downes devoted a column to the film adaptation and felt that Menotti would have had greater success had he composed an opera especially for the film medium—something, by the way, that Menotti is still longing to do, if given the chance.

CHAPTER
9

Menotti's brush with filmmaking took a somewhat unexpected turn when an offer from MGM came his way during the run of *The Medium* on Broadway. Almost simultaneously a call came from David O. Selznick, then running his own company. Both MGM and Selznick wanted Menotti to supply them with film scripts and/or music. The composer became thoroughly intrigued, although he had no experience whatever in Hollywood script writing. But riding on the crest of success, he felt altogether secure in the knowledge that the film medium would supply him with yet another creative challenge. The Hollywood machine did not intimidate him. He had heard enough about Hollywood contracts to know that they could tie him up both artistically and in terms of time. In a gesture of independence, he resolved to draw up his own contract, which he submitted both to MGM and to David O. Selznick. He had nothing to lose.

"I gave myself fabulous conditions," said Menotti. "And I drew up a contract consisting of ten points. I agreed to submit to them one or more film scripts, with or without music according to my judgment. They had fifteen days to decide on whether they wanted to use my work. If they refused my ideas, all the rights would revert back to me automatically. I also agreed to spend no more than three months in Hollywood. If after three months things would not get started, I would have a right to go back home and receive my salary there. If they accepted any of my scripts, I would have to be appointed director. They would have no right to change a single word in my scripts without my permission. I would be the composer of any music used in the films. They could not ask anyone else to write a score for them.

"I drew up this contract without the assistance of a lawyer, and when MGM received it, they thought I was completely mad. Still, they knew about Selznick's offer—the two companies were great rivals—and decided to accept my contract. And so I left for Hollywood with Robert Horan. Those were still the great years at MGM. There, and at the home of David O. Selznick (who quickly forgave me for having gone to the rival company), I met a stream of big stars—Elizabeth Taylor, who was still a young girl, and Marlene Dietrich, Charlie Chaplin, Frank Sinatra, and Judy Garland—as well as writers such as S. N. Behrman and Christopher Isherwood. I also struck up quite a friendship with Ira Gershwin. It was Arthur Freed at MGM who actually hired me. And when I arrived in Hollywood, I was treated like a king."

Menotti was given Irving Berlin's studio. He was given a car and was permitted to make use of every research facility available. Menotti would spend hours watching silent films, for which he had a special love. After a few days, he began work on a film script which he entitled *The Bridge*. Months earlier he had read a story in the *New York Times* dealing with a group of refugees. During World War II, they had left Austria and landed in Hungary. When the war was over, they tried to get back into Austria and had to cross a certain bridge that was at the frontier between the two countries. When they crossed the bridge, the Austrians asked for their passports, which they did not have. They pleaded for entry, insisting that they were in fact Austrian citizens who wished to return to their own country. But the authorities would not let them through. When they tried to return to Hungary, the Hungarians did not permit reentry, as the group of refugees did not have the proper papers. For an entire week, this group of people—some 25 in number—lived on the bridge between the two countries—neither of which would take the responsibility of accepting them as citizens.

About three-quarters of the way through the script, Menotti showed the results to Arthur Freed, who deemed the subject too depressing for a movie. He thought the subject would not appeal to the majority of moviegoers, who were tired of sad war pictures. Menotti abandoned work on *The Bridge* and offered to write a second script pointedly entitled *A Happy Ending*, which dealt with five young children and their grandmother.

MGM liked the story well enough and even went so far as to begin casting it. Ultimately, however, the powers that be considered the ending of *A Happy Ending* to be much too negative. The people in the Middle West would never go see such a film. Menotti lost patience and returned home. He had had a good time in Hollywood, and the experience actually proved invaluable, for it was through his writing of *The Bridge* that Menotti conceived the idea for his next major work—*The Consul,* which he began writing in Hollywood.

The inspiration for *The Consul* was a *New York Times* item that appeared on February 12, 1947. It read as follows: "IMMIGRANT A SUICIDE. WOMAN DENIED ENTRY TO U.S. HANGS HERSELF ON ELLIS ISLAND. Mrs. Sofia Feldy, a 38-year-old Polish immigrant, who was refused admission to the United States by a board of special inquiry at Ellis Island, Febr. 6, committed suicide by hanging at the Ellis Island detention room, the Immigrant and Naturalization Service announced yesterday. Mrs. Feldy was denied admission to the country, after her husband, Antoni Feldy of Chicago, testified he had divorced her in November, 1940, on grounds of desertion. Mrs. Feldy, who came here January 19 with her daughter, declared she had received no notice of the divorce which her husband claimed he sent to her in Poland. Mr. Feldy agreed to accept his daughter, who was admitted on that basis, but his former wife was excluded by a vote of the board."

In reading of this tragic incident, Menotti found his leading character. Sofia Feldy became transmuted into Magda Sorel, the heroine of *The Consul.*

It took Menotti some three years to write his new opera. When he returned to Capricorn, he found a letter from the Curtis Institute asking if he would come to Philadelphia and teach composition. It was a perfect opportunity for Menotti to regather his resources in a quieter, academic milieu. He had had his fill of the social whirl and was anxious to resume work.

He returned to Philadelphia and the Curtis in glory. He had become a famous alumnus and had achieved renown through *The Medium,* an opera that, in effect, liberated the young American composer from the belief that to compose operas was an unrealistic and unattainable goal. *The Medium* proved a major breakthrough in a field American composers felt loath to tackle. With its success, they took courage and began writing short operatic works, which often shamelessly echoed Menotti's style. It was now possible to venture into opera, and any number of interesting works were written in this new spirit of creative daring.

Menotti was not a stranger to teaching. In 1943 he had returned to the Curtis to teach a course called "dramatic forms." *Amelia Goes to the Ball* and *The Old Maid and the Thief,* the latter another highly influential work, convinced the school that Menotti could impart some of his dramatic secrets to select students. One of these was the eighteen-year-old composer Ned Rorem, who subsequently won the Pulitzer Prize for music in 1976. Rorem had come to the Curtis on the strength of a number of his early compositions. Like Menotti and Barber before him, he studied with Rosario Scalero. The young composer did not entirely profit from his work with his composition teacher, whom he considered far too pedantic. But he enjoyed his course in dramatic forms with Gian Carlo Menotti.

"I automatically enrolled in it. There was one other composer in the class, plus a whole bunch of singers and performers. The other composer's name was Wainright Churchill. Menotti was far more interested in Churchill than in me. Anyway, we were both asked to write short dramatic pieces which would be performed in the class. I set an extract from Flaubert's *Temptation of St. Anthony*. I also set a speech that Huysman used in *Against the Grain*, which I did for two voices and piano. It was performed in Menotti's class by my fellow students Ellen Faull and Kenneth Remo. I remember developing a crush on Menotti. I thought he was the most glamorous man in the world. I had never personally come into contact with a person from Italy. I had known Italians, but not native-born Italians. He was dashing, charming, and I figured out all sorts of ways in which I could contrive to be on the same bus with him, or perhaps the same train with him coming to New York."

Rorem, who finally became friends with Gian Carlo Menotti, spoke of the significance of *The Medium*'s success:

"Whether you like his music or not, the fact exists that due to Menotti, and only Menotti, the whole point of view of contemporary opera in America, and perhaps in the world, is different from what it would have been had he not existed. If he had not existed—and if only Benjamin Britten had existed—there would not have been an upsurge in opera in America. Menotti wrote operas that were not only operatic, but wonderfully theatrical. Also they were easy to produce. They had small orchestras and they were singable. After the success of *The Medium* every composer in America said, 'If Menotti can hit the jackpot, so can I.' Everyone in the middle 1940s was writing operas like mad. And yet nobody made it the way Menotti has made it. People have aimed higher than Menotti, but they've also fallen lower.

"The reasons for his success are interesting to speculate on—the most obvious being his Italian origin and background. He was raised with opera. I used to think that this would make no difference, except that it does. The fact that Menotti owed so much to Puccini is beside the point. Menotti has never written an original note in his life, and yet every note immediately has the signature of Menotti. The fact is, his music lasts. I think every note of *The Medium* is truly inspired. The first time I heard it was on the radio, and even on the radio I was caught in its ghastly net.

"The so-called musical intelligentsia always disliked Menotti's music because it was immediately likable. This is suspect. You see, the reason he was originally liked was for theatrical reasons. When people like Tallulah Bankhead, who was not known for her musical perception, went to see *The Medium,* and got down on all fours in front of Marie Powers and said, 'It's the only opera that's ever chilled my marrow and thrilled my guts,' it was because Menotti was writing things that appealed to nonmusical people. People remembered the tunes and all of that became suspect. In musical circles, likability is a suspect word, and it became more and more so in the fifties when the Boulezes of this world took over. Charm and grace, the very essence of that which is Italian, and which pervades Menotti's music, are villainous qualities in America. You can, nevertheless, get away with it in opera, and Menotti did."

Ned Rorem went on to shape his own career, becoming one of the country's most respected composers of songs and producing notable works in all genres. Ironically, Rorem joined the league of young American composers who, in their attempts to write opera, did not succeed in the way Menotti did. *Miss Julie,* commissioned by the New York City Opera in 1965, proved a noble failure.

Menotti taught at Curtis on and off between the years 1948 and 1955. Dozens of pupils attended his classes on dramatic forms, and composition and orchestration, but only two—Stanley Hollingsworth and Lee Hoiby—attracted some attention as composers. The two would also become lasting friends of their teacher. As it turned out, both Hollingsworth and Hoiby began their serious musical studies at Mills College in Berkeley, California. And it was through Hollingsworth that Hoiby, who hoped to make a career as a pianist, came to the Curtis to study composition with Menotti.

"I had applied to the Curtis in the hope of studying with Scalero," said Stanley Hollingsworth. "Actually, at Mills, I was working with Darius Milhaud, who was giving summer classes in orchestration and counterpoint. He was a beautiful man and I adored him. We worked together for two years—from 1946 to '48. Then I sent some of my compositions to the Curtis and received word that they wished to see a song—something I hadn't sent. They said Mr. Menotti was teaching classes and he wanted to see a song. And so I sent one and was accepted. I remember when I told Milhaud, my former teacher, that I was going to study with Menotti, he told me that Menotti was a twentieth-century composer who wrote bad nineteenth-century music. Some years later, I had occasion to tell Menotti. He laughed and said, 'Well, Milhaud is a nineteenth-century composer who writes bad twentieth-century music!'

"I had heard about Menotti but wasn't very familiar with his music. In the meantime, I enlisted in the army. I heard that Menotti's *Amelia Goes to the Ball* would be performed in Chicago, and I thought I would go and hear it because I wanted to know who it was I was going to study with. It was during that performance that I met Menotti. I was twenty-one, and when I was discharged from the army, I went straight to Curtis and began to work with him.

"I arrived at the Curtis and was surprised to find that Menotti taught very much in the Scalero style. For a whole year he would not look at any of our creative work. It was counterpoint and more counterpoint. I found he was a man of great craft, although he didn't sweat over it. I was really in awe of him. I was impatient to start showing him my compositions, but he wouldn't look at them. He would say, 'Anyone who has a gift—a real gift—is not going to be destroyed by craft.' So we were writing fugues and madrigals. It wasn't that Menotti was an academician; it was just that he believed the craft had to be there. And so I worked on craft. Only a year later he permitted me to show him my original work. After I graduated, Menotti asked Mary Zimbalist to commission an opera from me, and I wrote *The Mother*. Years later Gian Carlo put the opera on in Spoleto, with sets by Lila de Nobili and conducted by Julius Rudel. It was marvelous. And he also made it possible to have the opera published by Schirmer's.

"I was at Curtis for about six years and eventually taught there. In fact, I took over Menotti's classes when he became busy with *The Consul*. Of course, we developed a friendship. I consider him a dear friend, and I'm sure he's fond of me. But to be honest about it, it's always better between us when a third party is present. I think I make him rather nervous when we're alone. I think our sense of humor is different. I'm close to Gian Carlo, but he is never completely at ease with me. I don't really know why. He's always very charming, very considerate . . . it's an intangible thing. Anyway,

Menotti was very kind to me, and after the production of *The Mother*, he spoke to Sam Chotzinoff, who commissioned an opera for NBC—*La Grande Bretèche*—based on a story of Balzac. So he was good to me.

"I helped Gian Carlo with *his* operas. I coached the second cast of *The Consul*. I even directed the Turkish production of it. So I was Gian Carlo's assistant for some time, and I enjoyed that very much. I like his music. I feel Gian Carlo writes everything with great love."

It was through Stanley Hollingsworth that Lee Hoiby came to the attention of Gian Carlo Menotti at Curtis. "I expected to become a pianist," said Hoiby, "I had studied with Egon Petri and Grant Johannesen. Still, I was something of a 'closet composer.' Anyway, Stanley Hollingsworth showed some of my compositions to Menotti, and shortly thereafter he called me from Philadelphia saying Menotti had accepted me as a pupil at Curtis. I don't know why, but I dropped everything and flew to Philadelphia. I arrived there October, 1948. I loved Menotti right from the start.

"In class Menotti was very gentle. He never gave the impression of being an authority. Lessons were supposed to be an hour long, but they turned into two- or three-hour classes. Gian Carlo taught everything except sonata form, which, in a funny way, I always held against him. At any rate, the first year we did Palestrina counterpoint. We did the same kind of counterpoint that he had learned from Scalero, and that Sam Barber had learned from Scalero. We never discussed harmony—ever. Menotti never went into Bach-language, or figured bass. I learned how to sharpen my compositional tools by doing that strict counterpoint that he was teaching us. One really had to use one's mind. It was like doing push-ups to develop your muscles.

"Menotti had very inventive ways of teaching us how to approach the mysteries of the orchestra. I remember one day in a class we each took a piece of staff-paper and a piano score of Brahms' Third Symphony. There were four people in that class—Louisa Raymond, Leonard Castle, Stanley, and I. We were told to play the adagio movement on the piano. Then he played us a recording of the movement. Afterward he said, 'Now orchestrate that movement in the way you think Brahms did.' We worked with the piano score. When we finished we were absolutely dumbfounded: Brahms had so many things going on that we didn't know about—little clarinet arpeggios, subtle things you couldn't hear but which give it a richness. This is

Gian Carlo (first on the left) with his brothers and sisters.

Gian Carlo at the age of four.

Portrait by Amisani of
seven-year-old
Gian Carlo sitting
with his brother Tullio.

RIGHT: Gian Carlo's mother at
about the time of his birth.
BELOW: The house in Cadegliano.

LEFT: Gian Carlo's Italian driver's license.
BELOW: Gian Carlo as train bearer at his sister Amalita's wedding.

Gian Carlo with his mother, his sister Amalita, and his Aunt Emma in Cadegliano.

Gian Carlo with Samuel
Barber and Gama Gilbert at
the Curtis Institute.

Samuel Barber as a student
at the Curtis Institute.
(*Herbert Mitchell*)

Capricorn.

Robert Horan at Capricorn.

Mary Curtis Bok Zimbalist.

From left to right, Chandler Cowles, Efrem Zimbalist, Jr., and Gian Carlo at the time *The Medium* was produced on Broadway. (*Dan Weiner*)

Marie Powers and Leo Coleman in *The Medium.* (*Mili Studio*)

TOP: Francis (Chip) Menotti in the French television version of *The Medium*.
BOTTOM: Menotti directing *The Medium*. (*Pierre Lelièvre*)

A scene from the first act of *The Consul*, with Marie Powers, Leon Lishner, and Patricia Neway at the table. (*Mili Studio*)

LEFT: Another scene from *The Consul*. BELOW: Menotti with his teacher Scalero after the premiere of *The Consul* at La Scala. (*Erio Piccagliani*)

A scene from *Amahl*, with Andrew McKinley and Chet Allen in the foreground.

The painting by Milena that inspired *The Saint of Bleecker Street*. It was used as the cover for the published vocal score.

George Tooker's set for the third act of *The Saint of Bleecker Street*. (*Erio Piccagliani*)

Thomas Schippers at the time he was coaching *The Consul*.

Menotti on the beach at The Lido.

just one example of the interesting things Menotti asked us to do.

"Another thing pops into my mind which I'll never forget. I took the first five pages of my first big orchestral piece. I had orchestrated it the best way I knew how. Menotti started with just the first bar. I can remember him saying, 'Put your nice trombone down here in B-flat.' I remember the word *nice*. Menotti had affection for his instruments. He always thought of them as friends, as part of the family, as something you respected and loved. So Menotti taught me to respect and love the orchestra. He was a real teacher. He gave tremendously of himself, so much so that at the end of the day he was just a wreck.

"The other thing that comes to mind is how Menotti led me very subtly into writing operas. I would never have done it otherwise. I hated opera. I still hate opera. But one day Menotti said, 'I want you to write a little scene for voices and small orchestra and we'll perform it in the opera class.' I didn't want to do that. I rebelled. However, I went ahead just to please him. Well, that's how I found out I had the gift to set words to music. He was very encouraging and later on gave me a real push. He suggested to Mary Zimbalist that she commission me to write an opera, and that's how I wrote *The Scarf*. Ever since then I've written mainly operas.

"Menotti never tried to influence us stylistically. I had met other students of composition who had studied with Hindemith or Milhaud or Copland. They all sounded like little Hindemiths, little Milhauds, little Coplands. Actually, at the beginning, I came out sounding like a little Menotti. But it wasn't his doing, it was my doing. I couldn't help it because his personal style is so strong. In class he would warn me about that. He would also warn me when I started sounding like Prokofiev or Poulenc. He'd say, 'Prokofiev has that particular trick—you shouldn't do that.' On the other hand, he never tried to dictate my style. I think he took me on at the Curtis because he felt a musical kinship of our inner instincts—they were very kindred.

"In the classroom, he was someone you couldn't take your eyes off. When he walked in, the whole room lit up. He captivated people by the way he talked. You were spellbound with everything he said. It didn't matter whether he was talking about the range of the flute or the oboe, or about the mysteries of counterpoint. He had an easygoing feeling about his own knowledge. I think he is a master of orchestration.

"I've heard it time and time again that the reason for Menotti's great success was because of his remarkable theatrical instinct. But I think the word 'theatrical' is very deceptive in Menotti's case. I think it is the musical impact of his operas that had never happened before. I began to assist him after I got out of the Curtis. I worked with him on *The Consul*. Of course, Gian Carlo is not very distinguished when it comes to meeting deadlines. He always gets into pickles about that. His ability to postpone is rivaled only by his dedication to aristocratic society. I think he likes to be a social butterfly. He likes to experience the *douceur de la vie,* as Sam would say, and he hates the *chagrin de la vie.* I'm afraid writing music comes more under the heading of *chagrin* than *douceur.* For me Menotti was a touchstone. He really taught me something. He was an important influence."

Gian Carlo Menotti's association with the Curtis Institute of Music had been a long and loving one. He enjoyed teaching and a return to Curtis seemed to be a nourishment—a replenishment for both his soul and his musical productivity. He had already begun *The Consul* in 1948. But one year earlier he and Samuel Barber had received a commission from Martha Graham to compose music for a ballet. Barber embarked on a work that would eventually be entitled *The Cave of the Heart.* This was Graham's epic dance based on the legend of Medea. Both the score and the ballet proved an enormous success, and it remains in the Graham repertory to this day. Menotti was not as successful with *Errand into the Maze,* although the work is still in the Martha Graham Company's repertoire. He recalled his meeting with Martha Graham:

"I met Martha Graham through Robert Horan, who was then a member of her company. She was a frequent visitor to Capricorn, and it was during one of these visits that she asked Sam and me for dance scores. To work with Martha was both very exciting and very frustrating. As other composers will tell you, she begins by giving you a very detailed scenario of what the dance is going to be. She gives vivid descriptions of its general mood. Martha has the extraordinary gift of inspiring her composers by throwing them all sorts of visual images. Often she does this in a rather inarticulate way, but somehow through her great effort to express herself, the ideas become even more suggestive.

"*Errand into the Maze* is the story of Ariadne. I followed Martha's instructions scrupulously, but during the very first rehearsals I realized that the dances she was weaving over my score had nothing or very little to do with what she had planned originally. This was unnerving because in my music I tried to keep in mind the visual images she had given me. Still, I soon found out that Martha had a magical gift for going to the more abstract core of the music—that she could enrich it with her own highly evocative personality. At first I thought she was turning my music into something other than it was intended to be. When she finished creating the ballet, it seemed quite appropriate. Although I can't help thinking that if I had known in advance the sort of dance she finally conceived, I would have given her a different and perhaps better score.

"It was both exciting and easy to work with Martha—as long as you kept a certain distance from her during rehearsals. Martha could become dangerously tense. The ballet had sets by Noguchi. I shall never forget how, during a rehearsal of *Errand into the Maze*, Noguchi had come in to object to the use of one of his props. Martha went into rage. She suddenly slapped Noguchi in the face, and quite hard, I may add. Poor Isamu! He stood stock still for a few minutes in the middle of the stage, then moved away as if nothing had happened. Evidently he knew his Martha and forgave her anything.

"The premiere of the ballet was not as successful as it should have been. The boy who danced the Minotaur had an unfortunate mishap. He makes his entrance with a big leap. On extending his legs, one of his testicles shot up into his groin—his dance belt was much too tight for him, and he was obviously in great pain. Somehow he managed to finish dancing the work, but it was a painful performance, to put it mildly.

"After Robert Horan left Capricorn I saw less and less of Martha Graham. We did have a few meetings during which we discussed the possibility of a dance based on the essence of fairy tales—a sort of surrealistic collage that would show the psychological, symbolic, magic, and poetic aspects of fairy tales. Sadly enough, nothing ever came of it. Perhaps the idea will become an opera one day."

CHAPTER
10

"To this we've come; that men withhold the world from men.
No ship nor shore for him who drowns at sea. No home nor
grave for him who dies on land."

(*The Consul*)

On March 15, 1950, the curtain rose at the Ethel Barrymore Theater on Broadway, unveiling Gian Carlo Menotti's three-act opera,
The Consul. When the curtain fell on this presentation, the audience
sat stunned, then burst into frenzied applause. They had witnessed
a work that would transform the American operatic scene and
would bring total and unqualified success to its composer. The press
was unanimous in its praise, and the rewards for Menotti were stag-
gering. No other composer in America achieved his celebrity and no
other celebrity was so honored.

New York in the 1950s boasted some six newspapers. Each one
vied for adjectives to celebrate the magnificence of *The Consul*.
Olin Downes of the *New York Times* led the accolades: "*The Consul* by Gian-Carlo Menotti . . . had an unquestioned and over-
whelming success. All rejoiced in this fresh discovery of Mr. Menotti's unequaled power of expression in the lyric theater. He has
written, composed, and directed this creation. He has produced
an opera of eloquence, momentousness, and intensity of expression
unequaled by any native composer. This opera is written from the
heart, with a blazing sincerity and a passion of human understanding. It is as contemporary as the cold war, surrealism, television, the
atom bomb. It is torn out of the life of the present-day world, and
poses an issue which mercilessly confronts humanity today. And this
is done with a new wedding of the English language with music in
a way which is singable, intensely dramatic and poetic by turns, and
always of beauty."

Virgil Thomson, writing in the *Herald Tribune,* commented: "*The Consul* is all Gian Carlo Menotti's—the play, the music, the casting and stage direction—a one-man music drama concentrated and powerful. To report on it as merely a piece of music would give no idea of its real nature. To recount it as drama would not experience its intensity. It is a play of horror and deep pathos, but these qualities in it are as much a result of musical stylization as they are of dramatic exposition."

The press as a whole was dazzled by the thirty-nine-year-old Italian-born composer, who had produced a new American genre and who had done so without the help of a librettist or stage director, a practically unheard-of phenomenon at that time.

But Menotti was not the sole object of acclaim. Patricia Neway, a relatively unknown soprano, became an overnight sensation in the role of Magda Sorel. Marie Powers, who had reached stardom through Menotti's *The Medium,* received unqualified praise. Interpreting the role of the mother, she abandoned the bizarre qualities inherent in her role as Madame Flora and provided poignant believability in a heartrending role.

The Consul takes place in an unnamed demogogic country— which has been variously interpreted as Communist or Fascist. The plot deals with Magda Sorel's desperate and hopeless efforts to join her husband, a haunted political exile, and her struggle against the human impassivity of the bureaucracy which keeps them apart. Most of the action takes place in a foreign consulate, which is also left unnamed, but is more often than not identified as home-grown.

The opera ends in the desolate Sorel home, where Magda asphyxiates herself by putting her head in the oven. The telephone rings on and on, as the consul's secretary tries, too late, to reach her and be of help.

The lives of other characters are woven through the plot; a number of them were inventions of pure imagination, but others were drawn from actual encounters in Menotti's past. The role of Magda was conceived after Menotti had read the *New York Times* article about the woman who had been detained on Ellis Island and there killed herself. The small role of Anna Gomez was inspired by the strange woman the young Menotti had seen in an Italian hotel dining room who shouted the word "no" while nervously running her hand through her hair. The role of the foreign woman was brought to life through Menotti's meeting with an old Italian peasant woman who had been on the plane with him and was visiting her daughter in the United States. Although Menotti's distaste for bureaucracy may have stemmed from his childhood in Cadegliano, when he had to produce a passport each time he swam in Lake Lugano (which is half Italian and half Swiss), it was surely the tragic fate of his Jewish friends in Austria and Germany which fired his indignation so eloquently.

The original cast of *The Consul* included, in addition to Patricia Neway and Marie Powers, Cornell MacNeil as John Sorel, Leon Lishner as the chief of police, Gloria Lane as the secretary, Maria Marlo as the foreign woman, Maria Andreassi as Anna Gomez, Andrew McKinley as the magician, and the voice of Mabel Mercer, singing the opening—unfinished—song on a record. Scenery was by Horace Armistead, choreography by John Butler; Lehman Engel conducted, and Thomas Schippers acted as musical coordinator.

The evolution of *The Consul* brought together a series of people whose lives would become entwined with Menotti's. Chandler Cowles and Efrem Zimbalist, Jr., who had produced *The Medium* and *The Telephone* on Broadway, were again the prime arbiters in the production of *The Consul*. Cowles recalled the early history of the opera:

"During the run of *The Medium* I went to Gian Carlo and said, 'How about another one?' And he said, 'Well, I do have an idea for a new opera. It's called *The Consul*.' I thought he said, 'The Council,' and I said, 'Why don't I commission it?' This was quite funny because, at the time, even though *The Medium* was a success, Menotti was broke. For some reason he needed two hundred dollars. I told him that I would give him two hundred dollars in return for which he would give me the new opera. Menotti agreed immediately. I wrote up a little piece of paper which said, 'For two hundred dollars, which I acknowledge receiving from Chandler Cowles, I hereby give him my next opera, presently called *The Consul*.' And it was signed Gian Carlo Menotti. I gave him the two hundred dollars and we both promptly forgot about the piece of paper.

"Two years later *The Consul* became ready to produce, and I had to go to Schirmer's to negotiate the contract. At the time, Heinz Heinsheimer was new at Schirmer's, and he was trying to make a tough deal. I happened to have mentioned to my lawyer that I had commissioned this work. And I showed him the little piece of paper —which I remembered about. It turned out that Gian Carlo had sold me the copyright for two hundred dollars. Had I been a tough guy, *The Consul* would have belonged to me and not to Schirmer's at all.

This whole business raised an explosion at Schirmer's. Finally I said, 'I don't really want to publish it. I want to produce it.' So Schirmer's gave me a nice contract and I gave them the piece of paper."

When Cowles and Zimbalist took *The Medium* to London in 1948, Menotti had already begun work on *The Consul*. Upon arrival in London, he took a small suite at Claridge's that had an upright piano in it. Menotti continued composing and Cowles would often badger him to sing some of the arias in the new opera.

"Gian Carlo sat at that little rinky-dink piano and sang me Mr. Koffner's scene. To this day I've never heard it sung better. Hearing this music and these words, I just knew that *The Consul* would be a great work, and more and more I knew that Menotti was a great artist. And so from then on, I would hear bits and snippets of the whole opera. Sometimes I would give little suggestions about a word sounding wrong, and Gian Carlo would always be very good about this. He trusted me. You see, we were very good friends, although I was never really part of the charmed circle. I had a certain stability as a friend. Anyway, in 1949 we began hunting for a cast and started to hold auditions at the St. James Theater on Broadway."

Among Menotti's greatest concerns for the production of *The Consul* was that its musical direction be impeccable. Chandler Cowles suggested that Lehman Engel be engaged to conduct its premiere. Engle had by this time made a considerable name for himself, both as a conductor and as the director of a small group of chamber singers called The Madrigal Singers. Menotti had heard Engel conducting his chamber group and was once moved to write him a fan letter. Throughout the years the two musicians had also met casually at social gatherings.

Lehman Engel remembered the circumstances of his being engaged as conductor for *The Consul*:

"Chandler Cowles called me one day and asked me to have lunch with him and Menotti at Sardi's. I was flattered to be asked because in my career I was deflected from what I really wanted to do, which was to work in the field of opera. I had seen *The Medium* and *The Telephone* and loved them. At any rate, I was thrilled and told Menotti and Cowles that I would happily accept the job, but that I had a problem with dates. I could only conduct *The Consul* for the first three weeks in New York, after which I had other commitments.

"After our lunch, I remember asking Gian Carlo when he would play me the score. He laughed and said, 'Never!' He told me that the composer was dead, and that I was speaking to the stage director.

He said, 'You will have to do the playing of the score, because I want you to create the performance.' I laughed and told him, 'Look, Gian Carlo, I've worked with a lot of composers, and I know you'll start screaming, because the tempi won't be what you want, and the dynamics will be different from what you have in mind. If you don't tell me these things, how will I know them?' Well, he said to me, 'No. I swear to you, I will never say a word until after the first public performance.' Of course, I believed that like I believed I could fly to the moon on a broomstick.

"But I will tell you that it was really true. I don't know how it was true, but it was absolutely true. Now, what really happened in the whole process of things was that he was, of course, very busy staging The Consul himself, and that meant daily rehearsals with the singers. Secondly, he was orchestrating the work at the same time. So he was incredibly busy.

"When I came into rehearsals, Thomas Schippers had already been hired. Tommy proved invaluable. He had been coaching the singers and I could easily tell that he was a consummate musician and a superb pianist. He and Gian Carlo had become very close friends. I went in and rehearsed with the singers and Gian Carlo was never present when I did. I, on the other hand, was never there when he was directing. Tommy was there all the time because he played for the rehearsals—my rehearsals and Gian Carlo's rehearsals.

"My memory of The Consul is practically a love song. My relationship with Gian Carlo was absolutely marvelous. He was an absolute angel. Tommy Schippers was a great help throughout. The only upset had to do with Marie Powers. It was during a rehearsal. You see, Marie had thought that because of her success in The Medium, she had the leading role in The Consul. When it began to emerge in all its glory that Pat Neway was, by far, the leading performer, Marie suddenly got it into her head that she knew a way of changing the sequence of things so that she would emerge the star. It occurred to her that there was a way for her to sing the big 'papers' aria. She told Gian Carlo that there was a way that she could sing it instead of Pat Neway. Well, he told her definitely no, and he shrieked at her and she shrieked at him—and they did most of that in Italian. I remember she said something so absurd that we all laughed. She said, 'It means so much to me, caro, that I have taken sacred vows that if you will give this aria to me, I will never again drink, I will never again smoke, and I will never again have sex.' At this, Gian Carlo screamed with laughter and shouted,

'It's not worth it, Marie. It's not worth it!' Finally he took the only stand that he could, and that was to tell her that the aria was definitely going to be sung by Pat Neway—that it had not been written for her."

The out-of-town opening of *The Consul* in Philadelphia brought many friends from New York. "I remember that Lincoln Kirstein came backstage afterward," recalled Lehman Engel. "Kirstein told Menotti, 'Well, of course, you must throw out the last scene—all that nightmare stuff.' You see, everybody had come for the sole purpose of saving the show. Gian Carlo, through it all, was long-suffering and patient. He listened to everybody and would say, 'Oh, yes, that's very interesting.' He was calm and nice, after which he proceeded to do absolutely nothing. He did not change a note of music and not a word he had written. I think he worked with John Butler on the choreography of the last scene, somewhat. He altered Jean Rosenthal's lighting a little bit. That's all he ever did. As far as he was concerned the work was finished."

When he died at the early age of forty-seven in December 1977, Thomas Schippers was the music director of the Cincinnati Symphony. A man of extraordinary and dashing good looks, the conductor undeniably owed much of his brilliant success to Gian Carlo Menotti. This is not to say that Schippers would not have risen to prominence without Menotti's guidance and help. There is no question that this young conductor showed unusual talent from the first, as pianist, organist, and conductor, but his meeting with Menotti proved a major stepping stone in a career that made him one of the most sought after and successful conductors of his time.

Born in Kalamazoo, Michigan, Schippers started piano lessons at four and played in public at six. At fourteen he became an opera coach and accompanist. A year later—it was 1945—he entered the Curtis Institute in Philadelphia. In 1950 Schippers settled in New York, conducting the Lemonade Opera Company, while coaching singers on the side. For several seasons during the early fifties, Schippers conducted repertory at the New York City Opera Company. Then, in 1955, with his Metropolitan Opera debut, Schippers became the second youngest (he was twenty-five) and the third American-born conductor to be engaged by the company. When in 1966 the Metropolitan moved to Lincoln Center, it was Schippers who opened the new opera house with the world premiere of Samuel Barber's *Antony and Cleopatra*. By that time Schippers had conducted in virtually every major opera house throughout the world, becoming a special favorite at La Scala. It is safe to say that Thomas Schippers' unequivocal artistic rise was in great part triggered by his fourteen-year relationship with Gian Carlo Menotti who, in 1958, made his young protégé the music director of the Spoleto Festival of Two Worlds.

The chance meeting with Menotti in 1950 proved a turning point in Schippers' life:

"Among the students whom I coached was a young bass, who came to me one day and said that he was going to attend an audition for Gian Carlo Menotti's *The Consul*," said Schippers. "Now, I had a pact with all my students that I would coach them but would not serve as their accompanist in recitals. Of course, I felt I was much too grand to serve them as an accompanist for things like auditions. At any rate, the young bass went to the theater where *The Consul* auditions were being held, and suddenly he telephoned me in desperation saying that his wife, who usually played for him, had been taken to the hospital that morning to give birth to their child. He would be losing a chance of a lifetime if he failed to audition and he was there without an accompanist. Well, I took the subway and rushed up to the theater. For some reason, the piano had been placed in the wings. And so I played unseen for the bass, who stood in the middle of the stage. It was awkward for me because not only was the piano one of those mini-instruments—there was no full keyboard—but there was no chair for the piano. I stood to accompany him in the dark. So, the audition was held and I left the theater. On the way out, I was stopped by a secretary and was asked to give her my name, address, and telephone number. I was very surprised, but I gave her the information.

"The next morning I received a call from Gian Carlo Menotti. He asked, 'Was it you who played for the young bass yesterday?' I said yes. He said, 'Would you prepare *The Consul* for me on Broadway?' Of course I was terribly excited, but I had a commitment to go to South America and tour with Eileen Farrell. In fact, I was to leave that very day. I told Menotti this and he said, 'Oh well, it doesn't matter, because I haven't finished the opera anyway. We can certainly wait three weeks for you to get back.' The terrible thing was that my plan was to tour across the country as a pianist when I got back from South America. I didn't dare tell Gian Carlo this. What I did was—I lied.

"I went to all the rehearsals, which would take up the morning and early afternoon, and then I would have cars waiting for me to take me to the airport to fly me wherever I had to play in the evening, and I would return every day in time for the *Consul* rehearsals next morning. This went on for three weeks. Neither Farrell nor Menotti knew any of this. Finally I was able to dedicate myself fully to Menotti."

While *The Consul* was having its pre-Broadway engagement in Philadelphia, Lehman Engel had to absent himself from the pit for a day. Thomas Schippers was advised that he would have to take over for that evening's performance.

"I was given ten hours' notice that I was conducting that night. Well, I had conducted at the Lemonade Opera, which had two pianos, but I did not call myself a conductor. I thought of myself as a composer and as a pianist and an organist—but not a conductor. Anyway, I remember Chandler Cowles saying, 'You're going to conduct,' and I said, 'But I don't know how to conduct.' I quickly realized, however, that he meant business. And so I was given the orchestral score, which I had never seen before. Mind you, I had ten hours notice. I went through all those pages all day long, and, of course, got sicker and sicker. I was in such a state of nerves that I had to be carried across the street from my hotel room to the pit. And that's how I came to conduct *The Consul*. Then Lehman Engel came back, and he continued conducting in Philadelphia as well as in New York."

Schippers recalled Menotti of those days:

"Gian Carlo was always an artist. When I met him he had already had a great success with *The Medium*. But he was too much of an artist to be carried away by his success. When I first saw *The Medium*, I did not, as so many others did, fall for it. But then I sat in the last row of the balcony. Perhaps I couldn't hear it properly. Anyway, I couldn't understand the enthusiasm of Toscanini or of anybody else for *The Medium* and *The Telephone*. It was one of the many times I was wrong, because I later realized what a masterpiece *The Medium* was. I must also insert here that I was one of the few people in the world who did not fall for Gian Carlo's so-called charm. Everybody fell for it—not just men or women, but dogs as well. I didn't fall for it because of my very boring blood—Dutch-German, very much from the north. That Mediterranean thing never captured me. But I could see it working on other people, like dropping salt on water.

"What did get to me in those early days was this mountain of sensitivity, and the fact that he was truly a great artist. I respect him more than anyone else in the world for his music because I happen to know it better than anybody else. Gian Carlo will tell you how many conductors have fallen on their behinds conducting his music. They assume that his works are very easy to handle. Well, *The Medium* is one of the most difficult works in the world to conduct. And so is *The Consul*. I think that's one of the reasons why today Gian Carlo doesn't receive many first-class performances of his works. People have the mistaken notion that they are facile. The fact is, conductors have never taken his music as seriously as I did."

When *The Consul* opened at the Ethel Barrymore Theater in New York, the first-night audience was nothing if not glittering. Arturo Toscanini was there. And the evening was given added luster by the presence of Leopold Stokowski and Dimitri Mitropoulos. Lehman Engel recalled that Toscanini was the first person backstage, embracing Menotti, Patricia Neway, and Marie Powers.

This was Lehman Engel's only association with the works of Gian Carlo Menotti, although he was the conductor for the original-cast recording of *The Consul*, for which he won a Tony award. "I've had occasion to see Gian Carlo a million times after *The Consul*,"said Engel. "He was lionized, feted, and adored by everyone. After *The Consul* he became incredibly famous and *Time* magazine did a cover story on him. I saw him everywhere, and every time we met, he was always extremely cordial and very pleasant. This may be a terrible thing to say, but I have a feeling that I'm not one of those persons that fascinate Gian Carlo. But I think he has affection for me. I didn't know a time when he didn't immediately embrace me if I walked into a room."

With Lehman Engel's departure from *The Consul*, all musical responsibilities fell on nineteen-year-old Thomas Schippers. *The Consul's* producers, Chandler Cowles and Efrem Zimbalist, Jr., were delighted with their new young maestro. "He was an extraordinary musician," said Cowles, "he was fantastic. At the time, his ears stuck straight out and he had bad teeth. Within a week, he had his ears operated on and his teeth were capped. And then, of course, began the great friendship between him and Gian Carlo."

For his part, Menotti looked upon the young Schippers not only as a friend, but as perhaps the most sensitive and intuitive interpreter of his works. "The thing that touched me more than anything about Tommy," he said, "was that from the moment he played my music he seemed to understand it so thoroughly. I hardly had to give him any tempi. It was really such an immediate understanding of my music. This moved me very much. He read through *The Consul*, which was still in manuscript, and guessed all the tempi and made all the right *rallentandos* and *accelerandos*, so essential to the interpretation. For many years I considered him by far the best interpreter of my music. The first time Tommy disappointed me was with *The Last Savage*, at the Met. He conducted brilliantly, but not with that same understanding. Or when he did *The Saint of Bleecker Street* in Spoleto, I didn't feel that sense of communion."

Among the scores of interpreters who have sung in Menotti's operas, none have had the remarkable success of Patricia Neway, who exploded on the musical scene with her shattering performance in the role of Magda in *The Consul*. If the critics were all of one mind over Menotti's new work they were no less unanimously ecstatic about Miss Neway's performance. An imperious, big-boned woman with large, blazing eyes set in a mobile and expressive face, she held the stage by dint of a strong and moving presence. Her voice, opulent and lustrous from high to low register, projected pathos and drama that lent poignant life to Menotti's searing arias, ducts, and trios. There was enormous credibility in her acting, and the role of Magda would henceforth be tied to the name Patricia Neway.

Menotti did not have Miss Neway in mind for Magda when she came to sing at an open audition for *The Consul*. Chandler Cowles remembered that Menotti had wanted a Viennese opera star for the role. He *did* consider Neway for the role of the secretary. After repeated auditions, however, it became clear that no one could more thrillingly justify the leading role than Patricia Neway.

The soprano was born in Brooklyn, New York, then moved with her parents to Staten Island, where she was schooled. There was little in the way of musical background in her family, although her mother loved good music and her father had quite a good tenor voice. Their child always had an urge to sing and was drawn to the pop songs of the day. When she began attending a private Catholic school, she sang in the choir and was given a number of solos. In time, Neway moved to Manhattan and trained with various voice teachers. She did not attend any particular music school but did go to college, where she earned a degree in science. But singing was in her blood, and she joined sundry choruses, including Robert Shaw's, and took a number of opera classes. In 1949, Benjamin Britten's *The Rape of Lucricia* was produced on Broadway. It was not a commercial success, but Neway garnered professional stage experience, as well as several good reviews. When Britten's opera closed, *The Consul* was beginning to hold Broadway auditions.

"I had been singing in Chautauqua," recalled Miss Neway, "when my agent called to say I should come to New York and audition for a new opera by Gian Carlo Menotti. I came back and sang some Verdi and other arias, and when it was over, Menotti called me down to the footlights and said, 'I don't know what I'm going to use you for, but I'm going to use you for something.' I auditioned three more times. Finally I sang one of the arias from *The Consul* and I was told that I could sing all the Magdas for the backers' auditions, until all the money was raised. Mrs. Zimbalist was the main backer, but I think we had to raise $75,000 more. These auditions were quite petrifying because the audience was always very select. I remember at one of them I had Toscanini sitting under my nose. Well, we did this for about two months, and I was never really told whether I would get the role of Magda or not. Finally Menotti had a gathering at Capricorn, and I decided to go up to him and say, 'Mr. Menotti, do I or do I not have the role?' He said, 'But of course you have the role.' We raised the money, we went into rehearsal, and little by little we all knew we were into something terribly, terribly exciting.

"We played in Philadelphia for ten days, and it was a raving success. When we came to New York, we never dreamed it would also be a commercial success. But *The Consul* turned out to be fantastically successful, and it paid off in four months.

"Of course, there are very few roles that are that fabulous. The role of Magda contains the qualities of great humanity, and to sing it was one of the greatest experiences of my life. Menotti directed me with great care. He usually inspires people, more than giving them specific direction. He would say things that were very specific but, at the same time, would allow his singers to look into themselves. Anyway, it was a rich, rich experience. We ran on Broadway for about eight months, before touring with it everywhere, including Europe."

Patricia Neway was no novice as far as performing was concerned. But she had never had to hold onto her identity and responsibility quite so much as when confronted with a co-star as powerful and egomaniacal as the temperamental Marie Powers:

"My memories of working with Marie had mainly to do with taking care of myself. I always considered her as a sort of rock on stage. However, if you bumped against that rock, you'd get awfully big bruises. Thank God I had a lot of stage-worthy things that I did instinctively. For example, I could easily upstage anybody, if anyone tried to do that to me. And I was often put in that position with Marie. Of course, she had her innings when she did *The Medium.* I was very careful to be professionally friendly toward her, and personally uninvolved. But on stage I had to be totally aware of her every move. When she was in a belligerent frame of mind, she could do things that were considered a little, shall we say, tacky. I mean, she would blow her nose real loud just when I had a quiet moment, say, after the baby's death—things like that. So I had to protect myself. Still, she had remarkable things to offer. I never complained to her personally. It would only have made waves. With Marie, I played it very cool."

Patricia Neway sang the role of Magda some 550 times during the course of some twenty years. Her last experience with the opera occurred in 1966 when *The Consul* was revived by the New York City Opera. It was a performance that found Neway not quite as vocally arresting as in earlier years. Menotti, who directed the opera on that occasion, seemed unhappy with Neway and indicated as much to the performer.

"Gian Carlo had not directed me in it in a long, long time. The older one gets, and the more experience one accumulates, the more one develops a technique that is uniquely one's own. Anyway, Gian Carlo falls in love with particular phases of your performances. And he wants you to repeat them. He would come backstage and say, 'But you did thus and thus back in Philadelphia!' Well, to make a long story short, Gian Carlo and I had a bad, bad time together in 1966. We were really at odds for the first time in all those years. He finally got quite angry with me and came into my dressing room right before the performance—I wasn't even quite clothed. Well, I threw him out royally. For the longest time, both Gian Carlo and I thought we'd never work together again."

But Patricia Neway did continue to perform in Menotti's works, albeit seldom directed by the composer. With the passage of the years, the luster and sheen of her voice diminished, and by the early 1970s she performed less and less. Patricia Neway had sung many Menotti roles after her triumph in the Broadway premiere of *The Consul.* She created the role of the mother in *Maria Golovin* and sang leading roles in *The Medium, Amahl and the Night Visitors,* and *The Death of the Bishop of Brindisi.* Throughout her career, she also directed several works by Menotti, including *The Medium, Amahl, The Old Maid and the Thief, The Telephone*, and portions of *The Consul*. In 1970, she assumed a leading role in Menotti's play *The Leper*. It would be her last association with Gian Carlo Menotti. In assessing her relationship with the composer, Neway said, "To me Gian Carlo is essentially an Italianate aristocrat. Practically everything about him fulfills that kind of role. Not that he plays it, but that it's essential to him. He is very childlike and very childish. He is very warm, very ebullient, full of humor of a certain kind, but he's also terribly self-centered. His concern is mainly with himself—it's an habitual self-involvement that often proved painful to me, because he doesn't really assess himself. He is captivated by the idea of being in love, and by love in general, in the romantic sense. When he was young he *talked* about love a great deal. I was never in his social circle, but I owe a great deal of my life to his creative genius."

The Consul won the Drama Critics Circle Award for the year 1950. Together with Carson McCullers' *Member of the Wedding* and T. S. Eliot's *The Cocktail Party, The Consul* went on to win the Pulitzer Prize. Menotti was enjoying an unprecedented success, and as Chandler Cowles said, he adored his fame. "Of course, Gian Carlo was always a gregarious man," said Cowles. "He liked his success. He loved little supper parties and dinner parties. Naturally it's a double-edged sword, because that sort of acclaim has its dangers. Being a very intelligent man, Menotti always knew that he ought never to compromise himself."

Menotti talked about *The Consul:*

"Of all my works, *The Consul* was written the quickest. I was very much inspired. The aria 'Papers, Papers' was written in one night. The orchestration of *The Consul* is very sparse. Every conductor who has ever done it has urged me to enrich the orchestration. They feel that for a large opera house, where it is generally given, it needs a richer sound. But I rather like the sparseness, which allows the text to be understood.

"As you know, the opera starts with a popular song, sung in French, by Mabel Mercer. In the opera the song is never sung to the end. I purposely left it unfinished. I've had many offers to finish it, so that it could be made into a pop song. Even Mabel Mercer herself, for whom I wrote it, begged me to finish it, so she could use it in her nightclub appearances. But I hate nightclubs, and so I never agreed. I might add, parenthetically, that I have an absolute loathing for musical comedy. I hate musicals, especially those with operatic pretensions, such as *My Fair Lady*. But I do love revues —old-fashioned revues—the sort Noël Coward and Bea Lillie used to present. I must confess, however, that I was most impressed by *West Side Story*, because it was musically very inventive and the dances were wonderful.

"So many critics have said that my music sounds like background music. And because of that, I've had endless offers to write film scores. One of them was for the movie based on Hemingway's *The Old Man and the Sea*. But background music doesn't interest me in the least. I could have made pots of money with it but I've never sold my soul for money. I *have* sold myself, but only for what I really wanted to do.

"But to get back to *The Consul*. It carries on in the tradition of *The Medium*. By that time my recitatives began to have a very definite style. Of course, thematically and musically *The Consul* is much stronger than *The Medium*. It's much richer melodically. I felt that in *The Consul* I was able to give instant life to my characters, which I think is very rare in opera."

The Consul proved a triumph wherever it was staged. Its Paris premiere was particularly brilliant. Not only was Menotti hailed as a new young genius of opera, but Patricia Neway became the toast of the city. Subsequent to the Paris run of *The Consul*, the soprano was engaged by the Paris Opera and caused a sensation in the role of Tosca. Stories about *The Consul* abound. But Menotti was particularly fond of the opening night adventure he experienced during the gala premiere in Paris.

"We were very nervous about presenting *The Consul* in Paris. First of all we didn't know whether it should be sung in English or in French. We decided to give it in both languages, and so the cast alternated, singing it in French one night and in English another night. At any rate, we opened at the Champs-Elysées and *le tout Paris* attended the opening night. We had inserted a note in the program that no applause should follow the first two acts. Of course, Pat Neway always got a huge ovation after her big aria. At any rate, when the third act began, everything had gone very well. At the end, Pat Neway stuck her head in the oven and 'died.' Schippers struck the last chord and held it. At this point, the curtain was to fall slowly. To my horror, the curtain wasn't coming down. The trumpet and the trombone players were getting blue in the face holding their notes. Still no curtain. Pat sat with her head in the oven for what seemed an eternity. I was standing in the back of the house—frantic. Tommy finally stopped the orchestra. Still no curtain. There was complete silence. I couldn't believe it. I ran from the back of the house down to the stage and collared the first stagehand I found, telling him to bring down the curtain. He looked at me perplexed: 'That's not my job.' I took the man by the neck and said, 'I don't care if it isn't your job. Get that curtain down.' It turned out that the man who was to work the curtain had gone across the street to have a beer and had miscalculated the time. Anyway, after minutes and minutes and minutes, the curtain finally came down. I remember how Pat Neway burst into tears—she was hysterical. I was in despair and thought the whole thing had turned into a disaster.

"Well, the first person who came backstage was Jean Marais. He was ecstatic. He said, 'Menotti, ce silence à la fin! Quel genie!' Needless to say, we didn't continue with 'ce silence.' *The Consul* was a huge success in Paris. Pat Neway made headlines in *Le Figaro*. She was compared to Réjane and to Sarah Bernhardt."

Once again, *le tout Paris* feted Menotti, and endless wires and notes of congratulations came his way, praising a work that had riveted and thrilled even the most avant-garde of French writers. Wrote Jean Cocteau: "My dear Gian Carlo Menotti, You have created the most beautiful work that can be seen in a theatre. It uncurls itself like a plant. It opens to the light and closes at night. I wept in the presence of a perfection which every second held my attention and which overwhelmed me."

In London, *The Consul*, presented by Sir Laurence Olivier, was equally acclaimed, as it was all over Europe. But in Italy, where Menotti had received an invitation to stage the work at La Scala, acceptance still eluded him. First was the problem of finding a suitable Magda, because Patricia Neway was, at this point, touring with *The Consul* in America.

"Victor de Sabata, La Scala's artistic director, felt that *The Consul* should not be sung by foreign singers, but that Italians should be cast in the roles. La Scala's general manager, Ghiringhelli, said there was no one in his company who could compare to Patricia Neway in dramatic intensity. He suggested that I go out and audition in Italy. He told me he would take anyone I chose. So Wally Toscanini, who knew about this, told me that there was a young singer who was singing Isolde one night and *Il Turco in Italia* the next, at the Eliseo in Rome. 'She's absolutely fantastic,' Wally said. 'Hardly pretty and very fat, but she's an incredible artist.'

"So I went, and I heard her, and immediately realized what a great artist she was. We met at the Hotel Quirinale, and I told her I would like to have her sing *The Consul* at La Scala. She said she would gladly do it, but that she didn't want to go there just as a guest artist and be thrown out again. So I said, 'I'm sure they will take you into the company.' I called up Ghiringhelli and told him who my choice was—this girl called Maria Callas—and he said, 'I'm sorry. Any singer but *that* singer. I can't stand her!' And then he continued, 'If you insist that I keep my promise, I will take her for *The Consul,* but I will not take her on as a regular at La Scala.' When I told that to Callas, she said, 'Then I cannot accept. But one day I'll make Ghiringhelli feel sorry for this.' I finally settled on another very gifted singer, Clara Petrella."

Tom Prideaux, writing in *Life* magazine, described the turbulence surrounding the Italian production of *The Consul:*

"Optimistically [Menotti] accepted an invitation to stage *The Consul* at La Scala. To celebrate the opening, he bought new full-dress evening clothes, his first since he was seventeen years old. A dozen members of his family, who had never been much impressed by the reports of his success, were coming to observe Gian Carlo's gala night.

"Menotti plunged into his job of directing rehearsals, which went on daily for almost two months. . . . It was hard enough to on large *The Consul*—an intimate opera on Broadway—to fill the vast La Scala stage. It was harder to challenge centuries of operatic tradition. The singers were cooperative but dumbfounded when Menotti asked them to act intensely on stage, even when they were not actually singing.

"But before opening night, there were darker mutterings in the musical circles of Milan. Many Italians were resentful that Menotti had won his fame in the U.S. The Communists resented the libretto, which they already knew to be scornfully antitotalitarian. And then came a final omen of disaster—the white doves that the magician was supposed to release in the second act had been delivered to the singer's apartment; the cook had baked them for dinner.

"Just before the overture, a leading critic of Milan's *Il Tempo* [Giulio Confalonieri] stalked into a box with seven friends, all equipped with whistles. They were upholding the tradition of La

Scala, where even Verdi and Puccini had faced boos and critical brickbats, and where many Italians still consider opera important enough to fight over. The curtain was barely up on *The Consul,* when whistles began to toot. While the singers strained their lungs, and Menotti paled in the wings, the audience began its obligato of boos and bravos.

"Shrieked one woman, 'Down with Americans! Long live Italy! This is a dirty mess!'

"One of La Scala's conductors, defending Menotti, stood up in the audience and roared, '*Cretini! Stupidi! Ignoranti!*'

"The performance continued. So did the uproar. And after the composer and cast had taken eleven curtain calls to the applause of the many in the audience who liked the opera, the tumult spilled into the streets; amid the flying fists, two music lovers were arrested. Next morning, most critics continued their attack in the newspapers, calling the opera 'old fashioned' and 'impotent.' The controversy went on through *The Consul's* subsequent four performances in Milan."

It is interesting to note that critic Giulio Confalonieri felt so strongly about his opposition to Menotti beforehand that he turned in his complimentary press tickets and paid out of his own pocket for the two boxes he and his friends occupied, so that he could feel free to blast the work. Years later, however, Confalonieri felt that he had judged Menotti unfairly. One day, to his great surprise, Menotti received an apologetic letter from him, asking for a tête-à-tête. The two lunched together, and from that day until his recent death, Confalonieri was one of the staunchest defenders of Menotti's music.

If the tumultuous reception at La Scala weren't traumatic enough, Kinch Horan reappeared in Menotti's life at the same time.

"One day before the dress-rehearsal," said Menotti, "I suddenly received a call from Taormina, from Truman Capote. He told me to come to Sicily immediately, because Kinch was seriously ill. I was desperate, I didn't know what to do. At the time, one couldn't just take a plane; one had to take a train, which would take a whole day. It was left that I should call back to find out how Kinch was. Well, Truman called again and said that Kinch was out of danger, but that he couldn't be responsible for him any longer. Knowing that I was staging *The Consul,* Truman volunteered to bring Kinch to Milan.

"I got a room for them in my hotel and went to see them after my rehearsal. Truman left, and Kinch was behaving very strangely. I had a very long talk with him. I said, 'You should go back home. You should have someone to take care of you. You should go to a psychiatrist.'

"Finally we decided Kinch must return to California where his family lived––that I couldn't help him anymore."

Composer Charles Turner, who was in Milan with Samuel Barber at that time, recalled the turmoil.

"It was Sam who took the initiative regarding Kinch," said Turner. "The situation could have gone on for years. During his stay in Europe, Kinch had not written to Gian Carlo, except for postcards saying, 'I've run out of money.' Gian Carlo would send him the money, and Sam would say, 'Stop doing that.'

"So Sam and I took Kinch to Zurich, and he was never told that we were going to put him on a plane to New York. He went on the plane reluctantly, and that's how he got to New York and finally back home to California.

"Gian Carlo's attitude about Kinch was that he should be responsible for him forever, but Sam's attitude was that that's what ruined Kinch, and that if Kinch had any chance for survival, he would just have to be on his own. And that's what Sam brought about."

Indeed, Horan himself realized that leaving the Menotti-Barber establishment would prove to be the healthiest thing he could do.

"I was, in fact, never to see Capricorn again, except later, as a guest," said Robert Horan. "I recall Gian Carlo telling me, 'Remember, Kinch, this house will always be your home to live in and return to wherever you are. It is yours as much as it is ours.'"

CHAPTER

11

"Hell begins on the day when God grants us a clear vision
of all that we might have achieved, of all the gifts which we
have wasted, of all that we might have done, and we did not
do. The poet shall forever scream the poems he never wrote.
The painter will be forever obsessed by visions of the pictures
he did not paint. The musician will strive in vain to remember the sounds which he failed to set down on paper. There
are few artists whom I can imagine resting in heavenly peace
—Leonardo, Michelangelo, Goethe, and a few minor artists
who have merited that peace. But for the weak, the lazy, the
damned, their torture shall be in proportion to the greatness
of the genius they have wasted. For me, the conception of
hell lies in two words: Too late!"

Menotti in *The Saturday Review*, April 22, 1950.

After the vociferous controversy aroused by *The Consul* in Milan,
the composer returned to America and all too happily moved back
to his retreat, Capricorn. Both Menotti and Barber were enjoying
the fruits of their labor, receiving prizes, awards, and the attention
of the music world and of the public. But there is no denying that,
of the two, it was Menotti who was the recipient of the greatest
share of adulation. Menotti had become a major force in the operatic world and, because of his great personal magnetism, enjoyed
the sort of celebrity that eluded the more somber and unyielding
Barber. Nonetheless, the two friends maintained their close relationship and continued sharing Capricorn. The house bore witness to
hard work and to many festivities and soirees.

In 1950 Menotti's friend and protégé, Thomas Schippers, and the
young composer Charles Turner, who had become the close friend
of Samuel Barber, were frequent guests at Capricorn. Turner remembered how life was spent in those early years following
Menotti's great success with *The Consul*:

"I met Sam first. I was introduced to him by Gore Vidal. It was in 1950, shortly after *The Consul* was done in New York. I had been in Paris the year before, studying with Nadia Boulanger. In Paris I met Gore, and he asked me if I would like to meet Samuel Barber. Very shortly thereafter I met Gian Carlo. Sam and Gian Carlo asked me up to their house in Mt. Kisco quite often. It was very stimulating—intellectually and artistically. Sam had just had great success with his Piano Sonata, which Horowitz had played, and Gian Carlo had just had *The Consul*. The parties at Capricorn were marvelous. Gian Carlo and Sam had fabulous people out. I was part of all that. Laurence Olivier and Vivien Leigh came out, and Shostakovitch and Marcel Duchamps, and God knows how many other 'names.' Of course, Tommy Schippers was usually there. Horowitz came often to their house—he would come for weekends. Naturally, everyone wanted to hear him play, and I was used as a sort of patsy. Sam would ask me to start playing something by Chopin, and Horowitz would inevitably take over. He would come up to the piano and say, 'No no! Here's the way it should go.'

"One of my memories of Gian Carlo is the stream of secretaries he has always had, none of whom lasted very long. And there was a long list of housekeepers at Capricorn. The housekeeper situation was always a bone of contention between Sam and Gian Carlo. Gian Carlo tended to befriend them, spending time in the kitchen asking them to tell him their joys and sorrows. Of course, they often developed tremendous crushes on Gian Carlo. Sam, on the other hand, tried to run the house efficiently and was often considered the ogre, because he simply wanted meals to be properly served, on time and all that."

Charles Turner claimed that Barber's attitude toward Menotti had always been rather complaining and difficult in those years. "Gian Carlo seemed to take all this in his stride. It never fazed him, he never got angry. He tolerated it. It just never bothered him at all. I mean, Sam would always complain about the running of the house or about the people Gian Carlo had invited to Capricorn. For example, Sam would say 'Why did you invite *her?*' and Gian Carlo would say, 'I *had* to invite her. She's the leading lady in my opera.' And Sam would say, 'I can't stand her,' and he would go off and slam the door and stay in his room."

Charles Turner was in a position of observing at first hand the working methods of both composers. "Sam was very organized. Gian Carlo, as long as I've known him, always wrote things at the last minute. Very often he didn't really start writing the music down until rehearsals had almost begun. And so it went from opera to opera." The impression of last-minute creation is not truly accurate, however; Menotti works mentally for months on his ideas until he feels they are ready to be set down in a precise form.

The four friends—Menotti, Schippers, Barber, and Turner—would at times spend summers away from Capricorn. In 1953 it was decided that the summer would be spent in Brooklyn, Maine.

"It was one of the nicest summers we had ever spent together. Sam had arranged it all. He found a house not far from Blue Hill. It was a funny, old-fashioned Maine farm house, with four little parlors. Each of us had a parlor of his own. This was all the year before Gian Carlo's *The Saint of Bleecker Street* was produced. Sam had started writing *Vanessa*—he wrote the first act of it there. Tommy was conducting *Salome* at Tanglewood that summer, so he was singing away in German preparing for it. And I was writing my first orchestral piece.

"All of this required four pianos. Two of them were in the house. One of them was used by Sam, the other by Tommy. Gian Carlo found a piano in a school house, and I put one in an abandoned hotdog stand nearby. We'd work during the day. We had a very nice housekeeper, a black woman by the name of Edie Piper. She cooked for us and kept the house. We'd all get back by four o'clock, and we'd play tennis or go sailing. We all learned how to sail that summer. We were taught by Ethelbert Nevins' granddaughter. The evenings were partly games. Gian Carlo has always loved games and so did Tommy and so did I. Sam never would play any games. He would read a book and usually go to bed early. And so the three of us would play word games. We didn't invite many people to visit us that summer and we got a lot of work done."

Charles Turner described Menotti's friendship with Thomas Schippers. "They were like two boisterous boys who liked dashing each other about, a bit. There was a lot of wrestling, a lot of horse-play. Most of Gian Carlo's close friends, except for Sam, behaved like that—lots of joshing around, playing pranks on each other. Gian Carlo was always amused by that. If you squirted him all over with shaving cream, he thought it was just great fun."

Another summer of the early fifties was spent by the foursome in Italy. "We thought we'd have an Italian summer," recalled Turner. "We decided to go to Capri. Gian Carlo found two houses next to each other. We decided to take Edie Piper, our housekeeper, along with us, and Edie turned out to be quite an attraction on Capri because there weren't any other blacks there at that time. She was a striking-looking woman, and young Italians would follow her on the street. We went on a working schedule, but it was a little difficult because Capri was very noisy. I remember there was an outdoor movie theater rather far away from us, but you could hear every word of the dialogue at dinner. They'd show the same movie every night for a week. There was one week when they were showing *Marie Antoinette* with Norma Shearer. Just about the time dessert would be served, we'd hear the guillotine come down. Another time they showed an Italian movie—something with gladiators. We'd hear the screams of '*L'assassino! L'assassino!*' during dinner.

"Sam was very nervous that summer. He was picking on Tommy a great deal. He was trying to make Tommy seem less important, because he was *only* a conductor while the rest of us were composers. Gian Carlo would seldom defend Tommy because it was assumed that Sam would always do this sort of thing and he always did. Of course, Sam could also be wonderfully charming."

In 1951 Menotti had begun work on *Amahl and the Night Visitors*, which would become a television and stage staple for all the Christmases to come. As Charles Turner put it, "ever since *Amahl*, Gian Carlo took over Christmas as his day. Christmas was always a great occasion at Capricorn. Gian Carlo was always extraordinarily generous with presents. He had more money than the rest of us and he always wanted to give us pleasure—he gave us paintings, beautiful books, really precious gifts. And there were wonderful Christmas parties with music all day long.

"I also recall something about *Amahl*. The opera was scheduled to be done on television for Christmas of 1951. Halloween came and Gian Carlo hadn't yet decided what to call it. He kept asking us what we all thought would be a good title for the opera. He kept coming back to *Amahl and the Night Visitors*. Well, nobody liked that title except Gian Carlo. Finally I remember on Thanksgiving Day after dinner he decided to call up Sam Chotzinoff, who had commissioned the opera for NBC. Gian Carlo said to him, 'I'm going to call the opera *Amahl and the Night Visitors*.' It was only then that he set about to compose it. On that same evening he had done the first three or four pages and rehearsals began a week or so later."

Amahl and the Night Visitors, barely an hour long, was written for a small stage, although it was also the first opera written specifically for television. Menotti has always resisted what he terms "a mechanical theater." The trappings of television did not really appeal to him, and so he made certain that the work could also be performed on the stage. *Amahl* is an opera for children, but it is enjoyed by people of all ages the world over. Much of it is written, rather refreshingly in this day and age, in the major key. The melodic pattern was kept very simple, and as in his previous works, *Amahl* is almost a continuous recitative. The composer has written poignantly on the genesis of *Amahl*:

"This is an opera for children because it tries to recapture my own childhood. You see, when I was a child I lived in Italy and in Italy—before it became Americanized—we had no Santa Claus. Our gifts were brought to us by the Three Kings, instead.

"I never actually met the Three Kings—it didn't matter how hard my little brother and I tried to keep awake at night to catch a glimpse of the Three Royal Visitors, we would always fall asleep just before they arrived. But I do remember hearing them . . . the weird cadence of their song . . . the mysterious tinkling of their silver bridles.

"My favorite king was King Melchior, because he was the oldest and had a long white beard. My brother's favorite was King Kaspar. He insisted that this king was a little crazy and quite deaf. I suspect it was because . . . Kaspar never brought him all the gifts he requested. . . .

"To these Three Kings I mainly owe the happy Christmas seasons of my childhood, and I should have remained grateful to them. Instead, I came to America and soon forgot all about them. . . .

"But in 1951 . . . I had been commissioned . . . to write an opera for television, with Christmas as a deadline, and I simply didn't have one idea in my head. One November afternoon as I was walking rather gloomily through . . . the Metropolitan Museum, I chanced to stop in front of *The Adoration of the Kings* by Hieronymus Bosch, and as I was looking at it, suddenly I heard again . . . the weird song of the Three Kings. . . . They had come back to me and had brought me a gift.

". . . I must confess that in writing *Amahl and the Night Visitors*, I hardly thought of television at all. . . . To me, cinema, television, and radio seem rather pale substitutes for the magic of the stage. This is why . . . I intentionally disregarded the mobility of the screen and limited myself to the symbolic simplicity of the stage."

Another important recollection not mentioned here by Menotti must have influenced the creation of *Amahl*. During a brief period in his childhood, he himself became slightly crippled, and was taken by his despairing nurse to the sanctuary of Sacro Monte, near Cadegliano, where a much-venerated Madonna was reputed to work miracles. His leg was blessed in front of the holy image, and it healed shortly thereafter; he has walked normally ever since.

Samuel Chotzinoff, who commissioned *Amahl*, had previously commissioned *The Old Maid and the Thief* for NBC radio in 1939. When Menotti's *The Island God* opened at the Metropolitan Opera House in 1942 Chotzinoff's enthusiasm had cooled. With the productions of *The Medium, The Telephone*, and *The Consul*, however, the producer's opinion again warmed to his former admiration. In addition to producing *Amahl*, Chotzinoff was later responsible for persuading NBC to back Menotti's 1958 opera *Maria Golovin*, which was given its first performance at the Brussels World's Fair; and in 1963 a second television opera—*The Labyrinth*—was offered by the network.

According to the Central Opera Services Directory of 1972, *Amahl and the Night Visitors* was the most frequently performed opera in the United States. In the six years between 1966 and 1972, *Amahl* had received 2187 performances, more than twice the number for any other opera. It is interesting to note that after *Amahl* the most often performed operas were *La Bohème, The Marriage of Figaro*, and *The Barber of Seville*. In 1969, Hans W. Heinsheimer, Menotti's publisher at G. Schirmer, confirmed that 70 percent of their mail order business was for *Amahl*. During that year, there were 350 productions of the work, and as many continued to be mounted in the years following. Some 50,000 scores of *Amahl* were in circulation during 1969. When one considers that these figures only include performances in the United States, it is dizzying to speculate on *Amahl*'s popularity throughout the rest of the world. The opera is performed on all continents, in all languages, and has become a universal Christmas fixture. *Amahl* is Menotti's most beloved work, and with its harmonic simplicity, its melodic clarity, and the way in which it touches the emotions, it will no doubt endure.

The original production premiered over NBC on December 24, 1951. Its cast included Chet Allen as Amahl, Rosemary Kuhlmann as his mother, Andrew McKinley, David Aiken, and Leon Lishner as the three kings, and Francis Manachino as the servant. The television director was Kirk Browning, and the stage director, Gian Carlo Menotti. The production was designed by Eugene Berman and was conducted by Thomas Schippers. Choreography was by John Butler, and among the production's dancers was the New York City Ballet's Melissa Hayden, as well as Glen Tetley.

In an unprecedented front-page review for the *New York Times,* Olin Downes wrote: "Mr. Menotti with rare art has produced a work that few indeed could have seen and heard last night save through blurred eyes and with emotions that were not easy to conceal. It may be said at once that television, operatically speaking, has come of age. . . . The music is written often in recitative but with intensifying beauty at the climactic moments. . . . The choruses of the approaching and departing shepherds and other ensemble pieces are always poetic and atmospheric, never obvious or banal . . . [a] tender and exquisite piece . . . [an] historic event in the rapidly evolving art of television."

These sentiments, in one form or another, were echoed throughout the New York press and all major papers and weeklies throughout the country. If there was any contention by reviewers, it centered on the sets created by Eugene Berman, which were thought by many to be out of key with the childlike fantasy of the story. But the acclaim was unequivocal and complete. Menotti's champion, Arturo Toscanini, once more sang his praises. "I think it is the best opera you've done," he told him.

The opera's first stage production was given in April of 1952 on a double bill with Menotti's *The Old Maid and the Thief* by the New York City Opera. It proved a huge success. The productions were conducted by Thomas Schippers, making his New York City Opera debut with these works.

Of the endless productions of *Amahl and the Night Visitors,* Menotti was particularly fond of its Italian premiere, which was presented in 1953 at the Pergola Theater in Florence. A first-class cast and orchestra were conducted by no less a personage than Leopold Stokowski. (Thomas Schippers served as coach on this occasion, and the choreography was devised by the equally illustrious George Balanchine; the role of the mother was sung by Giulietta Simionato.)

Menotti recalled his serendipitous meeting with Balanchine:

"The one thing that worried me about the first Italian production of *Amahl* was the little dance of the shepherds. No choreographer had as yet been appointed, and as it turned out, Balanchine happened to be in Florence. As he was very cordial and in a very good mood, I took the courage and asked him if it would amuse him to choreograph a small Italian dance for the production. To my great surprise he accepted immediately. His only request was that the three dancers to be used—two boys and one girl—would at least have had some American ballet training. Fortunately we found such dancers, and the result was a most charming 'introduction and tarantella.' It was very Italian, very inventive, quite perfect for *Amahl*. At the time Balanchine and I struck up a fairly close friendship. We used to lunch and dine together almost every day. Then, as the years passed, we saw very little of each other and never worked together again. I fear that he never forgave me for having invited Jerome Robbins rather than him to inaugurate the Spoleto festival in 1958.

"I might add here that despite my great admiration for Jerome Robbins, I have always found it difficult to be his friend. He hardly ever trusts anybody. He's always so suspicious. I like him and we get along together, but I never have been very comfortable or relaxed with him. I think I make Jerry nervous, and he certainly makes me nervous. Although he has come to Spoleto repeatedly, our meetings are always very brief, rather tense, and we are both sort of relieved when we leave each other."

Menotti, who likes to have a strong hand in the presentations of his operas and who usually directs his major stagings himself, could obviously not be in control of *Amahl* once its enormous popularity was established. Fearful that directors would oversentimentalize the role of Amahl, he has continually let it be known that the boy cast in this role should not be sweet and angelic. "I like my Amahl to be a naughty little boy—a little devil. The character should be impish. He tells lies, he is disobedient."

Even so trusted a friend as Samuel Chotzinoff, who continued to produce *Amahl* on television (the 1951 production was live, while later productions were taped), incurred Menotti's displeasure over one particular broadcast of this work. In a heated exchange of correspondence in 1963, Menotti wrote Chotzinoff that he was dissatisfied with the latest television presentation of *Amahl*. Menotti wanted it postponed until he could come to direct it himself, rather than trust it to the director Chotzinoff had engaged.

As it turned out, the producer took umbrage at Menotti's strongly stated request and answered the composer, saying that the new production of *Amahl* was set and could not be postponed. He told Menotti that if he felt so strongly about being present, then he could easily take a plane and spend some days in New York to supervise rehearsals and make necessary changes. Barring this, he could convey in writing what changes, "musical or otherwise," he desired. "Frankly,'" concluded Chotzinoff, "I do not understand your hysteria about this third production of *Amahl* (I am sure it won't be the last), and I must tell you that I find your lack of faith in my judgment and experience most disappointing."

Menotti, busy staging the world premiere of his *The Last Savage* at the Opéra Comique in Paris, could not have been more surprised at the recalcitrant tone of Chotzinoff's letter. In his answer can be read his overriding concern for the quality he wished maintained in productions of his work.

"Dear Chotzie, I am most shocked by the hostile tone of your letter," wrote Menotti. "Evidently our friendship has not yet reached that degree of sturdiness that withstands complete frankness. What is so 'hysterical' about a composer asking to be present at the taping of one of his operas, particularly when it may well become the definitive performance for years to come?

"It seems to me shortsighted on the part of NBC, when the composer is still alive, not yet quite gaga, and not such a bad stage director besides, to choose for the taping a date on which he cannot possibly be present. . . .

"I do not say this in a spirit of recrimination, as I am well aware that in the theater it is almost impossible to obtain everything one may wish. Also, I am well aware that you have always tried to give me the best that is available at NBC. What I am trying to impress upon you is that the way in which I like to stage my operas cannot be quite the same as that of other people. I did sincerely admire the way *you* staged *Amahl*. Still, it is not *completely* my way—how could it be? As *Amahl* is particularly dear to me it is natural that I would like to have it recorded as nearly as possible to the way I conceived it. . . .

"This taping of *Amahl* could and should be not only a good production but, should *Amahl* by any chance outlive me, also be a document of the composer's and librettist's wishes.

"All this *if* you feel that the composer's wishes have any value at all. If, however, you think (as Toscanini often did) that the composer is his own worst interpreter, go ahead your own way—don't ask me to be happy.

"As you see, I'm not 'hysterical' about it. I simply assume that friendship is a safe climate in which to be truthful. I only hope you feel the same."

As it turned out, this production of *Amahl,* minus the presence of the composer, proved erratic, so much so that Menotti chose to end his relationship with NBC.

"I finally decided not to renew my contract with them. Actually it was up to my publishers, Schirmer's, and without my permission they gave NBC one more year. I was so angry I threatened to leave Schirmer's and I had a terrible fight with Hans Heinsheimer—we almost came to blows. I told him, 'If you sign again with NBC'—and they'd offered a lot of money—'I'll leave Schirmer's.' So they had to say no to NBC. And then NBC got mad and said to me they'd never perform *Amahl* again. I offered to do a version of *Amahl* for nothing, and to get the singers to do it for the union's 'minimum.' But they didn't take me up on it. RCA, which had recorded *Amahl,* stopped recording my music. NBC never did *Amahl* again after 1964. People *think* they've seen it recently, because they still remember the earlier productions, but *Amahl* has not been seen on television for many, many years."

Some two months after the premiere of *Amahl,* a controversial exchange took place between Menotti and Boris Goldovsky, the well-known opera coach and producer, who for many years also doubled as the host for the Metropolitan Opera's national Saturday afternoon broadcasts. Goldovsky asked Menotti to be the intermission speaker during the Met's presentation of a new production of *Carmen* on February 16, 1952. It was, no doubt, Menotti's huge success with *Amahl* and the fact that the Met had presented his first two operas that prompted the invitation.

In a gesture of misguided benevolence toward contemporary composers, yet fully aware that the Met had not presented a contemporary work since 1947, namely Bernard Roger's *The Warrior,* Goldovsky opened his intermission talk with a self-congratulatory speech centering on the fact that the Met's talks usually concerned themselves with composers of the past—dead composers—and almost never with live ones. This time, however, he was delighted to have with him "a real live opera composer." After a brief and effusive description of Menotti's past successes, the "real live composer" took the microphone.

"Thank you for such a glowing introduction, Mr. Goldovsky, but may I add that I would feel much happier if, instead of asking composers to come and *speak* at the Metropolitan, the Metropolitan would ask them to come to hear their operas *performed* here. I personally have nothing to complain about, and my works have already been performed more than they probably deserve, but I find it rather depressing that the most important opera house in America seems interested in having living composers heard only during intermissions."

"Now, now, Mr. Menotti," Goldovsky sputtered, "you don't really mean that?"

For the next twenty minutes, the nation listened as Menotti gave what amounted to an impassioned plea for the American composer, blaming the Met for having neither the confidence nor the farsightedness to encourage native talent. Goldovsky countered by saying that financial considerations made it impossible to mount unknown operas by unknown composers. He reminded Menotti that they had, however, taken a chance with his own work and that Stravinsky's *The Rake's Progress* would be presented by the Met the following season.

"Yes, I was very pleased to hear that," Menotti answered. "But once again, this opera was first tried out somewhere else."

"Well, what of it?" Goldovsky said. "This will be its first performance *in America,* isn't that something? But regarding contemporary operas in general, how many do you think there are—and particularly, how many reasonably good contemporary *American* operas do you think there are—available for production?"

Menotti quickly replied, "I really don't know. But I doubt that the Metropolitan knows either, or has ever bothered to find out."

The interview went on in this fashion, with Menotti finally calling the Met cowardly in its attitude toward commissioning new works. "Small opera companies with an even more limited budget seem to take chances, but poor little Metropolitan prefers to be a museum rather than a creative artistic institution."

After the broadcast, hundreds of letters poured in from all across the country, congratulating Menotti on his daring to speak out or condemning him for abusing so venerable an institution as the Met. Some weeks later Menotti, feeling that the Metropolitan Opera's General Manager, Rudolf Bing, might have interpreted his interview as a personal attack rather than an attack on the longstanding policy of the Metropolitan, decided to send him a veiled apology for his outspokenness.

Mr. Bing replied that he shared Menotti's views, but that he was disappointed with the way that the composer chose to present his case. He considered it "hostile" and "unfair," claiming that Menotti had "blissfully ignored" major factors involving the issue. "Your leaving out any mention of these important factors," wrote Bing, "could lead only to the conclusion that you were deliberately and, if I may say so, unfairly attacking the Metropolitan Opera." Admitting that while his name was not mentioned on the air, Bing nevertheless felt that an attack on the Met was, necessarily, an attack on himself. "I would not mind in the least if it was delivered fairly and objectively," Bing's letter concluded, "but not on the basis of uninformed and cheap phrases."

Clearly Menotti was being treated condescendingly, for he was well acquainted with the topic of that intermission talk. What seemed to have offended Bing, and some of the Met's listeners, was Menotti's candor and his absolute conviction that the Met had never been a friend of contemporary composers. As it turned out, it would take six years for the Metropolitan Opera to mount a new American opera—ironically enough, Samuel Barber's *Vanessa*, with a libretto by Gian Carlo Menotti. As for a new opera by Menotti, it would be eleven years before the Met presented *The Last Savage*, originally commissioned by the Paris Opera. In short, precisely twenty-two years after the Met's production of *The Island God*, they deigned to produce another Menotti opera, a period during which Menotti had written no less than eight operas.

Gian Carlo Menotti's orchestral works have never received the kind of recognition that attended his works for the stage. The public responded to Menotti's theatrical genius and could easily relate to the visual and musical dramas he so instinctively created. Menotti, minus the stage, seemed deprived of his most fluent medium. To this day, his Piano Concerto (dedicated to Robert Horan), Violin Concerto, and other nontheatrical works receive few performances, but the purely orchestral works have great merit, are skillfully composed, and contain passages of rare melodic and harmonic richness. Immediately after his commission for *Amahl and the Night Visitors*, Menotti was asked by the well-known Italian conductor Victor de Sabata to compose a large orchestral work, which de Sabata wanted to premiere during his American concert tour.

This became known as *The Apocalypse*. As its title implies, it is a bravura piece for orchestra. Menotti maintains that when it is performed conductors tend to make it sound more "apocalyptic" than he intended. "Whereas most of us think of the Apocalypse as a description of a future catastrophe," wrote Menotti, "I found inspiration in the more lyrical, ecstatic and mystical pages of the writings, including, besides the well-known Apocalypse of St. John the Divine, the versions of Baruch and Enoch."

The Apocalypse has a particularly beautiful second movement, which is based on Gregorian chant, harking back to Menotti's early studies with Scalero at the Curtis. The last movement is somewhat weak and recalls Respighi at his most overflowing.

Menotti's Violin Concerto, composed in 1952, was written on commission for Efrem Zimbalist, the violinist who was then head of the Curtis Institute of Music. It received its premiere in that year with Zimbalist and the Philadelphia Orchestra, under Eugene Ormandy. "I'm rather fond of that work," said Menotti without elaboration.

The definitive performance of the Violin Concerto is given on a recording by violinist Tossy Spivakovsky and the Boston Symphony Orchestra conducted by Charles Munch. The work treats the solo instrument with singular reverence, giving it a prime thrust over the orchestra, which is supportive in the best sense of the word. Filled with themes of great radiance, the work is never less than a superb vehicle for the solo violin. As in *The Apocalypse*, the Concerto's second movement is particularly haunting and meditative. The work's chief asset is its unpretentiousness. Once more Menotti wrote straight from the heart and in the romantic tradition. Based on a classical formula, the Violin Concerto is one of the composer's most felicitous works.

Menotti wrote a work for two cellos and piano on commission from Gregor Piatigorski; a Triplo Concerto a Tre; also the song cycle *Canti della Lontananza*, based on seven of his own poems, on commission from the soprano Elizabeth Schwarzkopf. One lone song, "The Hero," is the only work of Menotti's that did not use his own words. It was a setting to a poem by Menotti's friend Robert Horan. This small output of non-theatrical works will no doubt be enlarged in the years to come. At the time of this writing, Menotti was working on his first symphony, as well as a cantata and a Capriccio for cello and orchestra. It is safe to assume, however, that the weight of Menotti's talent will forever rest upon his operatic works.

Menotti was never the darling of the world's musical intelligentsia. The musical avant-garde considered his work entirely too accessible and deemed both the man and his work superficial. As he was not an atonalist or a daring experimentalist, and because he did not break new musical ground, he was not accepted by the so-called innovators of his time. Even his American contemporaries—men like Aaron Copland, Virgil Thomson, Roy Harris, Roger Sessions, among others, who were members of the League of Modern Composers—considered Menotti a musician apart, something of a European intruder in the guise of an American composer. They were more inclined to accept Samuel Barber, whose American heritage was undisputed and whose stylistic outlook seemed more in keeping with the going trends. Menotti, for all of his musicianship and training, seemed an anomaly within the group. His success also proved suspect, and there is little doubt that an element of jealousy colored the attitude of his fellow composers.

Despite this professional opinion, Menotti was allotted sufficient respect at least to be tolerated by New York's "serious" musical circles. Because he stood as a voice that celebrated all that was human and traditional in music, he was often called upon to express his views in broadcasts, musical conferences, and panel discussions. Among the latter was Juilliard's Sixth Annual Symposium of Composers, held at the Juilliard School in New York on March 25, 1952. The subject at hand was "A Composer's Approach to His Music." The panelists on that occasion included Roy Harris, Ernst Krenek, and Gian Carlo Menotti. Each composer made a lengthy speech bearing directly on the subject. It is worth quoting Menotti's words, for they sum up his strongest beliefs about music and its creation:

"At the risk of sounding paradoxical, I would venture to say that for me there is no 'approach' of the artist to his art. . . . Too many people . . . approach art armed to the teeth with all sorts of beligerent attitudes, as if art were some kind of dragon to be slain. . . . All of these attitudes are symbolized by the very strange expressions that have entered our daily vocabulary. One of them is that contemporary music must be 'modern,' thus implying that art should be subjected to fashion, and that whatever is not 'modern' is inevitably oldfashioned. . . .

"One of the essential ingredients for music to sound modern, for example, is the constant and unrelieved use of dissonances. I don't know why dissonance per se should be more exciting or interesting than consonance. . . . There are people who consider it essential for contemporary music to be nervous and intense. Again, why should tension be more interesting than complete serenity?

"There are composers who insist that they are writing for the future, and only then will their music be understood, with the implication that art is a sort of commercial product which automatically improves as the years go by. Actually, we have no guarantee that the audiences of the future will be more understanding or sensitive than those of today. If anything, all indications point to the fact that our audiences are getting duller and duller. The passage of time does not improve art, nor develop it. . . .

"Artists struggling to be original seem to be unaware that there is only one way: to be honestly and candidly oneself, as there are no two people alike in the world, even if one cannot totally escape family resemblances. The only unoriginal artists are those who assume the traits of other personalities, whether they feel akin to them or not. . . .

"I have no patience with artists who say, 'Well, it satisfies *me!*,' as art should be an act of love and not a form of masturbation. . . . Our inner discovery, to become a work of art, must be communicated and shared. We shall soon learn that people are interested in the more painfully hidden side of our character rather than in our polished social manner. But to be able to reveal ourselves for what we are, we must also accept *what* we are, which at times may prove embarrassing. It takes the courage of a genius to face one's public in complete nakedness. . . .

"I am convinced that composition is more an act of discovery than of creation, and it *must* possess a quality of inevitability. To paraphrase what Michelangelo said in one of his sonnets: 'There is nothing in the mind of the artist which is not already contained in the piece of stone before him. All that he has to do is to get rid of the superfluous.' This is what I mean for: *inevitable* . . . and only when I feel I have reached the inner chambers of my heart, I'll know that I've become an original composer."

CHAPTER

12

"Who by God's love is wounded
and by its tide encircled
is then forever drawn
into its tumultuous vortex "

(*The Saint of Bleecker Street*)

When, in 1953, Gian Carlo Menotti at the age of forty-two began
work on his most elaborate opera, *The Saint of Bleecker Street*, the
inner man felt the pangs of various subtle emotional stresses. From
early youth Menotti had been subjected to the doctrines of Catholi-
cism. The church and its canons were irrevocably part of the fabric
of his emotional makeup. His faith, however, was continually in
question. Upon his arrival in America, Menotti still clung to the
beliefs that were so melodramatically implanted in him by his contact with Don Rimoldi, the eccentric parish priest in his native
Cadegliano. Yearning to believe, the young Menotti encountered a
progressive sense of doubt. As his intellect flowered and deepened,
these doubts increased, and with the onrush of his professional success his spiritual side became increasingly troubled. In its place and
almost without warning, strong feelings of guilt made themselves
felt. They would rise to the surface at unexpected moments, plunging the composer into depression. No doubt the seeds of guilt were
already present in Menotti the child, for the concept of sin and
retribution was a strong element in his Catholic upbringing. No
doubt the notion of faith was an ever-present source of inspiration
to the composer; from his earliest operatic compositions, faith was
the subtext of his librettos. From *Amelia Goes to the Ball* to *The
Consul*, it was the element of faith—of belief, whether spiritual or
mundane—that informed the actions of his characters.

With the exception of *The Island God* and *Amahl and the Night Visitors,* none of Menotti's works prior to *The Saint of Bleecker Street* dealt directly with the spiritual. Faith made itself known primarily through the symbolic or psychological implication of the plot. Religious belief was there by implication or allusion. With *The Saint of Bleecker Street,* however, religious faith became the central motif.

The undertaking prompted Menotti to requestion his own spiritual values. With characteristic curiosity, he sought to test his seeming loss of faith.

"When I began writing *The Saint,* I felt emotionally disturbed," said Menotti. "I felt a great impatience—a great need to find my faith again. Before I actually wrote the opera I felt I *should* know a saint. I asked to meet Padre Pio [Father Pio de Pietralcina]. Do you know about him? Padre Pio was an Italian Capucine monk who recently died. He was an extraordinary little man and was a great problem to the Catholic church, because the church is very suspicious of such people. The fact was that Padre Pio bore the stigmatas. Well, the church didn't quite know how to handle him, how to treat him. Also, he had a very difficult personality. He was a rather rough and uncouth man. The Italian clergy tried to hide him in a little village in Apulia, at San Giovanni in Rotondo, where they thought people would forget him. Instead, thousands of people poured into the little village to see Padre Pio. Now, Padre Pio never claimed to be a saint. He had always said he was a poor sinner and was rather embarrassed about his stigmatas."

Menotti recounted how Padre Pio would hold mass very early in the morning—just before dawn. He hated the idea of people coming to see him. Nevertheless, whenever mass was served, one could barely get into the church. It is said that he could cure the sick, and indeed, Padre Pio founded a hospital in San Giovanni in Rotondo, where the maimed and ailing would come to receive the Padre's spiritual and physical cures. "He kept saying he couldn't cure anyone," said Menotti. "But as it turned out, he did achieve many, many miraculous cures."

Menotti arranged to visit Padre Pio. "I went to stay with a friend, a very charming girl. We got up very, very early. We went into the church. It was an extraordinary experience. My friend and I stood there for hours, because we wanted to be very near the altar. The church was crammed full—there was an awful smell of sick humanity. But what was extraordinary was that when Padre Pio came in from the sacristy, the smell suddenly changed. People talk about the odor of sanctity—well, it really exists. Suddenly there was a new odor, not a perfume, but a mixture of perfume and disinfectant which seemed to purify the air. When he came out, the people surged toward him. He wore gloves to hide his stigmata. They tried to touch him. But he would kick and push them away from him, protesting in rough peasant language that one could hardly call saintly. That's how he made his way to the altar. Then he recited the mass, very slowly. It took hours. Everybody stood. It was so hypnotizing, because in the middle of the mass, he would go into a trance. He would stand for five or ten minutes without moving, as if he were seeing something. Of course, when he said the mass, he would remove his gloves, and every time he would open his arms to say 'Dominus vobiscum,' you could see these huge bleeding scars on both sides of his hands. He kept a little towel hidden behind the missal with which he would wipe the blood away. It was said of Padre Pio that he always ran a temperature and lived in great pain. It was also said of him that he had the gift of ubiquity.

"When the mass was finished, I walked out of the church by myself. I was so preoccupied and was assailed by so many conflicting emotions that I fell into a great unhappiness. I can't even tell you *why* I was so unhappy at that moment, but the whole scene was very disquieting. I remember it was in the middle of winter. It was very dark and the sun was just beginning to rise. Finally I had an audience with Padre Pio. He said to me, 'Do you believe in the Church?' And I said, 'No, I'm afraid I don't believe in the Church.' He asked, 'But who do you think gave you this great gift and talent that you have?' I replied, 'I did not say I did not believe in God, I only said I did not believe in the Church.' Padre Pio looked at me for a time, then said, 'Why did you come to see me, then? *I* believe in the Church, and if *you* don't believe in the Church, then you must think I'm an idiot.'

"In a sense he was right," continued Menotti. "But he should have gone beyond. I didn't need to hear what he told me, because it was so obvious. You see, I didn't really know why I came to see him. That was the mystery. Somehow, I wanted him to tell me why I came to him. At any rate, Padre Pio failed me. The point is that he needn't really have said anything to me. I mean, if he had simply taken me into his arms, I would immediately have gone back into the arms of the Church. Part of me has *such* a need for that. Still, it was quite an experience—one I never forgot. I remember talking to one of the monks and telling him how moved I was by the mass but how disappointed I was by my audience with Padre Pio. The monk said to me, 'I understand all that. But you will never forget this visit. Padre Pio will always be in your thoughts.' With it all, I did have the feeling that I *had* met a saint."

Menotti, at the age of sixty-three, continued to question his religious beliefs while simultaneously yearning for a spiritual answer. He again touched on the problem at Yester House in Scotland—in the home that he claimed would be his last.

"I am definitely *not* a religious man. All the same I am haunted by religious problems, as most of my works show. Why? I can hardly explain it to myself. Can one be a secular mystic? Since the age of sixteen I had broken away from the Catholic Church, and I very much doubt, as some of my wishful religious friends predict, that at the last minute I shall ask for extreme unction and the holy sacraments.

"However, it is undeniable that the intense and incandescent faith which nourished my childhood and my adolescence has seared my soul forever. I've lost my faith, but it is a loss that has left me uneasy. I often feel like a runaway, who suddenly finds himself wondering if he has not left home too rashly or too soon. A certain nostalgia for my years of grace is, I believe, the knowledge that faith cannot be attained, but can only be given by God as an act of grace. But alas, or fortunately, depending on how you look at it, my mind is much too rational to abandon itself to faith. I am a would-be Voltaire, yearning to be Tolstoy, if you know what I mean. And it is this very duality in my character, this inner conflict, which I have tried to express in some of my operas. First in *The Medium* and then, and foremost, in *The Saint of Bleecker Street.*"

The Saint of Bleecker Street was commissioned by the City Center for Music and Drama under a grant-in-aid from the Rockefeller Foundation. Lack of funds prevented it from being produced during the regular opera season of the City Center, but Chandler Cowles brought the work to Broadway at the Broadway Theater on December 27, 1954. Menotti again directed his opera; Thomas Schippers conducted; and the principal roles were sung by David Poleri, Gloria Lane, and Leon Lishner. Visual production was supervised by Lincoln Kirstein. The sets were designed by Robert Randolph and were inspired by the paintings of George Tooker.

Against the colorful but sinisterly superstitious setting of Little

Italy, the plot deals with the conflict between saintly Annina (mysticism), her unbelieving brother (cynical realism), and his mistress Desideria (earthly love). In the effort to convert each other, they succeed only in destroying one another, for their unshakeable beliefs lead them along opposite paths to seemingly unavoidable destinations. In a curious way *Saint* reasserts the symbolic values of *The Medium;* Annina corresponds to the clients, the brother to Baba, Desideria to Monica. Only Toby is absent, his physical presence being replaced by the abstract presence of God.

The press welcomed *The Saint of Bleecker Street* and found it to be a work of substance and importance. Olin Downes of the *New York Times* wrote: "This opera, as human drama and first-rate theater, gives one the feeling of a masterfully integrated whole." Walter Kerr, in the *New York Herald Tribune,* called it "dynamic and dazzling. Everywhere the dramatic structure is forceful, cunningly inventive, courageous in its abandoned use of melodrama. . . . Technically the work is a powerhouse; emotionally it keeps its distance."

There were grumblings here and there over the melodrama of its plot and the "garishness" of its music, but in general critics of both music and drama decided in its favor. Indeed, it received the Pulitzer Prize for 1954 and ultimately found itself in the repertory of the New York City Opera, which had already presented Menotti's *Amelia Goes to the Ball, The Medium, The Telephone, The Old Maid and the Thief, The Consul,* and *Amahl and the Night Visitors*.

Musically, Menotti became more conscious of the play between tonalities during the writing of *The Saint of Bleecker Street.* His orchestration became richer and harmonically more complex. The choral writing became more interesting.

"I think that melodically *The Saint* is an improvement over *The Consul,*" said Menotti. "A weakness of my early music was that it had a certain 'shortness of breath.' In *The Saint* my melodic line acquires more powerful lungs."

The Saint, Menotti's most ambitious undertaking to date, was a critical but not a commercial success. It ran on Broadway for some four months and, as Chandler Cowles put it, was a labor of love.

"You see, it was such a big production," said Cowles. "There were fifty-eight in the orchestra, we had a cast of thirty and a chorus of thirty. It was just too big for Broadway. We lost all our money."

Menotti, while disappointed by the commercial failure of the opera, was undaunted as to its merit. In an interview given after the closing he said, "The ready-made audience that patronizes opera is a microscopic one. . . . Someone may ask, 'Why bother to convert the general public to operatic art? . . . and I must answer that such an attitude . . . is an absolutely fatal one. For I firmly believe that art should be an act of love toward humanity, not a specialized message to the initiated few. . . . If I insist on bringing my operas to Broadway, it is simply because of the letters I receive which begin, 'Dear Mr. Menotti, I had never seen an opera until tonight. . . .' "

Looking back on *The Saint*, Menotti maintained that the work somehow pinpointed the psychological and religious ambiguities that had always dwelled within him. "I have been accused of leaving the theme of *The Saint of Bleecker Street* unresolved. On whose side am I? Michele the unbeliever, or Annina the saint? But of course, I cannot take sides, because I am both. I am Michele, who envies Annina. That is why I have depicted their love as almost incestuous. The opera symbolizes my own inner conflict—the split in my personality—the impossibility of being both."

Menotti's next major work, *The Unicorn, the Gorgon and the Manticore*, premiered in 1956. Commissioned by the Elizabeth Sprague Coolidge Foundation in the Library of Congress in Washington, D.C., *The Unicorn* was first performed under the sponsorship of the foundation in the Library of Congress on October 21. The New York premiere was given by the New York City Ballet on January 15, 1957, at the New York City Center of Music and Drama.

"I am very fond of *The Unicorn*," said Menotti. "It makes me smile, because when I wrote it I knew that people who generally don't like my music would like it. Inspired by Orazio Vecchi's *Commedie Armoniche*, and scored for nine instruments, ten dancers, and chorus—all in a kind of very sophisticated wrapping—it had too many of the snobbish ingredients that attract the fastidious listener to fail with critics and musicologists."

The Unicorn, the Gorgon and the Manticore, with the subtitle *A Madrigal Fable*, was choreographed by John Butler, conducted by Paul Callaway, with decor by Jean Rosenthal, and costumes by Robert Fletcher. The New York City Ballet cast included Janet Reed, Roy Tobias, Nicholas Magallanes, Arthur Mitchell, Eugene Tanner, Richard Thomas, John Mandia, Wilma Curley, Jonathan Watts, and Lee Becker.

As Menotti had predicted, the critics and New York's musical intelligentsia found *The Unicorn* entirely enchanting. *Time* maga-

zine called it "a singular and engaging combination of ancient contrapuntal harmonies and tart, modern, dramatic values. Its orchestral
underpinning, on a chamber music scale, was fresh and spare. . . .
As the last notes died away, the tough audience of musical pros
leaped to its feet and called for one curtain call after another."

Looking back on its extraordinary reception, Menotti was wryly
amused. "I got some incredibly rapturous reviews from people who
have always hated my music. Stravinsky himself, who had never
liked my music much, came backstage after one of the performances
and told me how very much he enjoyed *The Unicorn*. The performance given at the Coolidge Hall in Washington was the one I
liked best. When it was produced at the New York City Ballet, it
lost some of its charm. Lincoln Kirstein was responsible for its
being done there, although Kirstein never had much use for John
Butler as a choreographer. I believe it was the one and only time
Butler was allowed to set foot in the City Ballet."

Talking about *The Unicorn*'s symbolic meaning, Menotti said that
the work is aimed against the dilettantes in art, who go along with
fashion and trends but don't really have the courage to feel or to
make their own judgments. "Sam Barber once said to me: 'A dilet-
tante is someone who loves art without humility.' How right he
is! At any rate, the three monsters in the piece are Youth, Middle
Age, and Old Age. What I am trying to say is that everything an
artist does is equally important to him, even his failures. An artist
has to be judged in his entirety, not just on the basis of one work
which might be popular or fashionable. His quest for beauty and
aesthetic truth is represented by everything he does, not only by the
works that succeed. I was trying to say something about the artist,
the life of the artist, the difference between real feeling and the
mimicry of feeling."

CHAPTER

13

"It is never my enemies I wish to see dead,
but often the people I love."

(from Menotti's notebook)

The year 1958 proved seminal in Menotti's life. It was the year
that saw the birth of the Spoleto Festival of Two Worlds, and also
the year of *Maria Golovin,* Menotti's ninth opera, a full-scale work
commissioned by NBC and given its world premiere at the Brussels
World's Fair.

Maria Golovin once more centered on the highly theatrical subject—the unfulfilled love of a blind youth, whose passion for an
older married woman ends in tragedy. It was the first of Menotti's
operas that dealt directly with the theme of love. "I wrote *Maria
Golovin* because I always wanted to write an opera about love,"
said the composer. "In *Amelia Goes to the Ball,* I made fun of love.
In *The Old Maid and the Thief,* I am very cynical about love. *The
Consul* certainly isn't a love story. Neither is *The Medium.* The
incestuous love in *The Saint of Bleecker Street* is symbolic. So
in *Maria Golovin,* I wanted to write purely about love. But it's very
funny, because instead of writing about love—and that again is a real
give-away about me—I wrote about jealousy. Like Proust, I cannot
separate love from jealousy. It's curious . . . but the things I've
been most ashamed of in my life were those I've done out of
jealousy. I've done things that are unworthy, even of the more un-
scrupulous side of my character. I mean steaming letters open,
looking through keyholes. Like all jealous people, I followed the
usual pattern. I hoped to be betrayed so that I could feed that
horrible monster called jealousy, because jealousy is a hungry
monster which, however, never dies of hunger. Fortunately, I now

think I've killed the monster in me. But for a long time it was the great shadow in my life. It made me lose so much time!

"So, when I wrote what I thought would be a tender love story, it turned out to be an agonizing story of jealousy. To begin with, I conceived the hero, Donato, as a blind man, not because I wanted to elicit pity for him, nor because 'love is blind,' but because for me jealousy is a form of blinding sickness—and I surrounded him with many symbols of his captivity such as cages and prisoners. The whole opera is about his fight against this double darkness in himself. That is why the ending, which is of the utmost importance to the plot, shows him freeing himself, not by actually killing Maria Golovin, which he does not, but by shooting at the ghost of his jealousy. In other words, he never actually sees the *real* Maria Golovin, but only an obsessive image of her which he has created within himself. He has to kill his obsession, the thing he *imagines* to be Maria Golovin, in order to kill his love and regain his sanity.

"*Maria Golovin* is one of my favorite works. I feel very close to it, because it reflects very much a part of my past, my character, my suffering. People who have never felt the pangs of jealousy feel the opera much less than those who do. Not everybody understands that concept of love."

Menotti considers *Maria Golovin* his "unlucky" opera. What was unlucky about it were the many complex professional and personal circumstances surrounding its production. When the work premiered in Brussels (it was conducted by Herman Adler, with a cast that included Richard Cross, Franca Duval, and Patricia Neway), it received mixed notices, although the public seemed to respond to it favorably. Among those in the audience on opening night was the Broadway producer David Merrick. During those years, Merrick enjoyed an unprecedented success with Broadway plays and musicals. Upon seeing the work, he offered to produce *Maria Golovin* on Broadway. Menotti was encouraged to accept this offer by both NBC and his publisher, Ricordi. They felt Merrick would give the production lavish and preferential treatment. The composer seemed taken by the prospect of working with so hugely successful a producer and sealed the commitment. In his heart of hearts, however, Menotti also knew that by accepting Merrick, he was somehow betraying the good faith and long-standing support of Chandler Cowles and Efrem Zimbalist, Jr., who had, in fact, promised Menotti to produce *Maria Golovin* on Broadway themselves.

Menotti overrode these feelings, and on November 5, 1958,

Maria Golovin opened at the Martin Beck Theater under the banner of David Merrick. The "unlucky" opera closed on Broadway after five performances. "I couldn't believe it," said Menotti. "Merrick told me he *loved* the opera . . . that it had moved him to tears. Granted that the reviews were half-good and half-bad, I'm sure that if Merrick would have allowed it to run for a least a full week it would have survived. But I was told that he got an offer to produce a musical called *La Plume de Ma Tante,* he needed a theater, so he closed *Golovin.* What was so awful was that he gave me no warning. He closed it while I happened to be in Washington. Well, that, of course, gave the opera a black mark and everybody thought it was a failure. For a long time nobody would perform it."

Chandler Cowles commented on *Maria Golovin*'s demise. "I wanted to bring the opera to Broadway, but Gian Carlo was suddenly dazzled by David Merrick. Naturally I thought it was bad for Gian Carlo to do this, because I knew that Merrick wouldn't really understand him. And he didn't. I was furious, and when Merrick closed *Golovin,* Gian Carlo felt very guilty. Later he apologized. It didn't really hurt our friendship, but in a way it broke the umbilical cord between us. It was a good thing for me to break away from Gian Carlo because I had been very much under his influence. In retrospect I don't regret it at all. I grew up at that moment."

Maria Golovin is among Menotti's most richly melodic operas. Its faults lie not so much in its musical expression as in its delineation of character. The people in the opera seem oddly one-dimensional, and their relationships are neither fully developed nor entirely believable. While *Golovin* remained unperformed for several years, it nevertheless received major productions in Europe, notably in Marseilles at the Paris Opera and at La Scala. Today it stands as one of Menotti's major works. With all its faults, the drive and beauty of the music continues to enthrall the public.

CHAPTER
14

"The better it is, the sooner you try."

(Labyrinth)

Why and how did Gian Carlo Menotti start the Spoleto Festival of Two Worlds? The answers are manifold; an entire book could be written on the subject. Whatever the reasons, one major fact emerges. With the inception of the yearly festival, Menotti's life changed dramatically. The flow of his music diminished under the pressures and demands that such an undertaking imposed on his creative faculties. Menotti the composer was suddenly transformed into Menotti the organizer, the fund-raiser, the administrator, the talent scout, the secretary, the dealer in minutiae, the father-confessor, and the politician. His time was spent in courting the rich, in charming the talented, and in pursuing an ideal that by twentieth-century standards seemed positively childish. He wanted to create a Utopian city, a place where the creative spirit would reign unimpeded by commercial, political, or social considerations. He wanted to build bridges upon which a massive flow of international artists could walk hand in hand, combining their gifts for the glory of Art.

Such visions have their price. While the Festival did not block Menotti's talents as a composer, it seriously limited his sense of concentration and played havoc with his working habits. But in 1958 Menotti turned forty-seven, and his life was at midpoint. He had enjoyed unqualified success in America and had fulfilled his early promise. He had become a celebrated composer and perhaps the only living twentieth-century operatic composer known the world over. Something in him demanded a new perspective; something visionary prompted a gesture that would override personal success. It was time to do something that would bring into focus his quest for a world in which the artist held sway, where the intellect would dominate, where the creative act would find release.

Looking back on it, Menotti voiced his reasons for Spoleto. "Actually the Festival satisfied a very selfish need. I became so completely disenchanted with the role of the artist in contemporary society. I felt useless. Art had become what Sam Barber calls 'the after-dinner mint of the rich.' I felt that the artist should become part of society—a *needed* member of society rather than just an ornament. That's why I started Spoleto. I wanted to feel needed, and I wanted to see whether with my music and my knowledge I could help to recreate a so-called ideal city. My dream was not really to create a festival, but to create a small city wherein the artist would thrive and be one of its most essential members."

That was one reason Menotti gave. At one point he expressed it differently. "I don't really know why I started Spoleto. In America there is always the tendency of asking why people do things. Well, all of a sudden I wanted to do a festival, and I did. I didn't ask myself *why*. Perhaps like the man who was asked why he wanted to climb Mount Everest, I did it 'Because it was there!' Actually, every time anyone asks me why I did the Festival, I generally give different answers. Sometimes I say it's because of the young artists who need to be discovered, or need a push or whatever. Sometimes I say it's to help myself, because I felt a need for it. Tommy Schippers says I did it for *him*."

When the Festival was founded, Thomas Schippers had been Menotti's companion for eight years. In an interview in 1973 he did not hesitate at the suggestion that Spoleto was all his doing:

"Spoleto was not Gian Carlo's idea. It was *my* idea. We had done *The Consul*. We had done *Amahl*. We had done the Piano Concerto and the Violin Concerto. Then came *The Saint of Bleecker Street*— my favorite of Gian Carlo's operas. Well, when *The Saint* closed, it was a tremendous blow to me, and a deathly blow to Gian Carlo. I said to him, 'Look, you're an Italian. I am an American. Being an Italian, you must have some influence in Italy. I have some influence in America. We can't afford to put on *The Saint* in America. Why don't we do it in your country?' And that was the kernel of Spoleto. Nobody knows that. Even the title of the Festival was mine. It wasn't just the Festival of Gian Carlo and Tommy, but it was the Festival of Two Worlds—of Italy and America.

"And so we began looking for a place to hold the Festival. We made three trips together. It took us three summers in Italy to find Spoleto. Our trips were very well organized. Every theater in Italy knew we were coming, every town that was on the schedule knew. We visited at least sixty different places, especially in the middle and northern part of Italy. Strangely enough, Spoleto was the first place we visited and I fell in love with it. The Teatro Nuovo was a functional theater, and the Caio Melisso, the smaller theater, didn't need much fixing up to be in working order. I thought that if we came to Spoleto, we would have two theaters at minimum expense. Gian Carlo was against the Teatro Nuovo—he thought it was too big. Also, he had fallen in love with the theater in the nearby town of Todi. He kept saying, 'I want my operas done in a small theater, and I want Todi.' He doesn't mean it, but he still says, 'I wish we had gone to Todi.' Finally we settled on Spoleto. So you see, Spoleto was my idea."

Chandler Cowles claims that Menotti began the Spoleto Festival because of his disillusionment at his encounter with Padre Pio, who had not, after all, converted the composer back to the Church. "Gian Carlo told me that Padre Pio had given him a good scolding," said Cowles. "He told me that Padre Pio had said to him, 'Now listen, Menotti. You're a spoiled and selfish man. God has given you a great gift. And you are wasting yourself in self-indulgence. You must do something for other people.' Gian Carlo told me that it was this admonishment from Padre Pio that gave him the compulsion to start Spoleto. That it would be done for the sake of other artists. He may deny all of this now, but that's what he told me."

Oliver Smith recalled that Menotti, during a fund-raising session at Capricorn in Mt. Kisco, had announced that the Spoleto Festival would be a great democratic thing for all the poor people of America. "Poor American students could go to some lovely place and perform, and there were to be no titled people and no terrible snobbism," said Smith. "There would be none of that. It was to be a great intellectual commune. Of course, I thought it was a lot of nonsense. I might add that Sam Barber agreed. Finally, though, Gian Carlo was right and we were wrong. He made a marvelous thing out of Spoleto. Still, only rich people can afford to go there. It's not something for poor people."

The official reason for starting the Spoleto Festival was stated in the elaborate program that announced the first Festival of Two Worlds, dated June 5, 1958. "Why this festival?" wrote Menotti. "In

this age when few actions are planned without purpose of material
gain, it is difficult for me to answer this question and be believed.
Still, this is the only truthful answer: for the joy of it.

"To say that this Festival was planned to teach and help young
artists is only partly true. For, more often than not, one is taught
by youth, and is helped by its enthusiasm. The chance to work, the
modest material help, and the opportunity for renown that our
Foundation is offering our young guests, are but meager tokens of
what we expect to receive in creative and expressive ideas.

"Our only merit, perhaps, is to have discovered a peaceful and
beautiful corner of the world where young artists may express themselves freely, unhampered by political creeds, preoccupation with
aesthetic fashions, or by autocratic directors.

"Indeed, this Festival (fortunately, I may add) does not necessarily mirror my personal tastes. The four youthful directors to whom
the artistic reins of the Festival have been entrusted were allowed
all possible freedom—and that same freedom was given to the
artists whose participation they solicited.

"We hope, therefore, to have gained enough diversity of attitudes
and ideas to make our first season a provocative one.

"Spoleto offers no nightclubs, no fashionable beach or gambling
casinos. Only the tourist who is genuinely interested in the arts
will be happy among us. For these visitors, and for the young
artists who will participate in the Festival, we hope that Spoleto
may in time become the 'ideal city.'" (Some twenty years later—
on May 25, 1977, to be exact—when Menotti launched the first
Spoleto Festival U.S.A. in Charleston, South Carolina, he continued
to hold fast to the notion of an "ideal city." "An international festival
can have a deep meaning and give art the dignity of social and
political message," read Menotti's official statement to the world
press. "This is why the Spoleto Festival was first called the Festival
of Two Worlds, with the hope that one day Spoleto would find, as it
finally has, its other-world counterpart. It is a much needed sign of
hope in this age of suspicion and mistrust when two beautiful
towns, so different and so far away from each other, through the
common quest for beauty unfurl the flag of friendship.")

The "four youthful directors" of the first Spoleto Festival were
Thomas Schippers, for music; Jose Quintero, for drama; John Butler,
for dance; and Giovanni Urbani, for fine arts. The first general director on the Italian side was Anna Venturini; on the American side,
Chandler Cowles. The first president was Menotti; the treasurer was

William H. Diekman. There were four vice-presidents: Jerome Hill, Prince Alberico Boncompagni Ludovisi, Laurence P. Roberts, and Baroness Alphonse de Rothschild. On the board of directors were: Mrs. John Nicholas Brown, H. Bartow Farr, Gian Carlo Menotti, Lawrence P. Roberts, and Mrs. Mary Curtis Zimbalist. There was an honorary council made up of various individuals and foundations. There was an honorary advisory committee made up of some thirty-five individuals. Some one hundred sponsors and about twenty foundations and organizations also contributed money to the Festival foundation.

At first, Menotti had no trouble raising money, and the Festival was gloriously on its way. The events of that first three-week Spoleto Festival of 1958 were impressive. Thomas Schippers conducted a brilliant production of Verdi's *Macbeth,* directed by Luchino Visconti, with sets and costumes by Piero Tosi. John Butler brought a company of dancers that included Carmen de Lavallade, Buzz Miller, and Glen Tetley. Jerome Robbins created his Ballets U.S.A. Jose Quintero directed O'Neill's *Moon for the Misbegotten,* starring Colleen Dewhurst. There was a French production of Alphonse Daudet's *L'Arlesienne*, with Bizet's incidental music. Lee Hoiby, one of Menotti's pupils at the Curtis, was represented by a one-act opera, *The Scarf*, starring Patricia Neway. There was a new play by a young author-director, Patroni-Griffi, and other minor events. This was a meeting of the American, French, and Italian arts, presented under hectic and primitive conditions. Menotti remembered some of the turmoil:

"I was in a state of panic because things were very disorganized to begin with. The directors of the various productions were fighting for the stage—for rehearsal time. We had a very small crew. I was completely unprepared to face all the tremendous complications of that first Festival. But somehow, everyone lent a hand. Visconti and Robbins and Quintero and everyone else helped each other. We had a fabulous opening, but curiously enough the Italian press was incredibly hostile. Still, everyone came. The idea of me, this mad composer, starting this Festival, amused everybody. Ironically enough, I found myself surrounded by the very audience I was trying to avoid. People came from Rome, Paris, New York, London. There they were! All the same old faces! Still, it was a very exciting evening.

"But I couldn't believe the Italian press! They were positively poisonous. You know, whenever I'm asked the difference between

Italians and Americans, I always say the fundamental difference is
that the Americans like success. If you are a successful person,
Americans like you. If you are a down and outer, they try to avoid
you. The Italians are just the opposite. If you're successful, everybody hates you, and they'll try everything to do you in. If, on the
other hand, you are sick with the most revolting disease, or if you're
dying, they all come running . . . *poverino!* If a girl in an Italian
family marries a handsome boy, all the relatives are furious and say,
'He smells' or something. But if she marries a poor hunchback they
all say, '*Così simpatico!*' And so it was with the Festival. The
Italians just couldn't bear the idea that it was a success. During our
second year I was accused of having a festival of and for homo-
sexuals. A very well known Italian stage director and a stage designer hired a plane and dumped obscene leaflets on Spoleto. The
leaflets showed a bull with a huge erection, saying something like
'We *real* men salute the Festival.' This was only one of many Italian
sabotage maneuvers against us."

In its eighteen-year history, the Spoleto Festival of Two Worlds
has survived the devastating setbacks that might have doomed it to
an early death. Its success must be attributed to Menotti's incredible
tenacity and to the fact that against all odds he managed to actually
fulfill his dream of bringing together playwrights, actors, directors,
composers, conductors, musicians, painters, sculptors, designers,
choreographers, dancers, poets, and writers from many parts of the
world, all of whom pooled their talents to make the Festival one of
the most forward-looking and invigorating summer events anywhere. Unlike other Festivals, it combined the genius of well-
known artists with the adventurousness of promising newcomers.
More than any other festival in the world, Spoleto has spawned innumerable young talents, who were given their first international
platform there.

The list of "firsts" is endless, and one can only cite a few examples.
It was in Spoleto, for example, that stage director Frank Corsaro
made his debut as a director of opera, as did Patrice Chereau. It
was at Spoleto in 1961 that film director Roberto Rossellini directed
his first play. Soprano Shirley Verrett sang her first *Carmen* at
Spoleto in 1964 with Antonio Gades as its *premier danseur*. Maurice
Bejart's Ballet of the Twentieth Century came that same year, and
Arthur Mitchell offered his first choreographic effort for the opera
Salome.

Spoleto saw the world premiere of Tennessee Williams' *The Milk*

Train Doesn't Stop Here Anymore in 1962, starring Hermione Baddeley, and the European debut of the Alwin Nikolais Dance Company. In 1963 such playwrights as Edward Albee, Jules Feiffer, and Eugene Ionesco had their plays performed. The Paul Taylor Dance Company's European debut took place in Spoleto in 1964. Rudolf Nureyev created his version of the full-length ballet *Raymonda* for Spoleto, and French film director Louis Malle directed his first opera—*Der Rosenkavalier*—that same year. The young Justino Diaz sang in Rossini's *Stabat Mater* in 1964.

Henry Moore created his first stage set and costumes at Spoleto for Mozart's *Don Giovanni* in 1965, and Leroi Jones presented his *Dutchman* and Harold Pinter his *A Slight Ache*. The poet Ezra Pound turned composer for a work called *La Mort de Villon*, performed with choreography by John Butler. John Cranko brought his Stuttgart Ballet for the Spoleto premiere of its *Romeo and Juliet*, danced by Marcia Haydee and Richard Cragun.

In 1966 novelist Saul Bellow presented his play *Under the Weather*, starring Shelley Winters and Jack Warden, and Menotti undertook what he considers his best directorial effort, Debussy's *Pélleas et Mélisande*, starring Judith Blegen, with a superb set by Rouben Ter-Arutunian. Jerzy Grotowski brought his Polish Theater Laboratory to Spoleto in 1967, and Buckminster Fuller erected his Spoletosphere, a geodesic dome, for the Festival.

Menotti, having long eschewed the presentation of his own works at Spoleto, resigned as artistic director of the Festival in 1968 and allowed one of his operas to be presented: *The Saint of Bleecker Street*. He also undertook to direct his first Wagner opera—*Tristan and Isolde,* with brilliant sets and costumes by Luigi Samaritani. In 1968, Edward Albee returned with his *Box-Mao-Box.* Joseph Chaikin's experimental Open Theater came to Spoleto, and Israel Horovitz's *The Indian Wants the Bronx* was also performed.

The year 1969 brought Eliot Feld and his company with the young conductor Christopher Keene as its music director. (Keene would play a major role in the Festival in subsequent years.) The boisterous and highly experimental theatrical production of *Orlando Furioso,* conceived and directed by Luca Ronconi, was a major hit of the 1969 Festival.

In 1970 the La Mama Experimental Theatre Club presented its avant-garde fare, and the Merce Cunningham Company made its Spoleto debut. The following year brought Andre Gregory's daring *Alice in Wonderland* and the first European visit of Arthur Mitchell's

Dance Theatre of Harlem, while Christopher Keene conducted his first major opera, *Boris Godunov*, directed by Menotti.

Lar Lubovitch and his dance company came in 1972, and 1973 saw a superb production of Puccini's *Manon Lescaut*, directed by Visconti and conducted by Schippers. Jerome Robbins conceived of *Celebration: The Art of the Pas de Deux*, bringing together world-famous dancers from Italy, France, the U.S.S.R., England, and America. The following year saw the Spoleto premiere of Menotti's opera *Tamu-Tamu*. Film director Roman Polanski directed his first opera, Alban Berg's *Lulu*. And another "first" was Robert Wilson's production of *A Letter for Queen Victoria*.

Originally the Festival was to have a single director who would tie together the American and Italian activities, and it was thought that Menotti should hold this pivotal post. But Menotti demurred; the job would be entirely too time-consuming. Instead, he asked his friends Dorle and Dario Soria to take over. This arrangement did not work out, and the Sorias were retained on an advisory basis. Menotti then engaged a brilliant woman, Anna Venturini, to head the Italian part of the Festival, and Chandler Cowles agreed to handle the American side. Throughout the years these posts would change, as would much of the personnel of the Festival. Three of the key posts, however, have been staunchly held by faithful and irreplaceable collaborators. Raf Ravaioli, who began as an assistant to Miss Venturini, is now the General Administrator of the Festival. Secondly, Renato Morozzi, who seems endowed with the gift of ubiquity, is in charge of productions. Finally, Lida Gialloreti is the General Secretary, as well as keeper of all the keys, gossip and secret dramas of the Festival.

Year after year there is a stream of assistants and secretaries, all eager to work with Menotti and anxious to be a part of the Festival's excitement and glamour. Because Menotti had enlisted the financial aid of the rich from both America and Italy, the Festival is usually inundated by members of the Italian aristocracy and American society. These Spoleto "Angels," primarily wealthy women, cluster around Maestro Menotti like moths around a flame. During the Festival's two- or three-week period, Spoleto is the scene of frantic comings and goings on the part of the Spoleto staff, who must attend to myriad details. But no day passes that Menotti's own time is not spent in supervising practically all of the details, from finding accommodations for the sudden arrival of a foreign dignitary to a *crise* with a leading actor or singer.

During the Festival Menotti shuttles between two residences, the rented Palazzo Campello and his own house on the Piazza del Duomo. Palazzo Campello, one of the tiny town's grandest homes, serves the composer as his official "residence." At Campello he holds elaborate luncheons for prospective Spoleto backers, political dignitaries, and the rich and famous. He throws large postperformance parties there and holds small and large meetings pertaining to the Festival. At the Palazzo at least three young secretaries attend to his correspondence and the endless phone calls that continually interrupt the flow of a day's work. Menotti meets each problem with relative calm. He is truly in command, and only when situations are stretched beyond their limits will he explode. But these explosions are short-lived, and should a secretary burst into tears or an assistant be given a dressing down, Menotti invariably forgives all and cajoles all back to their former good spirits.

Menotti's private residence on the Piazza del Duomo is a small fifteenth-century house with three floors. The first floor contains a two-room guest apartment, the second his bedroom and studio, and the third is a large, luxurious terrace overlooking the piazza. This is where Menotti relaxes, ending his hectic day with a small group of intimate friends who usually keep the composer company, sharing a midnight meal with him and sitting around reviewing the day's activities. Often they amuse each other with droll stories about this one and that one and, on occasion, play wicked truth games instigated by Menotti, who takes an odd pleasure in needling the people he loves and being in return outrageously teased by those close to him. At evening's end, his entourage sleepily returns to their own quarters, allowing Menotti to get some much-needed sleep. But the composer is incapable of actually falling asleep without first reading for a while, usually from a book whose subject is far removed from his everyday activities, such as history, of which Menotti is a passionate student.

The next day finds him rising at around eight. His devoted housekeeper, Agnese, prepares a modest breakfast, which is consumed while Menotti reads various international papers. He then dresses and prepares to face yet another Festival day. He appears at Palazzo Campello, where the phones have already begun to ring. A typical morning will find the composer dictating letters and alerting Giovanna, the cook, as to who will be coming to lunch and dinner and who will drop by for drinks. At one point he will leave Campello to look in on rehearsals taking place at the various theaters. He will confer with directors, choreographers, and conductors and will be collared by innumerable people, each with his own problem that "only Menotti can solve."

In the early years Menotti originated a Festival presentation he called "Album Leaves." This was a kind of intellectual cabaret in which any number of well-known playwrights, musicians, poets, etc., would devise brief sketches, some lasting two or three minutes, others ten or fifteen minutes, which would be performed in cabaret style and contain a wide variety of theatrical genres. Participating in this concept were, among many others, Jean Cocteau, Thornton Wilder, W. H. Auden, Robert Rauschenberg, Larry Rivers, Donald McKayle, Gregory Corso, Campigli, Rafael Alberti, Alwin Nikolais, Italo Calvino, and Dino Buzzati. Menotti himself was represented by a series of short plays, some of which were written under another name. There was a little overture by Aaron Copland, a short opera by Henze, a short opera by Samuel Barber (which has been published under the title *A Hand of Bridge*) and one by Lukas Foss called *Introductions and Goodbyes*. Menotti supplied the text for them both. "Album Leaves," an interesting and successful Festival highlight, was inexplicably abandoned within a few years.

Another Festival institution, begun in 1960, is the midday chamber concert, underwritten by Alice Tully, who gave Lincoln Center its first chamber music hall. From the beginning these concerts have been under the direction of Charles Wadsworth, and are one of the most successful institutions of the Festival. Visitors to the Festival usually begin their days by attending these noontime events, which last only an hour and bring together some of the world's greatest instrumentalists. They have given such artists as Pinchas Zukerman, Jacqueline du Pre, Emanuel Ax, and the Guarneri String Quartet their first public accolades, and well-known musicians such as John Browning and Sviatoslav Richter often contribute their services. This midday oasis of chamber music is regularly attended by Menotti, who sits in a box alone or with invited guests, and it is here that Festival visitors get their first glimpse of Maestro Menotti. The concert over, the chamber players walk across the piazza and entertain friends at informal gatherings in Menotti's private residence. If not pressed for other work, Menotti joins the chamber players and their guests. More often than not, however, he returns to Campello, where he lunches with official visitors to the Festival or with dignitaries who will be attending the evening events.

Luncheon over, Menotti busies himself with endless details to which he attends with speed and precision. While appearing to be in the midst of chaos and confusion, Menotti is nothing if not totally clearheaded and organized. Major and minor problems are solved on the spot, decisions are made quickly, and duties are relegated to the appropriate people.

Of course, the Festival drains Menotti's energies. During its run, there is no time for him to compose or to attend to his own career. Nevertheless, he has often placed his talents as a stage and opera director at the service of the Festival and goes to his tasks with enthusiasm and inventiveness. For eighteen years Menotti has used his resourcefulness and imagination to make the Spoleto Festival of Two Worlds a unique experience. Aside from having placed Spoleto on the international map, he has brought culture and commerce to the townspeople—the Spoletini—who have responded each year by rewarding Menotti with a huge public display of their love and admiration. On his birthday, which usually falls toward the end of the Festival, the townspeople and all the children of the town gather in the Piazza del Duomo to pay him homage. They come bearing gifts, holding banners, singing songs, creating a holiday atmosphere in praise of their extraordinary benefactor.

The Spoletini were not always that grateful. Menotti recalled his initial struggle with the city fathers. "At the beginning everyone in Spoleto was extremely suspicious and very bewildered. During the first years we had a Communist mayor—a charming, intelligent man, who at first was rather embarrassed by this sudden onslaught of talented young Americans. Still, he immediately understood the importance the Festival would have for the town. He helped us right away. But the man who really made me come to Spoleto was a well-known lawyer, Adriano Belli, who was himself a Spoletino. He wouldn't hear of my holding the Festival anywhere else. At the beginning he helped me in every way he could, and treated me as if I were his own son. Later, however, as the Festival became more and more successful, he began playing all sorts of nasty little tricks on me. As I had become rather fond of him by then, I was at a loss to explain his strange behavior. One day I finally cornered him at a reception and asked, 'Why are you doing this to me? You are the one who made me come here.' He suddenly burst into tears and, throwing his arms around me, said, 'I'm sorry, Gian Carlo, I can't help it. I'm jealous—*sono geloso!*'" Finally, all the nastiness and jealousy that had made itself apparent and all the terrible articles that were written about the Festival actually helped me to go on with the project. It brought out my stubbornness and gave me courage. But all my strength was needed because I soon began to run out of money. While it was easy to raise money for the first year, the second year was very difficult and the third year became impossible.

"Believe me, I don't regret Spoleto. I foresaw almost everything about the Festival. I was prepared for all kinds of struggles. The one thing I was not prepared for was the humiliating quest for money."

Spoleto's money problems have continued, and to some degree it has affected Menotti's creative and personal life. Menotti would accept commissions just to have a flow of cash that could keep at least part of the Festival going. More and more, money began to play a major part in the composer's life, although the acquisition of it had never been a motivating factor.

The question of money brought about a strain between Menotti and certain of the people closest to him. During 1973 the relationship between Menotti and Thomas Schippers was particularly difficult. To be sure, money was not the sole factor. Menotti and Schippers, inseparable friends for some fourteen years, had long ago drifted apart, although no amount of acrimony would keep the conductor away from his duties to the Festival. During 1973 Thomas Schippers occupied an apartment in Palazzo Campello, directly above Menotti's quarters. But the two men barely spoke to each other. Discussing this rift, Schippers commented on the progressive change in Menotti's character and touched on some of the reasons why their friendship had dwindled.

"I will tell you the truth. There's a big difference between the Gian Carlo of today and the Gian Carlo of twenty-five years ago. I must be honest with you. Gian Carlo and I don't see one another now. Either I'm too busy or he's too busy, or he's running around like he never used to. One of the things that Gian Carlo taught me a long time ago was never to perform for money. Call it idealism, or what you want, but that got into my system. It isn't that I'm not concerned about how much money I make, but I never in my life conducted for money in a place or with somebody that I didn't believe in. Now, Gian Carlo, today, is doing just that."

I asked Schippers to tell me something of his years with Menotti, of his relationship with Samuel Barber. In discursive fashion, Schippers made clear the complexity of these relationships.

"The fact is, none of the relationships are clear, and no one will be able to explain them to anyone. I mean, you will talk to Gian

Carlo and he will say, 'What is happening to Tommy?' And *I* say, 'What is happening to Gian Carlo?' If you talk to Sam he will say, 'I don't understand anything.' You will never get to the bottom of our relationships because *we* haven't. Why don't I see Gian Carlo? I don't know. Why is that over? It's very sad. I repeat, I don't know why it's over. And I'm sure Gian Carlo doesn't know. We should see each other more. But we don't. Of course, there was Nonie [the late Nonie Phipps, Schippers' wife]. Nonie, who adored Gian Carlo, and maybe even more Sam, knew how to deal with them. I think they both adored her. Sam and I have never really gotten along. He's a brilliant man. No one has conducted his music more than I. But our wavelengths have never met. I respect Sam to the hilt. He is one of the world's great composers."

The Spoleto Festival, frantic and time-consuming as it was and is, did not bring Menotti's composing to a halt. Several major works were undertaken even as the composer's time became more precious. No less than three works were completed in 1963: *The Labyrinth*, *The Last Savage*, and *The Death of the Bishop of Brindisi*. In 1964 came *Martin's Lie*, in 1968, *Help! Help! The Globolinks!* In 1971 Menotti wrote *The Most Important Man*. In 1973 came *Tamu-Tamu*. In 1975 he revised the libretto of Samuel Barber's opera *Antony and Cleopatra*.

Spoleto was less of a drain on his own creative powers than is generally assumed. It is true that the works took longer and longer to complete. On the other hand, throughout his career the "last minute" syndrome had always been a part of his working methods. If closely examined, Menotti's music during the advent of the Spoleto Festival did not really diminish in either technical finesse or melodic inspiration. Those who never had much use for Menotti's music continued to damn it, and those who admired it were simply disappointed that Menotti never chose to repeat himself, but attempted to broaden his musical scope. It is possible that the depth of *The Consul* or *The Saint of Bleecker Street* was not recaptured in most of his subsequent works. It is also possible that his librettos assumed a rather more simplistic and perhaps naïve point of view. Most great operatic librettos, however, are not noted for their intellectual content, and Menotti has always preferred to keep the flow of his texts as accessible as possible.

In 1963 *The Labyrinth* was commissioned by NBC, once more under the aegis and enthusiastic support of Samuel Chotzinoff. Like

Amahl it was written expressly for television, but unlike *Amahl, The Labyrinth* was a work that could *not* be transferred to the stage. Menotti made use of the medium of television in ways that explored and exploited its video possibilities. Surrealistic and somewhat hermetic, the work was not deemed a success. Menotti himself claims that it is musically weak. "It has some good thematic ideas," he said, "and it's well orchestrated. But *The Labyrinth* needs to be re-polished."

Menotti's next major opera was *The Last Savage*. Its libretto was written in Italian. Not since *Amelia al Ballo* in 1937 had the composer written a libretto in his native tongue. The work was commissioned by the Paris Opera, and negotiations for it had begun in the mid-fifties. At the time, Maurice Hirsch was director of the Paris Opera, and under his direction most Paris Opera productions were "spectaculars." Hirsch wanted Menotti to write in that same vein.

The composer was honored by this commission. No foreign composer since Verdi had had a work commissioned by the Paris Opera. There was Verdi's *Don Carlo* in 1867 and Menotti's *Le Dernier Sauvage* in 1963. Characteristically, the work progressed slowly. Only one act was completed by the promised delivery date. By that time the opera's administration had changed hands. Hirsch's successor set a new deadline but asked the composer to diminish the extravagant aspects of the work. Paris no longer wanted spectaculars. Menotti went back to work and once again missed his deadline. On his next trip to Paris he found that a third administration was in power at the Paris Opera, this one under the direction of the composer Georges Auric. Auric was happy to extend Menotti's deadline once more, but he felt that the opera would be more appropriate for the more intimate confines of the Opéra Comique. Again Menotti went back to work, and what had begun as a large-scale comedy ended up as a rather intimate opera buffa.

The premiere of *Le Dernier Sauvage* took place in Paris at the Opéra Comique on October 21, 1963. It was staged by the composer and presented by Hervé Dugardin, the Comique's director, and the man responsible for having brought Menotti's *The Consul* to Paris. Its cast included Gabriel Bacquier in the title role and Mady Mesplé, Adriana Maliponte, Solange Michel, Michele Molese, Xavier Depraz, and Charles Clavensy. The Italian libretto was translated into French by Jean-Pierre Marty.

The farcical plot deals mainly with Kitty, a rich American girl who is hunting the Abominable Snowman in India. To humor her, a maharajah arranges for one of his servants, a simple-minded peasant named Abdul, to play the role of The Savage, and let himself be captured in the jungle by the gullible, pretty hunter. Taken to Chicago by the triumphant Kitty, Abdul is so horrified by modern civilization that he flees back to India and hides in the jungle, becoming a real savage. Hunted down again by Kitty, who has fallen in love with him, he succumbs to her entreaties and, although she pretends to share his simple, primitive life, it is obvious by the end of the opera that she will trick him back into the world he has tried to escape.

The French press was less than enthralled by *Le Dernier Sauvage.* They considered both music and libretto well below the standards set by the composer's earlier works. They found the score muddled, the scenery unattractive, and the story altogether too intricate. Even the singers were deemed ineffective. Menotti was understandably crushed, but his spirits soon revived at the prospect of the work's Metropolitan Opera premiere, to be held on January 23, 1964.

No effort was spared to make the American premiere as glittering as possible. The New York production differed slightly from the Paris version; the first act was cut by twenty minutes, and an additional scene was given to the savage in the last act. The work was conducted by Thomas Schippers and staged by Menotti. New sets and costumes were designed by Beni Montresor; an English translation was provided by George Mead. A distinguished cast was gathered, including Roberta Peters as Kitty, Nicolai Gedda as the maharajah's son, and George London as Abdul, the savage. Others in the cast included Ezio Flagello, Lili Chookasian, Morley Meredith, and Teresa Stratas.

Opening night was a gala affair, but the next morning's reviews were entirely mixed. Since it was Menotti's first major opera since *Maria Golovin,* its New York premiere received wide coverage. Because the critics were so at odds about the opera's merit, the Metropolitan, in a rare gesture, took out a large *New York Times* ad with a bold headline reading "Which paper do you read?" Quotes from all the critics—bad and good—were reprinted. Harold Schonberg, of the *New York Times*: "What has this to do with music? Not much. . . . The very modest talent of Mr. Menotti is not enough to sustain his elaborate scheme. . . ." Louis Biancolli of the *World Telegram*: "Menotti . . . has written . . . probably the best opera buffa by a living composer." And so it went, with critics hating or loving Menotti's latest offering.

The following May finally saw the Italian premiere of *The Last Savage* under its original title *L'Ultimo Selvaggio*. The opera opened in Venice to instant success

But in America *The Last Savage* died an early death, and there was scathing disapproval from highly distinguished quarters. In the April 1964 issue of the now defunct *Show* magazine, no less a personage than Igor Stravinsky took umbrage at Menotti's latest work.

SHOW: But did you find merit in *The Savage* at all?

STRAVINSKY: I enjoyed one episode, the "dodecaphonic" string quartet. This was not very good, but it is the best music in the opera. I appreciate that Menotti intended it as a parody of Schoenberg-Webern, that in fact he meant to behave like a pigeon on the newest monument of Western musical tradition. But his wings would not carry him high enough to make even that gesture effective. A parodist must have a home style before he can expose other styles, but *The Savage* is only parody, or attempts at parody, and when one of the ensembles starts out with a rhythm from Verdi (the "Zitti, Zitti"), it invites and receives ludicrous comparison. I should add, too, that "modern life," at least the 1964 kind, cannot be mocked successfully with a technique derived from mid-Mascagni.

SHOW: Then you don't agree that the subject has possibilities?

STRAVINSKY: No possibilities at least for Menotti's equipment, for though he certainly qualifies as a "natural savage"—he claims the predicament of the opera as his own, in a program note—he completely fails to project the other side of the dilemma: "sophisticated modern life." His "opera" is without a hint of that. In fact, the only aspect of "modern life" *The Last Savage* does suggest is that certain low-level functions should now be turned over to a computer; or, in other words, that the latter two-thirds of this score should have been composed by feeding the first one-third to an IBM machine.

The "predatory female" might have possibilities, though—I am thinking of Mr. Robbins' terrifying ballet about her to the music of my string concerto—especially to a bachelor composer with great talents, like Britten or to Henze or Menotti. In any case, a frank treatment of that subject could hardly fail to result in a work of more tension. (I imagine a spooky piece with an unex-

plained dread, as in "The Turn of the Screw"—a roomful of the
bodies of sacrificed boys, for example.)

SHOW: But surely you will concede that Menotti has personality. Aren't such devices as the repeated "Oh Mother, Oh Mother"
in *Amahl* and the "Oh Father, Oh Father" in the *Savage*—aren't
they marks of personality?

STRAVINSKY: Hmm, well, they are Menotti's bread and butter
at any rate.

SHOW: But you must have liked the sets. *Everybody* liked the
sets.

STRAVINSKY: Well, there was that sun in the second scene. It
looked like a fried egg and made me hungry.

SHOW: In short?

STRAVINSKY: In short.

SHOW: An eye-closer?

STRAVINSKY: An eye-closer.

Menotti accepted Stravinsky's acid remarks in good humor. He
was, however, annoyed that the libretto of *The Last Savage* had
been quoted scornfully in English without any mention that it was
not the original, but simply a rhythmic translation. "How would
Stravinsky feel," asked Menotti, "if I should quote Auden's libretto
of *The Rake's Progress* in its Italian translation by such hilarious lines
as: '*Io vo lontan, ma s'io tornassi un dí, ogni albero appassi* . . . '?"
Ironically, among the highlights of Menotti's directorial career
was his staging of Stravinsky's *The Rake's Progress* at the Hamburg
Opera in 1967. "Rolf Lieberman, the director of the Hamburg
Opera, asked Stravinsky whom he would like as director for *The
Rake's Progress*," recalled Menotti. "To Lieberman's great surprise,
Stravinsky said, 'Menotti.' I was very surprised and flattered, al-
though a great deal of the music was certainly not my cup of tea.
Nevertheless, I accepted with pleasure. To my further surprise, Rolf
Lieberman commissioned me to write something specifically for
the Hamburg Opera. As you know, the Hamburg Opera has always
been the citadel of the avant-garde, and my name was anathema
there. Nevertheless, it was for the Hamburg that in 1968 I wrote
Help! Help! The Globolinks!"

CHAPTER
15

"Venus has moved into the house of Capricorn.
Ah me, for any man born in July!"

(The Saint of Bleecker Street)

When Samuel Barber was asked why Menotti undertook the Spoleto Festival, he said "You could say it's a need for having people around *all* of the time. A need for a certain amount of power."

A need for people and a need for power. Menotti undoubtedly thrives under the pressures of human contact. His gregariousness is among his great virtues, and he has the capacity for producing excitement around himself. Because of this, he can make people collaborate, even under the most trying circumstances, and he has a way of ameliorating the most impossible situations. Intuitive to an alarming degree, he can instantly pinpoint a person's foibles and can describe them accurately yet disarmingly. There is, of course, his famous charm. Countless individuals have fallen under its spell and succumbed to solicitations for time, money, moral support, and work. The Spoleto Festival would not be what it is without Menotti's unceasing ingenuity for making others do his bidding. Menotti has also earned the lifelong devotion of many. Acts of extreme kindness have tied such people to him and their gratitude knows no bounds. Although they are aware of Menotti's weaknesses, their love for him remains blind. A woman long in his employ—Agnese Bonechi—made clear her feelings for the Maestro:

"As far as I'm concerned, Menotti is the most human person that exists on this earth. I have never met anyone so kind. I have always been a maid, and I was always treated like a maid. Not Menotti. He made me feel as though I were the mistress of the house. The thing that really bound me to him was that two years after working for him and Maestro Schippers, my little son died. I knew my boy was

ill, but I didn't know how ill. I remember running back and forth
between my own house and Menotti's to take care of him. One
morning I knew that my child was terribly sick. I told Menotti and
he instantly got into his car to fetch a doctor. My boy had to be
placed in a hospital immediately. Menotti called every single hour
to enquire about him. Finally, my two-and-a-half-year-old son died
of diptheria. Of course it was a highly contagious disease and I had
been with my little son every moment. Menotti came to me, although I begged him not to come close. Nevertheless, he embraced
me many times in order to comfort me.

"After the tragedy I became even more attached to him. It was
Menotti who paid all the funeral expenses for my child and he also
paid for a large mass conducted for him. Menotti was the only one
who made the loss of my child bearable. It was extremely painful
for me to return to my own home, because everywhere I looked
I could see my baby. Menotti sent me money so that my husband
and I could move into another apartment. I have worked for Menotti since 1956. I have never seen the Maestro really angry. Of
course, he does a lot of screaming, but he is always good and always
gentle. He has many many people around him and especially many
women. All these women are jealous of each other—each one thinks
she is the one. The fact is, Menotti is sweet and charming to each
one of them, which makes them think that. Of course, Menotti is
also surrounded by a lot of artists and intellectual people. I find he
is really happiest when he is with very simple people—uncompli-
cated people. But even more than that, I think he is happiest when
he is alone. That's when he is the calmest."

One of the mainstays of the Spoleto Festival is the highly energetic Festival secretary—Lida Gialloreti. Born in Spoleto, but
brought up in Rome, Miss Gialloreti met Menotti in 1958.

"When Gian Carlo was starting the Festival, he was looking for
a person who knew Spoleto and who also knew how to speak
English. He also needed someone to cope with the problems of the
city. Well, a friend of mine recommended me to Menotti, although
I had no intention whatever of taking on this job. Nevertheless, I
agreed to meet the Maestro and I will never forget our luncheon. We
met at the only hotel in Spoleto—a third-class hotel with a squalid
dining room—and there was Menotti, seated at a very large table,
surrounded by a large entourage, something he is never without. We
were introduced, and my friend quickly added that I had no intention of working for the Festival.

"Menotti paid no attention to this at all. He called over a waiter, told him to bring a bottle of wine, and announced to everyone that he wanted to make a toast in honor of his new secretary. I protested vehemently. Again and again I said, 'I don't wish to work! I don't want any responsibilities!' The upshot was that within ten minutes I had fallen in love with Menotti, had become his friend and faithful servant. After lunch he led me to the Spoleto office, and I have been here ever since.

"Menotti is more than a friend. He is part of my family, someone I can count on for anything and everything. You know, there are things about Menotti that no one knows—that are never talked about—that have to do with the kindness and generosity he extends to everyone. To the boy who needs his teeth fixed but can't pay the dentist. To someone who needs glasses but can't afford them. To a young girl about to get married who has no money to buy a wedding dress. There are so many examples. Take the case of Lorenzo Muti. This boy born in Spoleto was discovered by Gian Carlo when he was six years old. Gian Carlo sensed his talent, even at that tender age, and gave him a role in his opera *Maria Golovin.* Today Lorenzo Muti is on the brink of a major conducting career. He has studied at the Juilliard school, and Menotti was responsible."

Lorenzo Muti, who created the role of Trottolò in Menotti's *Maria Golovin,* is the son of a Spoleto bus driver; his mother is a housewife.

"I was always very shy, very timid, but when Maestro Menotti began rehearsing *Maria Golovin* here in Spoleto, he chose me for the role of Trottolò. I was seven years old, but it was the turning point of my entire life. I went with the Maestro to Brussels, where the opera premiered, and then I was brought to New York with the same production. I repeated my role the following year in Milan. Then I returned to Spoleto and I was always somehow involved with the Festival. I would be in the chorus of *Carmen,* or do something in *La Bohème.* When I turned twelve, Menotti put me in Benjamin Britten's canticle *Abraham and Isaac.* I sang the boy soprano in it. I worked in the production of *Pélleas and Mélisande.* I was also in Menotti's *Martin's Lie.* I played one of the boys when it was first done in Italy.

"It was through Menotti that I was introduced to the world of music. He gave me my orientation toward certain goals. It was Menotti who helped me to decide on becoming a conductor. He sent me to the Curtis Institute of Music in Philadelphia when I turned seventeen. I studied there under Max Rudolf for three years. I should add that I was also very much influenced by my having met Thomas Schippers. Anyway, Menotti also helped me to get a scholarship at Juilliard, and I hope to be able to live up to Menotti's expectations."

Young Muti, being a Spoletino, was in an excellent position to describe the effect of the Festival on his home town. "Menotti had first wanted an even smaller town for the Festival. He did not want the Festival with a capital *F*, but something that would really be part of the city environment. At the beginning this worked out in Spoleto, but the Spoleto Festival was quite different from what it is now. The fact is, the Festival now has a great big *F*. To begin with, there was far greater participation of the population itself. It was all so new for them. Suddenly all these Americans came and all these things were happening. Then, little by little, their participation diminished. The fact is, not the entire population of Spoleto is in touch with the Festival. It is the structure of the city itself that has brought this about. You see, Spoleto is built on a hill, so you have the old town on top where the Festival takes place, and then you have the newer part at the bottom of the hill, which is detached from the Festival. So there is a dividing point. Still, the Festival has helped the town immensely—not only economically, but intellectually. You can't imagine how close-minded a town like this can be. So just for this reason alone, the Festival has been a boon to Spoleto. As for me, it has given me my life."

Much of the credit for organizing Spoleto as a Festival town goes to another "find" of Menotti's—Raf Ravaioli.

"I began to collaborate with Gian Carlo in October of 1957. The first problem was to organize Spoleto. To begin with there were no accommodations available for visitors. The most fatiguing and problematic work for me was to assess the hotel and apartment situation and to put into shape the various private homes which visitors could rent.

"Actually I met Menotti quite a long time ago—when I was twenty. Gian Carlo was in Rome to make the film version of *The Medium*. He asked me if I would like a small role in it. Anyway, Menotti thought that I could be helpful to the Festival. As I said, my job was to handle the mechanics of the Festival. I did all the dirty work. To begin with I worked with the Festival's Italian director, Anna Venturini. We worked during the winters. We attended to remodeling the hotels. I dealt with the city about permits, and I concerned myself with the comings and goings of various companies appearing at the Festival. When Anna Venturini died, her job fell to me and I've kept that position until today."

Raf Ravaioli commented on his quixotic employer:

"Of course, I find Gian Carlo extraordinary. But he can also be very difficult. For one thing, he loves to play games with people. To be quite honest about it, I doubt Gian Carlo's sincerity or esteem vis-à-vis those around him. Frankly I like Gian Carlo better during the periods outside the Festival, because during the Festival all those many people confuse and upset him. Almost automatically his personality changes. The only time Gian Carlo is happy during the Festival is when he is directing an opera for it. But this now happens infrequently. All he does is run around like crazy. All those women around him! Amusingly enough, Gian Carlo treats them as though they were part of a drama that he is directing. The fact is, I never go near Gian Carlo during the Festival. I never appear at Palazzo Campello or at his apartment in the Piazza del Duomo. All those lunches, cocktail parties, and dinners, with countesses, princesses, and rich Americans scare me to death. Besides, I firmly believe that if one starts living at night, one cannot very well live during the day.

"As for Menotti himself, I must confess I have never quite understood what he has asked of life. I don't really know what is most important to him, whether to write music, whether to write plays, whether to run the Spoleto Festival. To be quite honest about it, I feel that he is leading a life that is in total contrast to the life he *should* be leading. My vision of Gian Carlo is that of a man living in a small house, on the side of a hill, in the middle of the woods, composing music. That is when he is happiest. As it is now, he goes from year to year, doing all the things that take him away from himself."

What, if anything, has Raf Ravaioli learned from Gian Carlo Menotti?

"I have learned to lie—to lie without guilt. Having said this, Gian Carlo can count on my infinite and lasting friendship."

As a single man, Menotti has enlisted the aid of several "hostesses" —women who act as mistresses of Palazzo Campello during the Spoleto Festival. These are cultured, attractive, sophisticated women, possessed of great tact and charm. They help manage Menotti's hectic social life. These urbane and elegant women, usually in their forties or fifties, are fluent in various languages and put his guests at ease by being at once solicitous, entertaining, and practical. Throughout the years, they have watched over Menotti's guests as much as over Menotti himself. They adore the Maestro and will go to any length to make his life as easy as possible. Usually they donate their services during the Festival, content to be in Menotti's orbit, and therefore wield a certain amount of power. Each in her way commands the respect of Menotti, and each has been his friend for many years. Each also harbors strong personal feelings about him. One of these "hostesses" was the handsome Arabella Ungaro, an elegant Neapolitan woman, married to a lawyer, and the mother of three children. For a number of years, she represented large American film companies in Italy. After her marriage she devoted herself to being a wife and mother, and in 1959 met Gian Carlo Menotti.

"Menotti simply said, 'You're not doing very much these days, why don't you come and work for me?'" recalled Signora Ungaro. "At the time, there was no public relations office at Spoleto, and I organized one. I put some order into the theaters and arranged the distribution of tickets for Spoleto visitors. Later on, Gian Carlo asked me to officiate as hostess at Palazzo Campello. That meant organizing and running the place, and supervising the kitchen."

Arabella Ungaro, extraordinarily self-possessed, commented on her relationship with Menotti:

"Of course, Gian Carlo is a man of great charm. Everyone will tell you that. But people with great charm are very hard to judge, because with their charm they can fool you. He is the kind of man who can obtain anything out of anyone. I get along with him very well and pay little attention to the problems he can so easily stir up. You see, I'm not influenced by other people. I hate gossip, I hate scenes. As I pay no attention to these things, it's easy to get along with Menotti. What bothers me a lot about him is that he has become too concerned with trivial matters here at the Festival. He should be more connected with the creative part of it, and he's not. He spends his time looking for rooms for people. He worries about the restaurants in the town—things like that. I mean, when people go to Salzburg, they don't go to Herbert von Karajan to ask him for rooms. Another thing that bothers me is that he sometimes relegates great authority to people who don't know how to handle it. That's always been a problem.

"On the other hand, I've loved working for Gian Carlo. And I loved being around when the Festival started, because Anna Venturini was there to help run things. She was a wonderful woman, but then she died. When people die they are forgotten. Anna gave so much to the Festival! But when she died, Gian Carlo never gave her another thought. It was as though she never existed. He doesn't believe in regretting someone's death, or in recognizing their value. Something should have been done about this woman. Something should have been dedicated to her—Gian Carlo should have dedicated one of his works to her. But he did nothing. He's quite a cruel person, you know. Let me just say that I don't think Gian Carlo will ever get old. Still, as one gets older, all the things that you are come out—the sum of your life is somehow exposed. In America you have an expression about chickens coming home to roost. I hope in Gian Carlo's case, the chickens *won't* come home to roost."

Anna Milla, a member of the aristocratic Florence family, the Rasponis, has also served as one of Menotti's hostesses. She had been a piano student at the Florence conservatory and later held a job with an Italian music management concern. She arrived at Spoleto via Thomas Schippers, whom she met in Italy in 1959 and who invited her to run one of the theaters at Spoleto.

"I worked at Teatro Nuovo all day long," said Anna Milla. "And, of course, I met Gian Carlo. At the time, the Festival was very small and the staff was minimal. We all ended up doing everything. It was really quite exciting. At one point I worked for Gian Carlo as his secretary, when he directed the Spoleto premiere of *The Saint of Bleecker Street*. In the meantime I got married and was away from the Festival for several seasons. In the last few years I have helped the Festival by raising money for it from American corporations based in Italy. I managed to raise some twenty-two thousand dollars in that way."

Signora Milla, a woman of independent means and a sensitive observer of people, spoke of her relationship with Menotti:

"Menotti fascinates me. I like people who are complicated and multifaceted. Menotti is like that. I try to give him something he can use in some way. He has been very kind to me personally. But I am careful with Gian Carlo. I try not to get too close to him. You see, the moment one sticks too close to Gian Carlo, he makes a very quick choice. He can drop you very fast. I mean, you think you're in one place but then you're not at all in that place. Anyway, in recent years I have found that Gian Carlo has become much too social. I think he has chosen this role, because he always chooses what he wants to do. I find the social side of Gian Carlo regrettable. Suddenly there are all these rich women around him in Spoleto. He used to be at all the rehearsals. He used to know all the artists. He used to enjoy all that. But in the last two or three years all these women have come into his life. Maybe it's the search for money, because I know that basically he doesn't enjoy any of that. The thing I love best about Gian Carlo is his warmth toward simple people. It's a very rare quality. I look at that with great respect."

Yet another in Menotti's Spoleto life was Nadejda Stancioff. She had met Menotti through the Italian ambassador in Washington, D.C., in the late fifties. Miss Stancioff was a professional actress both in Italy and the United States. During a fallow period the ambassador suggested that she might like to work with Menotti in Spoleto—that her theatrical background would stand her in good stead.

"Gian Carlo asked me what I could do besides act, and I told him I could make costumes. So I did that for a while at Spoleto, but then I was put in the public relations department, since I was good at that too. I took care of the VIPs and ended up running around like an idiot, tending to finding people rooms and making ticket reservations. More and more Menotti turned his energies to the Festival rather than to his own work—his music. It just drains him. I think that the Festival gives him a certain satisfaction, that he's not completely fulfilled. Personally I find him delightful, witty, amusing, and very loving. He pretends to be vague, but he's not vague at all. Of course, he's incredibly kind. I remember becoming very ill one time, and Menotti invited me to the house he was renting in Switzerland. He paid for my trip, took care of all my expenses, and nursed me back to health. On the other hand, one can never get close to Menotti. If you're there, he adores you. Once you're gone, he forgets you—out of sight, out of mind! If you come around the corner again, he takes you in his arms and adores you once again. I would venture to say that Menotti has very few real friends. What's certain is that he has a million acquaintances. My regret is that in the early years the Festival was something of a family affair. Now that feeling has become diluted and that's sad. Menotti should concentrate more on his work. He is not producing the way he used to. Perhaps he is trying to escape from something."

One of the most active women in Menotti's life has been the American Priscilla Morgan. Energetic in the extreme, she has helped to raise quantities of American money for the Festival, and her dedication to Menotti has been all-consuming. Once an important agent with the William Morris Agency in New York, Miss Morgan gave up this position to give her full-time support to the "cause." Miss Morgan's drive was such that she brought not only money to the Festival, but important artistic and social connections as well. It was Priscilla Morgan who introduced Buckminster Fuller to Menotti, persuading the theoretician to erect one of his geodesic domes in Spoleto. She introduced Menotti to countless other people and became a sort of agent-in-residence for the Festival. Her role at Spoleto and in New York was an important one—a role she jealously and zealously maintained until 1975.

"When I became involved with Menotti, it meant involving my whole life," said Priscilla Morgan. "I represented Gian Carlo as a world figure, as a great creative talent. In a way, I ran the whole Festival with him. In a way, our meeting was like fate. I became enamoured of him—dazzled by his gifts. I would have done anything for him. I've known him since 1958. We've been through a lot together. Never in my life have I ever met a man of such consistency of disposition, of such kindness and charm. God knows there's an ebullience and temperament there. I mean, he is *all* drama. Still, no matter what goes on around him, you can always count on Gian Carlo to be a gentleman, in the true sense of being a civilized man. In these very dark times for the arts, I feel Gian Carlo represents the continuum. He leads toward the future. That's why so many great people keep coming back to Spoleto every year.

"Menotti has a very special attraction to women. He has a great feeling for them and often allows them to play the role of a wife. Many men who are living and functioning with women aren't really that emotionally involved with them. Gian Carlo really is. One *knows*, as a woman. Any woman who is a woman senses this about him. She also knows the point at which it stops. It doesn't mean that the feeling stops, or the love. But one doesn't go beyond. Knowing that, the relationship takes on a deeper dedication. You bring a different kind of energy to the relationship, and you begin to really understand the poetic sense of the man. You realize that he is an artist and an internationalist—truly a man of two worlds. So we, the real women around him, sense this man of many worlds, this man who can reach many worlds and bring people together."

Among the many people who have helped, off and on, with the Spoleto Festival of Two Worlds, such as Mrs. John Nicholas Brown, Mrs. Henry Heinz II, Mr. Robert Tobin, Mrs. Edgar Tobin, Mr. Frederick Koch, and Mr. Ernest Hillman, none have been more consistently generous than Jean Tennyson Boissevain and Alicia Paolozzi, both of whom came to Menotti's rescue when the Festival found itself in dire financial straits. Yet another guardian angel proved to be the ever supportive Alice Tully.

A figure of utmost elegance, Miss Tully is a yearly visitor to Spoleto and an honored guest with "permanent" lodgings at Palazzo Campello, where she can be in close proximity to her good friend Menotti. It is Miss Tully who has supported the Festival's daily chamber concerts and who has helped Menotti whenever financial disaster has struck. A trim, neat figure, Miss Tully is something of a fixture at the Festival and during the course of its run can be seen strolling on the Piazza wearing elegant silk prints and shielding her eyes from the sun with a silk parasol. Miss Tully, a person of great reserve, was willing to reveal something about herself and her long friendship with Menotti.

"I was born in Corning, New York," she said. "The glassworks were founded by my great-grandfather in Cambridge, Massachusetts. But then my grandfather moved it to Corning, and it was there it became a successful thing. I am only too happy and proud to say that it is thanks to Corning Glassworks that I could do what I have done for Lincoln Center, and for music generally. I considered it the greatest possible privilege to be able to say yes when I was asked if I would be interested in helping to build a chamber music hall for Lincoln Center, and was, of course, deeply honored when this hall was given my name.

"A lot of people think I'm dead. The fact is, I'm not. Many years ago I was a singer. I sang a little opera but mostly I did recitals. Unfortunately, when I was young and ambitious, American artists were not appreciated or wanted. It was very difficult. This is why I didn't have many engagements in America. But I was able to give recitals in quite a number of European cities—Paris, London, Vienna, Budapest, Prague. I lived in Paris for a number of years. It was a marvelous period."

Alice Tully first met Menotti after a performance of his first opera, *Amelia al Ballo*, given at the Met in 1937.

"Gian Carlo was very young, and we were introduced in the dressing room of the conductor Maestro Panizza. Then I did not meet Menotti again for many years, until a cousin of mine, Mr. Arthur Houghton, Jr., called me one day and said that Menotti had a Festival in Spoleto and wouldn't I like to talk to him. Well, Menotti came to see me that same day, and we had a wonderful talk. He looked very much the way he does now. The Festival had already started.

I would say we met in the spring of 1960. Menotti asked me to come and visit Spoleto, and I did. I was really enormously impressed. I was particularly impressed by the glorious chamber music concert, and thought Charles Wadsworth was doing a wonderful job. Ever since then, those chamber concerts have been my special interest.

"About Menotti. Well, he's absolutely in a class by himself. There's nobody in the world like him. What he's done with the Festival is tremendous. He acts like a magnet. He attracts people who understand what a wonderful institution it is. I think he's enriched the lives of everybody who has worked closely with him. The only sad thing is that Menotti is a little too trusting and optimistic about people. He often expects more of them than they are able to give—and he's disappointed. As for our relationship, I think he realizes I deeply love and appreciate him—at least I hope he does. I know he's always been supremely grateful for the help that I've been able to give. I am happy to be on the board of the Festival."

There are many other women who circle about Menotti. There is the Countess Alicia Paolozzi, an American who married into the Italian aristocracy. She has been the life-long friend and supporter of Menotti's every undertaking. There is Camilla McGrath, married to Earl McGrath, once a secretary of Menotti's. The list goes on and on. The Spoleto Festival's long-time secretary, Lida Gialloreti, claims that Menotti loves these women, but that he is also extremely fond of toying with them.

"One might say that if Gian Carlo weren't a man of enormous sensitivity and goodness, he might be called something of a devil," said Miss Gialloreti. "Menotti is very disrespectful, but not in a bad sense. He loves to place these women in a position of emotional conflict—he likes to pit them one against the other. You see, each one feels she is the 'prima donna,' and each one admits to no rival. Each woman wishes to dominate her own particular domain. Arabella Ungaro does not like anyone to meddle with her position as hostess of the Palazzo. Priscilla Morgan never permitted anyone to touch her area in the arts. When these women overreach their places, a spark is set off and Gian Carlo loves to set the spark on fire. He likes to do this so that he can laugh and joke about it. It amuses him enormously. The point is, he really likes to be the center of attention himself.

"Of course, these women are all of a certain age. But Gian Carlo also adores having young girls around him. He has all sorts of beautiful young secretaries during the Festival. Some come from noble

Italian families. We've had Marina Colonna, Claudia Ruspoli, Livia Lancellotti. There were many others. They are there because Gian Carlo goes around saying that he is getting old. This is, of course, a pose, because he's made a pact with the devil and will never grow old. So there they all are, keeping him company, answering the phones, taking care of little details. However, even with them, he likes to see the sparks fly.

"One of the favorite things is to play cruel games. For example, the Tower Game. He will ask you to name the two most important people in your life, then he will ask which one you would push off the tower if you were forced to get rid of one of them. Or he will ask everybody in the room what three events in their lives they are most ashamed of. These are mean truth games, designed to expose people's weaknesses. In a way, it's to get to the core of somebody. Gian Carlo wants instantly to know who he is dealing with."

CHAPTER

16

"An ideal to be ideal, must suffer treason;
even ideals listen to reason."

(The Old Maid and the Thief)

While Menotti runs the Festival in consort with his various directors and with the help of dedicated women friends, the closest of his associates have invariably been his secretaries, many of whom have played an important part in Menotti's professional and personal life. These were generally bright, intelligent, hard-working persons, only too willing and able to give Menotti their fullest attention. They enjoyed considerable power and were given commensurate authority. If particularly adept, they were permitted to handle contractual matters between visiting artists or companies and allowed to negotiate business terms. They acted as liaisons between Italy and America and were generally useful as buffers for the constantly put-upon Menotti. Aside from these duties, they served as Menotti's personal factotums, seeing to his comforts, attending to his wide traveling schedules, arranging his appointments, and keeping a sense of order in his busy life.

Some of these secretaries were given many opportunities to broaden their own horizons. Some were allowed to assist Menotti in the staging of his works. If they were particularly talented, they would be sent to various parts of the world to stage Menotti's works on their own. But these were exceptional cases.

The first of these secretaries was Richard Evans, a talented young painter, who is responsible for having helped Menotti to raise the initial money and to organize the first Spoleto Festival. Through the production of *The Saint Of Bleecker Street*, he later became one of Broadway's most respected stage managers. Other secretaries included Earl McGrath, Joel Honig, Wendy Hanson and Joseph LeSeuer. But perhaps the most devoted of all was Francis Rizzo, for whom Menotti became something of an obsession. Rizzo, who is currently artistic administrator of the Wolftrap Foundation, is a trim, darkly handsome man of unusual sensitivity and intelligence. He heard of Menotti during his middle adolescence, and as he readily admits, even from that early age, he was intent on working for him.

"My interest in Menotti began with the dawn of the LP era," said Rizzo. "At one point my mother bought me a recording of *The Medium* and *The Telephone,* which was one of the few recordings of complete operas on LP. That was in the late forties. That recording turned me on to Menotti. I had always been an opera freak, but I hadn't realized that opera could be a theatrical form until I became aware of Gian Carlo's works. Anyway, I played *The Medium* and *The Telephone* endlessly, and just about that time *The Consul* was getting ready to go on. It was 1950. My mother got me tickets, and it was my first New York outing alone. I recall that the performance I attended was a benefit for Casa Verdi, and Gian Carlo made a curtain speech. That was the first time I clapped eyes on him. Tommy was conducting and that was the first time I clapped eyes on *him.* So I saw *The Consul* and was absolutely wiped out by it. I remember when the curtain came down on the first scene, my hand was stuck to the program on my lap. I was transfixed. Anyway, I saw *The Consul* about six times during that original run."

Francis Rizzo's obsession with Menotti took full flower. He had decided that, in one way or another, he would become associated with "this wonderful person." Thinking on what he wanted to do with his life, young Rizzo decided he would like to direct opera, and that he wanted to direct opera just the way Menotti did. He eagerly followed the composer's career. While he attended Hamilton College in upstate New York, he made frequent visits to the city in order to see repeated performances of *The Saint of Bleecker Street.* He had, in the meantime, been mesmerized by the television production of *Amahl and the Night Visitors,* which he recorded on his tape recorder. He had also gone to see the film version of *The Medium.*

Upon finishing college, Rizzo entered the Yale Drama School. He also made a trip to Europe with a close friend—someone who, while not knowing Menotti personally, knew many people who did. In 1959 the two friends found themselves in Milan. They stayed in the

Hotel Duomo, and there, fortuitously, was Menotti. Rizzo's friend introduced himself to the composer and introduced Rizzo as Menotti's greatest fan.

"I was twenty-two at the time. Menotti asked me what I wanted to do. I told him I wanted to be a stage director. He said, 'If I put you in front of Marie Powers, could you direct her? I have a hard time doing it myself!' Well, I was crushed. I thought he had discounted me automatically as a stage director. Anyway, Menotti invited us to come to Spoleto. My friend agreed to leave me there, and Menotti found me a little job as an assistant stage manager for the ballet group, which included Nora Kaye and Herbert Ross. That was in 1959."

Rizzo remained in Spoleto for a short period, then returned to Yale, and a few months later learned that the latest in a series of Menotti's assistant directors and secretaries had been fired. There was an opening for a job. During that summer, Rizzo was at the Williamstown Theater with Nikos Psacharopoulos, and he met Nikiforos Naneris, whom Menotti had sent to Williamstown to be an apprentice actor. The two young men became friends—a friendship based on their mutual admiration for Menotti. Through Nikiforos, Rizzo attempted to return to the world of Menotti. He offered himself as Menotti's assistant.

"It was not easy to get back into his orbit. It became clear to me that he felt I was too superficial and not to be trusted to work for him. Then, around the time of *The Last Savage*, in 1964, I learned he needed a staging assistant, and I had one more crack at it. Menotti held me on a string for three weeks and then didn't follow through, which embittered and disappointed me tremendously. By now I was in my twenties. I hadn't done any work. Everyone thought I was very bright, but that was about it."

Intent on getting some sort of work, Rizzo offered his services *gratis* at the Santa Fe Opera. While there, he learned that the assistant Menotti had hired instead of Rizzo had proven to be a catastrophe. Rizzo sent off a letter. "This is your absolute last chance to have me as an assistant. After this I will never ask you again." The letter worked. He was hired by Menotti, but not as a staging assistant.

"I was hired because he liked the way I wrote letters. The one I had written was particularly effective. Actually this is a key thing with Gian Carlo. He is fastidious about literary style. Well, he encouraged all my worst excesses in writing. So I became his secretary, although I told him I typed with one finger. At last I was working for Menotti and it was marvelous. For many many months he was happy with my work, although he found a lot to complain about, as he did with anyone who worked for him. But he could see that I was fanatically devoted to him and I did my best. In time, he also made me his staging assistant. I helped him on *The Saint of Bleecker Street* when it was done at the New York City Opera. The first summer I worked for him, we staged *Martin's Lie* in Venice.

"I had emotional problems in connection with Gian Carlo. You see, I really idolized him in an unquestioning way. I would have marvelous fantasies about the fact that he would eventually have to die and that I'd be at the funeral service, red-eyed, and there would be thousands of people from all over the world. I pictured it all happening at Capricorn. I saw myself wandering down the garden path after the services and shooting myself. In other words, the moment he was dead there would be no more reason to go on living. So I was passionately devoted to him. But this devotion did not include any erotic element. I wasn't, as many people are, genuinely attracted to him physically. And this is ten years ago, when he was even better preserved than he is today."

Francis Rizzo was Menotti's secretary and, eventually, staging assistant from 1964 to 1967. He was given the opportunity of staging *The Consul* and *The Saint of Bleecker Street* at the New York City Opera. He helped Menotti stage most of the operas given at Spoleto and assisted him in the production of Stravinsky's *The Rake's Progress*, at the Hamburg Opera in 1967.

"Of course, working as an assistant director wasn't always a lark, because Gian Carlo would bring in lots of other types to assist him and I was jealous of them—I didn't want them around. This was a great problem. Basically I felt that Gian Carlo liked me around more as a secretary, because he knew it would be very hard to find somebody who could combine all of my qualifications."

Despite his devotion, Rizzo's feelings toward his mentor were ambiguous:

"There are times when I think that Gian Carlo must be the kindest, most compassionate man who ever lived. At other times I think there is something terribly wrong and sick in him, which is destructive to other people. Oddly enough I have never been comfortable with him on a social level. I could have spent twenty-four hours a day of *work* with him, and enjoyed it. But to be alone with him in a social situation seemed very artificial. I didn't feel a free and easy flow between us. I never have."

Being in close proximity to Menotti, Rizzo could observe the composer's relationship to Sam Barber and Thomas Schippers:

"Everyone automatically loves Gian Carlo. Sam is a lot harder to appreciate. People would enjoy knowing Sam because he was an important composer. He could be charming, and was a wonderful conversationalist, and was very, very witty. But Gian Carlo was the 'fun' one. And Gian Carlo was the one who got his picture on the cover of *Time* magazine, and one of the 'hundred most important people in New York.'

"One thing that was obvious right away, was that anyone who was Gian Carlo's body servant, as his secretary was, was automatically suspect by Sam. While Sam was intrigued and perhaps secretly touched by my complete devotion to Gian Carlo, he also resented it very much. He made fun of the way I would address Gian Carlo: 'Maestro Adorato.' Sam hated that. He'd say, 'Your Maestro Adorato is waiting at the station. Why don't you go pick him up?'—that kind of thing. So Sam would be hard on Gian Carlo's secretaries. Gian Carlo had warned me about this. From the first he said to me, 'Now you must understand that Sam is very possessive. He doesn't like people around me—especially the ones who are around me *all* the time.'

"That was one of the problems that the household at Capricorn had to face. That is, Sam would have *his* friend, who would loathe Gian Carlo. Of course, there were good grounds for complaining about Gian Carlo's behavior toward Sam. It was mostly financial. The house at Capricorn was maintained almost entirely by Sam. The improvident Gian Carlo would just about scrape by with his own expenses during the year, drinking champagne, eating caviar, and running around all over the world. Sam would be stuck with the taxes, the phone bills, the servants—everything! All the expenses of Capricorn fell on Sam. So, of course, whoever was Sam's friend at the time, probably seeing his own 'legacy' threatened, would be very rude to Gian Carlo. And Sam would then be rude to Gian Carlo's friends.

"To begin with, Capricorn was a fabled place. Both Sam and Gian Carlo love the country and isolation. Sam was much more fixed at Mt. Kisco because he doesn't have the career Gian Carlo has, which compels him to be in the outside world. But Gian Carlo certainly looked forward to getting back to Capricorn. When the place was sold in 1973, Gian Carlo was able to put up with the trauma a lot more easily than Sam. I don't think Sam knew what it would mean when he finally had to leave. It was very *Cherry Orchard*. But when it came to money matters, Gian Carlo was never any good at handling them. His whole attitude toward money is actually admirable. He's never had any insurance. He's never put anything away. He's never had stocks and bonds. He doesn't care about that. Sam, of course, is more conventional and prudent. Gian Carlo runs through his money like an adolescent."

In 1968 Menotti made Francis Rizzo general manager of the Spoleto Festival. Although Rizzo had little managerial experience and was less than successful at ways of raising money for the Festival, he threw himself into the job with complete dedication. He held this post through 1970, at which point things fell apart. "The Festival had a disastrous summer in 1970. At the time Robert Tobin was president of the board. The whole financial thing was in a state. I was dealing with a very capricious personality. It was Tobin and me, and we had a *folie à deux*. Things got way out of hand, and it became clear to Gian Carlo that something had to be done. As it turned out, I thought I was more important to Gian Carlo at the Festival than I actually was. This is another thing that people find out about him. He generally believes that no one is indispensable. Not even me. I had this feeling about myself that I was a rare talent at his disposal. That he *couldn't* destroy me. Well, at the time, Priscilla Morgan and other level heads started cultivating Harvey Lichtenstein, who was running the Brooklyn Academy in New York. When Gian Carlo realized he could have Harvey take the whole goddamn thing off his shoulders, he kind of dumped me. He did it on the sly, and in a way I found very wounding. Around Christmas of 1970, Gian Carlo finally broke the news to me that I was out. He said Harvey was taking over my job, and I was to arrange my life accordingly.

"When all that was over, I began to feel I was summarily rejected. Still, he continued to ask me to help him stage various of his works. I did *Amahl* in New York, and *Maria Golovin* in Marseilles. Then, when he came to New York to do *The Most Important Man*, I wasn't involved at all. In fact, he even asked me not to come to the dress rehearsal. From that point on I stopped having too much to do with him. And he wouldn't seek me out after that, except for advice. At one point he asked me to go to Houston to stage *The*

Medium and *The Globolinks*. And he asked me to go to Trieste to do *Maria Golovin*. So he would call on me only when he *really* needed me. These days I see Gian Carlo hardly at all."

As it turned out, in 1976 Francis Rizzo was once more called upon by Menotti to serve as director of one of his operas. In November of that year, Rizzo staged the New York City Opera's revival of Menotti's *The Saint of Bleecker Street*.

CHAPTER
17

The Spoleto Festival, plagued by financial problems, found Menotti becoming more and more immersed in fund raising. Nevertheless, year after year the Festival opened, becoming progressively more established, with countless visitors making the beautiful Umbrian village the highlight of their summer travels. Though plunged into the endless Festival details, Menotti continued to accept commissions. In 1963 he composed the cantata *The Death of the Bishop of Brindisi*. In 1964 came *Martin's Lie*. These two works once more reflect Menotti's concern with his still-ambiguous religious beliefs, while also making clear his very special affection for children, who figure prominently in both works.

The Death of the Bishop of Brindisi was commissioned by the Cincinnati May Festival and premiered in that city on May 18, 1963. Max Rudolf conducted the orchestra and a large chorus. The role of the bishop was sung by Richard Cross, and the part of the nun by Rosalind Elias. Menotti once more wrote his own libretto, this one based on the Children's Crusade of 1212, during which some 30,000 boys and girls were reported to have set out unarmed to liberate the Holy Land. Ultimately the children perished. The bishop, who encouraged the crusade, becomes haunted by the tragedy. On his deathbed he recriminates himself for having sent the children to their doom. In a series of flashbacks, the events of the crusade are recalled. The crux of the bishop's dilemma is captured in the questions, "What faith, what love can justify the man who makes himself the arbiter of other people's lives? Was it God's will or my own folly?" At the point of death the Bishop claims from God an answer: ". . . I pray not for eternal bliss or peace or immortality . . . no forgiveness can wash my guilt away, for without knowledge absolute there can be no paradise for me. No gates of heaven shall I enter unless it be revealed to me why I, who loved so purely, was cursed with such destructive love." The answer is given by the final chorus: ". . . you have not asked in vain. The tooth, the nail, the eye have a precise function. Nothing is purposeless, nothing. Then, why should God have given you in life a questioning mind if not to hand to you in death the blinding answer? Sleep, sleep at last, o gentle pilgrim. Sleep into the dawn."

The cantata was given a tumultuous standing ovation in Cincinnati; Menotti was impressed by the reception.

Speaking of *The Death of the Bishop of Brindisi*, Menotti reiterated his own contradictory feelings on religious matters. "Of course, this kind of metaphysical anguish, as I like to call it, includes the problem of ethics—of how far we must be held responsible for the good and evil we do. Is the bishop of Brindisi responsible for the death of the children? Is he a corrupter of youth? Is he a false teacher? Or is God only responsible for his mistakes? Surely the bishop is not an evil man, and acted in good faith. Why then does he bring disaster? Is the bishop only a tool of God? Or must he alone bear his guilt?

"Although I think that essentially I am a good person, I also nurse a secret feeling of guilt about my life, and the Augustinian problem of Grace had intrigued me long before I wrote *The Bishop*. You see, I could never be a halfway Christian. T. S. Eliot's compromise, preached in his *The Cocktail Party*, which was probably inspired by St. Basil's statement that "a man's imitation of Christ can only go so far as his vocation allows," would never satisfy me. Whatever I do, I like to do *all* the way. I am untouched by the Bible, but immensely moved by the teaching of the New Testament. One must, however, be a St. Francis to go all the way according to Jesus' teachings. So I have detached myself from the church, but I am still dangerously attracted to its history and to the lives of its saints. I never pray, nor go to church, except for purely sentimental reasons—like at Christmas or Easter—but I have a curious feeling of envy toward the lives of certain saints, like St. Theresa, St. Francis, St. John of the Cross, or even of St. Joseph of Cupertino, who often, upon hearing Mass, would fall into ecstasy and fly high above the congregation, throwing his little beretta into the air and uttering cries of joy!"

Menotti's questioning spirit again came to the fore in his church opera *Martin's Lie*, the theme of which is an attempt to untangle the complexity surrounding the concepts of truth and love. The work was first given in June 1964 at the Bristol Cathedral in England as part of the annual Bath Festival. The plot is set in a medieval European orphanage. It tells the story of a fourteen-year-old boy, Martin, who must make the choice between a truth which could cost a man's life (a man whom Martin has built into a father figure) and a love which forces him to lie and swear to a falsehood. Martin pays for his allegiance to love with his own life.

This choice between love and truth was deemed a shaky theology, and the Bristol Cathedral was criticized for harboring it. The opera was first commissioned by the Friends of Canterbury Cathedral, which, upon learning of its subject matter, turned it down. It was also turned down by the Welles Cathedral. It was at Yehudi Menuhin's urging that it was finally accepted by the Bristol Cathedral and included in the Bath Festival. At its premiere, particular praise went to Michael Wennick, who sang the title role. The role of The Stranger was sung by Donald Macintyre, the villainous Sheriff by Otakar Kraus, and William McAlpine took the role of the kindly Father Cornelius. The English Chamber Orchestra was conducted by Lawrence Leonard.

The critical reception of *Martin's Lie* was, for the most part, negative. The work was deemed too simplistic, its theatricality too overwrought, and its score, in spite of its severe sparseness, too Pucciniesque. However, when presented in Italy a year later, both in Venice and in Perugia, it was highly praised by the Italian press, and its American premiere at the Washington Cathedral confirmed its success.

Thinking back on *Martin's Lie*, which remains unpublished, Menotti claimed that the work needs some correction. "One day I will have to rework *Martin's Lie*. Basically I wanted to go back to utter simplicity. The opera is almost entirely built on recitative, much of it inspired—as in *The Death of the Bishop of Brindisi*— by Gregorian chant. There are no set pieces, and the orchestration, for thirteen instruments, is extremely simple. In it I have resisted the temptation to show off any virtuosity as an orchestrator (as Benjamin Britten often did, to the detriment, I feel, of musical clarity), and have tried to avoid gratuitous instrumental tricks for the sole purpose of color.

"When I wrote *Martin's Lie*, I was thinking of the many sins that I have committed in the name of love. Sometimes I feel guilty about them, sometimes not. But then you have to face the question: What is love? Do we invent the people we love? That is the question I asked in *Maria Golovin*. The question I ask in *Martin's Lie* is, How much must we sacrifice ourselves for the people we invent?"

Throughout the Spoleto Festival years, Menotti divided his time between rounding up money and talent for Spoleto and composing. Although his friends kept complaining that he was progressively drowning himself in trivial Festival details, the fact is that many of these details were highly imaginative and hardly trivial. Though not alone in seeking the best possible Festival presentations, Menotti often dared the impossible when it came to getting people to make any particular Festival attractive and adventurous. There were many instances when only because of Menotti's persistence would a particular artist ultimately capitulate and be seduced into the Festival.

A case in point was Menotti's attempt to bring the late sculptor David Smith to Italy so that he might produce one or two large works to be included in an open-air sculpture exhibit in Spoleto, called Sculptures in the City. Although most famous European sculptors, such as Henry Moore and Marino Marini, had readily accepted, Smith was a more difficult catch. In 1959 Smith had already achieved stature as one of America's most original artists, and his time was at a premium. Smith was also known to be a man of complex temperament and given to heavy drinking. Menotti had been warned that Smith would be the least likely candidate for what he had in mind. These warnings only served to spur Menotti on into direct action.

"I was told I was out of my mind to try to get him for Spoleto," recalled Menotti. "People said he would never accept, that he was extremely busy, and that he had just turned down a huge commission. Anyway, I was given his phone number in Bolton's Landing. When I called, this very gruff voice answered and kept saying, 'Who are you?' Again and again he shouted the question. Finally I shouted back and said I was a composer and that my name was Gian Carlo Menotti. 'Oh, Menotti!' he said. 'I want to see you, Menotti!' Well, I said I wanted to see him *too*. Of course, I couldn't imagine what he wanted to see me about. Anyway, I invited him to have a drink with me at—of all places—the Palm Court of the Plaza Hotel. Well, on the appointed day in walks this huge man with a big moustache and we sat at this tiny little table. All around us were these aging ladies sipping their tea. Smith immediately ordered a triple whiskey. The first thing he said—and in a very loud voice—was, 'Mr. Menotti, I want you to know that my wife is a bitch!' And he proceeded to continue to call her the most unbelievable names, much to the horror of the ladies around us. 'But,' he continued, 'I wanted to see you because I have two daughters who are absolutely marvelous and are the joy of my life. They adore your music. They love *Amahl,* and I want you to write a piece for them, or write down your name for them, or do *something* for them.'

"Well, I told him that I would dedicate one of my operas to his daughters, if he would come to Spoleto and do at least one or two sculptures there. I told him we were having a big sculpture exhibit for the Festival and that there was a steel factory in Genoa which would be honored to offer him any needed material and to house him as a working guest. To my absolute amazement he said, 'All right.' He wanted to know when he was to go. I told him, 'Next Friday.' He said, 'All right, send me a ticket and I'll go.' Of course, by this time Smith had already consumed several more whiskeys, and I had no idea whether he would remember anything of this conversation. However, we left great friends, and he was in a marvelous mood. Immediately I called the Spoleto office in New York and told them to send David Smith a ticket to Genoa instantly. We sent him the ticket special delivery, and true to his word, he left for Genoa that next Friday. Naturally we alerted the head of the factory of the arrival of David Smith. He was delighted at the prospect of housing such a distinguished guest, and not only offered him the use and cooperation of the whole factory gratis, but also promised to transport the finished sculpture to Spoleto at his own expense.

"Smith arrived in Genoa about six or eight weeks before the Festival began. Towards the end of his stay there, the head of the ironworks called me up in Spoleto and said, 'Mr. Menotti, we have a crisis. David Smith has created not one, but twenty-one sculptures —and is still working away. He keeps asking for cases of whiskey and won't leave the factory, not even at night. He has completely paralyzed our production. Please take him away. Furthermore, how are we going to transport twenty-one sculptures to Spoleto? It would take at least twelve trucks to get them there. Who will pay for it all?' At the urging of Giovanni Carandente, who was organizing the show, I called Smith, who was in a very high, jolly mood. He said he was very inspired, loved the factory—and threatened me with at least ten more works. To lure him away I said that he was urgently needed in Spoleto to choose the square in which to place his sculptures. I also succeeded in convincing the director of the ironworks to pay the transportation costs of the twenty-one sculptures, after Smith agreed to leave one behind as a thank-you note.

"So this huge procession of trucks left Genoa and arrived in Spoleto, and we had the biggest exhibit of David Smith, ever. We displayed the 21 sculptures in the amphitheater, and many of them were sold very quickly. Smith supervised the installation, and he couldn't have been nicer. We became great friends and I was greatly moved when he gave me one of his sculptures, which was about the height of a person. At the bottom of it he inscribed the names of his two daughters. Alas, I have not been able to keep my promise as yet, because the work dedicated to his daughters, *Martin's Lie*, is still unpublished. Before he left, David Smith told me, 'I know you are not particularly drawn to abstract art, Gian Carlo, and so, aside from giving you this piece, I am also giving you permission to sell it if you ever need the money. However, don't sell it for less than fifteen thousand dollars.' A few years later, I did have to sell it, unfortunately. It was again a question of not having enough money for Spoleto. I was very sad when David Smith died."

Another coup for Menotti and the Spoleto Festival of Two Worlds was his ability to persuade poet Ezra Pound to make an appearance in 1965.

"I had read somewhere that Pound had written a small opera based on some Villon ballads. Of course, after his political imprisonment he had chosen to live in Venice in complete retirement, having taken a vow of silence. He lived the life of a mute. His only companion was Olga Rudge, who had been with him for many years. Anyway, I decided to go to Venice and call on him. I told Olga Rudge that I wanted to obtain Pound's little opera for presentation at the Festival. She said that he had indeed written something, but it was not really an opera, that, in fact, it was difficult to know what it was. It was true, however, that the work employed voices. She gave me the manuscript, which I still have. Interestingly enough, this work, which was called *Le Testament*, was a rather sketchy piece of music. George Antheil made a new version of it, and it was once performed at the University of California. But Pound didn't like the Antheil version, and he wanted us to do another version altogether. So I asked two of my pupils, Lee Hoiby and Stanley Hollingsworth, to see what they could do with it. We went through the work and somehow put it together. We worked out a new orchestration based on Pound's own notes. Finally we presented it as a dance work called *Le Mort de Villon*, choreographed by John Butler and danced by Vera Zorina and Carmen de Lavallade. Pound observed the rehearsals and was very happy with it. He talked mainly through Olga. He would take a long time to answer anything. Sometimes he wouldn't answer at all.

"And so we gave the performance of *La Mort de Villon,* and that year we also held a Poetry Week in which people like Pablo Neruda, Salvatore Quasimodo, Allen Tate, Yevgeny Yevtushenko, and Barbara Guest appeared. This Poetry Week was organized by Stephen Spender, John Ashbery, Kenward Elmslie, and Charles Olson, and we thought that Pound should certainly be part of it. Well, to our astonishment, he accepted. He told me, through Olga, that he did not wish to appear on stage but that he would read from a box at the Caio Melisso. So we put up a microphone in the box and Pound sat there. Everyone read.

"Now, you understand, everyone knew that Pound had in a way taken a vow of silence, and this was a momentous occasion. When it was his turn to read, the whole audience rose and faced the box. It gave him the biggest ovation imaginable. Then came a long silence. Everyone waited. Finally out came these sounds from Pound. These were choking, unintelligible sounds. 'Rumph, aug, glaa, zreeg, erg.' This went on for fifteen minutes. Of course, no one understood a thing. When it was over, he received another enormous ovation. Later people came up to me and said, 'But what did he say?' I said, 'I don't know!' Then I found out from Olga Rudge that what he had read were some translations from the Chinese.

"Pound read again the following year and it was much clearer. In fact, he came three years in a row. I remember that he would attract huge crowds at the Piazza del Duomo. There were photographers and newspaper people all crowding around him. One time he and I sat at an out-of-door cafe having some refreshments. It was a beautiful day. Pound looked very handsome. Suddenly, out of the crowd, a young Italian jumped toward our table holding the *Collected Poems of Ezra Pound* translated into Italian. This young man turned to me and begged me to ask Pound to sign his book. He was incredibly persistent. He was practically in tears. He said, 'I am a poor poet. I have holes in the soles of my shoes. I've saved up my money just to buy this book. Please make him autograph it.' Well, I took the book from him and he handed me a pen. I opened the book to the front page and placed the pen in Pound's hand. Pound held the pen and kept staring ahead of him without stirring, as if he had not heard or understood what was wanted of him. 'You see,' I said to the boy, 'he is in another world. Leave him alone. He can hardly move, and doesn't even hear us.' But the boy persisted, 'Tell him my name,' and then blurted out an impossible name, something like Michelangelo Cocumerata delle Settefontane. 'My God,'

I said, 'Can't you make it simpler for the poor old man?' But as I was still speaking I suddenly noticed Pound writing on the open book, with secure speed, 'For Michelangelo Cocumerata delle Settefontane, with my best wishes.' He then closed the book abruptly, handed it back to him, and immediately fell back in his semi-coma, staring ahead as if nothing had happened. I was suddenly made aware that behind that wall of silence and show of senility there was still a very youthful, alert mind at work.

"Anyhow, Pound and I formed a close friendship. He was very affectionate with me. Every time he left Spoleto he would cry . . . he would embrace me and cry. Strangely enough, he hated most of the contemporary work in Spoleto. This was odd, coming from so revolutionary a figure. At the chamber music concerts, none of which he missed, he seemed to enjoy only baroque and romantic music. He showed definite distaste for most contemporary music, dance, theater—and he certainly didn't seem to like contemporary poetry. I must say that my own feelings about Ezra's poetry are very cautious. I find his poetry very captivating at times, and at other times irritating and unreadable. Also, I have strong reservations about the man he had been and his political beliefs. But the one thing which endeared him to me when I had the privilege of meeting him was his tremendous feeling of guilt and the painful self-abasement, with which he seemed to want to redeem his past. Every time anyone did the slightest favor for him he would always murmur, 'I am not worthy of it.' I am now told by friends who stay in my house that the first floor, where Pound lived, is haunted by his ghost. They hear him walking slowly up the steps and coming into the room."

In 1967 Henry Moore came to Spoleto. He had been persuaded by Menotti to do his first stage setting and costume designs—for Mozart's *Don Giovanni*. "Moore seemed nervous over the project and kept demanding endless alterations during the staging. He was very concerned with spatial relationships. The walls had to be cut lower or they had to be heightened. The statues either had to be smaller or bigger. It was never right. I was going crazy. Finally the boy who was actually executing all the sculptures for him gave me some advice. He said, 'Mr. Menotti, every time you come with Mr. Moore you sit in a different place in the theater, and of course, he sees the stage from a different angle. That's why he keeps changing everything. Why don't you make him sit in the same seat each time you bring him here. In that way he will always have the same perspective.' Sure enough, we made Henry Moore sit in the same seat every time he came to rehearsal, and the plot worked. He loved everything. He was a most charming man and most generous. Not only did he contribute his work without fee, but at the end of that Festival, instead of accepting our payment for his expenses, he gave *us* a check for a thousand dollars."

Through Priscilla Morgan, Menotti met Buckminster Fuller, who agreed to erect one of his geodesic domes in Spoleto. "That was an exciting thing, not only for Spoleto, but for Italy," said Menotti. "Many young architects came to help Fuller put up the dome. Bucky is a charming man, but a rather difficult guest, because as we all know, when he starts talking, he never stops. Also he had some incredible eating habits. For breakfast, for example, he would eat all kinds of fruits and drink all kinds of juices, then he would have eggs, bacon and ham, and on top of that a huge sirloin steak with potatoes! Anyway, after the dome was built, he asked whether he could give a ballet in it. He asked me to get him some young people—not necessarily dancers—and he would choreograph the ballet himself. So I asked a number of students to work with him. I got four boys and four girls. Then, of course, we announced this ballet by Buckminster Fuller! It would take place inside the dome. We drew a huge crowd. Everyone was fascinated by the idea. Well, Bucky improvised the whole thing as he was going along. He told some girls to 'stand there,' then he told a boy to put his hand on a girl's shoulder—to push her. He told the girl to resist him. So they were all pushing and resisting. He kept on talking and talking. Then he told one girl to divide the couples. Again he went on talking. One hour went by and then two hours. After three hours of this, Bucky was still talking, and the boys and girls still pushing and resisting. Little by little the audience had walked away. The only people left were Priscilla and three or four others. And still Bucky kept on talking. Finally I went up to him and said, 'Listen, Bucky, maybe we should go and eat something!' So he looked around, slightly bewildered, and saw there was nobody left. Anyway, that was Buckminster Fuller's *The Ballet of the Mind*. Let me add that I find him a very dear person and, taken in small doses, a fascinating one."

Buckminster Fuller's version of the event differed somewhat:

"I created *The Ballet of the Mind*. It was membered by a number of the dancers who were in Spoleto at the time. I had eighteen musicians and an equal number of dancers, actors, and singers. *The Ballet of the Mind* was completely spontaneous. I invented the ballet as I went along. I would tell the dancers what to do then and there.

"I don't think Gian Carlo quite understands my work," said Fuller. "I don't think he has a spontaneous interest in lightweight structures. You see, I'm interested in producing the most human environment with the least effort. I don't think Gian Carlo has the time to even think about what that sentence is saying. He likes me as a human being, but we do not have any intellectual exchange. We do not talk about what I am engaged in."

Isamu Noguchi, also a guest of the Festival in 1973, had met Menotti in 1946 when he had designed the sets for Martha Graham's ballet *Errand into the Maze*. Menotti had supplied the music. "I admire Menotti," said Noguchi. "I sympathize with him. I think he is a very serious person. Listening to his music, I feel a great sadness. His music is very moving. I feel his music reflects our time. He is very understanding and sympathetic to the sorrows of the world. Gian Carlo, like Bucky and myself, is an internationalist. When you are separated from your fellow man—me by circumstance, and Bucky by intellectual drive—you are very alone. We all have a sadness because we are alone."

Among the artists whom Menotti has helped, none seems more perceptive about the man or the composer than the young conductor Christopher Keene. In 1968 Menotti had heard Keene conduct while he was assistant to Kurt Adler at the San Francisco Opera. At the time, Menotti was looking for a conductor to assist Thomas Schippers in Spoleto, and he invited Keene to take on the job. His first assignment was to conduct a performance of *The Saint of Bleecker Street* when Massimo Bogiankino, the new Artistic Director of the Festival, broke Menotti's ten-year ban on his own music. The following year, Keene returned to Spoleto, this time as conductor for the Eliot Feld ballet, which was making its Spoleto debut. In 1970, Keene won the Julius Rudel Award and joined the conducting staff of the New York City Opera, making his debut with Ginasteria's *Don Rodrigo*. When Menotti's opera *The Most Important Man* was given its premiere at the New York City Opera in 1971, Christopher Keene was on the podium. Earlier on, Keene and Menotti jointly produced *Amahl and the Night Visitors* and *Help! Help! the Globolinks!* on Broadway. The venture did not prove a commercial success, but it brought the two into a even closer collaboration. It was Menotti who insisted that Keene conduct *The Most Important Man*, overriding Julius Rudel's reservations. Throughout the years, Keene has conducted various of Menotti's operas as well as his concert music. In 1974 Christopher Keene was named co–music-director with Thomas Schippers at the Spoleto Festival.

Speaking of Menotti's music, Keene enumerated its merits: "I like Menotti's music on three levels: a, I find it almost unfailingly beautiful; b, I find it honest; c, I find it skillful and full of craft—Menotti is a master orchestrator. His music is frequently very inspired, and it has a naïve faith, which is so touching. But there is something very sad. Benjamin Britten now has the total support of his country. The English are behind him. If Germany has not supported Hans Werner Henze emotionally, it has certainly supported him very well financially. But Menotti, as one of the great opera composers of these last decades, has somehow never found either an opera house or much less, a city, to back him solidly—to love him, no matter what he does. This, in spite of the fact that of today's opera composers, he is the most influential. In a way, he is a victim of his own success—of his own popularity—because so many people don't take him seriously.

"As a man, I find him infallible in taste and judgment. He is also an Italian schemer of the first degree. This incredible court he has of beautiful young things of both sexes is something about him I have never liked. But that's because I am an American Yankee—not a Puritan, but a Yankee. In a way you cannot predict what Gian Carlo is going to do. When he is putting one of his machinations into effect, it's like a stone rolling downhill. You can't predict where it will land. Actually Gian Carlo is as tough as nails. I mean, he is *really* tough underneath it all. On the other hand, just as he is about to cut somebody's head off and they begin to cry, he begins to cry too, because he's so compassionate. He's also a Renaissance man in that way—a kind of schizophrenic in the sense that there's a steely part in him, as you can see from his achievements, his career, his life.

"I owe my career to Menotti. As for my role at Spoleto, I would like to have the Festival resound with more music. I would like to see retrospectives of *living* composers—Milhaud, for example. I also want performances of music by very young and interesting composers from all over the world. Basically I want Spoleto not to be a repetition of other Festival towns.

"As for working with Tommy Schippers, I admire him enormously, but I don't know the man. We are not the same type. Of course, working with a man of stature and of recognized gifts is always a challenge. Finally, my allegiance is to Menotti. He's such a juggler! He's very concerned with how he appears—both to the public and to posterity. He's a man who should have had a family."

CHAPTER
18

"Why would God have sent me to you of all the children in the world, if you were not my son? Look into my eyes. No one has ever needed a son more than I do now. Please, Martin, help me, in the name of God. Be my son."

(Martin's Lie)

Gian Carlo Menotti is certainly a man who should have had children. Attracted to those in need of emotional sustenance, he has never stinted in supplying it. Generous to a fault, he has given time, money, energy, love, and professional help to those who seek it. He has often helped persons who were beyond help, sometimes to his own detriment. His great sense of compassion has led him into emotional quagmires from which he could barely extricate himself.

He is attracted to the helpless, the sick, the disturbed; characters in his operas often reflect this tendency. As Francis Rizzo pointed out, Menotti claims to like his "little lame ducks." "The masculine principle in his operas is almost inevitably incapacitated," said Rizzo. "The heroes are blind, or can't speak, or they limp. In a way, Menotti is projecting *himself* into the hero. Actually it's Menotti who's disabled—or imagines he is."

Given the complexities of Menotti's professional life, it easily follows that the psychological components of his personal life share in that complexity. Like all men of rarefied sensibility, Menotti is torn by drives and needs that must be as confounding to him as to those whose lives become entwined with his. Indeed, to analyze his relationship with men like Samuel Barber, Robert Horan or Thomas Schippers would mean to enter a province drenched in an ocean of ambiguity. The emotions having no reason, it is safe to assume that Menotti's personal ties have been the quasi-irrational results of pure instinct, a quality Menotti has heavily relied upon throughout his life. That he has so often veered toward individuals that have often caused him pain, must be put down to Menotti's perplexing and inexplicable sense of guilt and need for atonement.

Be that as it may, his search for personal happiness has led him toward involvements that, to put it simplistically, have been either passionate or paternal. Of the former may be counted his long relationships with Samuel Barber, Thomas Schippers and Robert Horan. Of the latter, Nikiforos Naneris, whom Menotti met in Athens, holds a very special place in his life.

Menotti traveled to Athens to mount a production of *The Medium* and there met a young Greek, Nikiforos Naneris, with whom he developed a strong and still treasured friendship. The composer talked about the boy:

"As I arrived at the opera house, I found to my great embarrassment that the casting director had assigned the role of Toby to the opera's *premier danseur,* a man well past middle age. To everyone's dismay I insisted that Toby should be played, as indicated in the libretto, by a young boy—preferably an actor. Such things in Greece become insurmountable problems. Who had ever heard of actors appearing in an opera? Impossible. 'All right, then,' I said, 'go out in the street and find me a few unemployed boys—there seem to be plenty of them in Athens; I'm sure I'll be able to teach the role to one of them.' They thought I was joking, but, to humor me, within a few hours they dragged in a bewildered group of six boys. I immediately stopped this one boy with great black eyes and a marvelously expressive face. He must have been sixteen. He wore pathetically shabby clothes, and looked both anxious and lost. He was my immediate choice.

"I soon found out that he was very poor indeed—he could hardly afford a change of clothes, had no education to speak of, and had never been inside an opera house—let alone know what an opera was. I also learned that his father had been an anarchist—had been condemned to death and shot when Niki was only eleven. Niki's last meeting with his father was in prison on the day he was condemned to die. His mother, a handsome woman from Crete, was left to raise her three children in utter poverty. Niki told me later how he often had to steal his food or look for it in other people's garbage.

"As we started rehearsals I soon became aware of Niki's great natural talent for the stage. Although I could hardly communicate

Lunching in Cannes with, from left to right, Thomas Schippers, Francis Poulenc, Aaron Copland, and Jack Kennedy.

Nikiforos Naneris.

Menotti and Samuel Barber at the White House with President and Mrs.
Kennedy.

Menotti with Margot Fonteyn and Rudolf Nureyev in Spoleto.

Menotti embracing Lida Gialloreti and surrounded from the left by Luchino Visconti, Raf Ravaioli, Bill Crawford, Jerome Robbins, Jerry Fitzgerald, Jorge Granados, Nikiforos Naneris, John Browning, and Sam Barber. The man in front of Lida Gialloreti is unidentified. Spoleto, 1963.

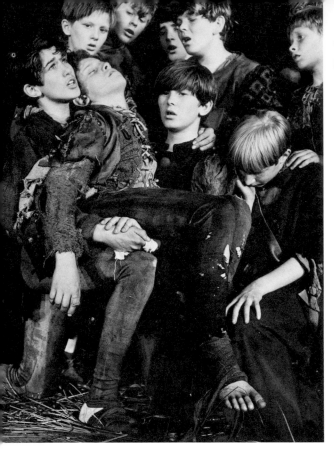

The final scene of *Martin's Lie* in Bristol Cathedral.

The final scene of *Don Giovanni,* staged by Menotti with settings by Henry Moore. (*Lionello Fabbri*)

to Gian Carlo Menotti   wishing him every good in the world (and in "Two Worlds") [poetis?] admiration and affection.

poreto 1965

Ezra Pound

Menotti with Ezra Pound. (*Werner Neumeister*)

Celebrating Gian Carlo's birthday in Spoleto.

The world premiere of *Help! Help! The Globolinks!* in Hamburg. (*Peyer*)

Gian Carlo. (*Nina Leen*, Life *magazine*)

Gian Carlo with his adopted son Chip.

Yester. (*Country Life*)

with him, for my Greek was limited to a few sentences and his English was nonexistent, he was astonishingly responsive to my direction. I also realized that the boy had become very attached to me and had pinned all his hopes for a better future on this unexpected debut as an actor.

"Every morning I would wake up, look out of the window of my hotel room, and there, across the street, would stand Niki, waiting for me to come down on my way to the rehearsal. In complete silence, as we had no way of understanding each other except through signs, he would take my briefcase and escort me to the theater.

"*The Medium* was a triumph in Athens. Niki had a personal success, and his picture was in the newspapers as a theatrical discovery. The next day, however, I was approached by my interpreter, a sensitive woman who had taken Niki's future to heart. What was I going to do about him? she asked. Frankly, I thought I had done enough. 'But Gian Carlo, once you are gone, who will look after him? He has no education whatever, doesn't speak properly, doesn't know how to behave. He got away with *The Medium*, because Toby is a mute—but what future is in store for him once *The Medium* has closed? You gave him a taste of success. Do you expect him now to go back to his former life?' I immediately realized how right she was. I offered to pay for his schooling, and I also arranged for him to be admitted into an important drama school in Athens.

"When I went to the airport to leave for Rome, Niki insisted on coming along. Don't forget that we had hardly ever exchanged more than a few words with each other. As I was about to kiss him goodbye, he suddenly held onto my sleeve and, bursting into hysterical sobs, wouldn't let me go. I knew then and there that I would love him for the rest of my life as if he were my own son. Fighting my own tears, I tried to tell him just that, with the help of my interpreter. I pulled myself away from him then, but I think we both knew that we would never lose each other. As you will find out, I always felt this terrible lack—this lack of a son of my own, a family of my own. The truth is, I'm always looking for a son."

A correspondence began between Niki and Gian Carlo Menotti. The composer learned that his protege was progressing as an actor and that he had won a role in a film directed by Michael Cacoyannis. Still, his lack of formal education threw him into vast depressions. Menotti learned that at one point the boy had tried to commit suicide. Menotti resolved to bring him to New York, and arranged a scholarship at the Actor's Studio. He also sent Niki to Columbia University so that he might learn proper English.

"This all happened just before I was to open the Spoleto Festival in 1958. So Niki came to New York on the very day I had to leave for Spoleto. I gave some money to a friend, which was to be given to Niki every week. As it turned out, being in New York on his own proved terrifying to Niki. By now he was eighteen years old, but still very naïve.

"I came back from the Festival in a rather depressed and worried mood. I was beset by many financial and emotional problems. It was Niki's presence in New York that saved my life. By then he could speak English reasonably well, and he soon found out that, as much as he needed me, I needed him. His unfailing loyalty and constant affection were great comfort to me during those days of anxiety and discouragement."

When *The Medium* was performed at New York's City Center, Menotti again engaged Niki for the role of the deaf-mute Toby, and again the boy scored a success. Niki realized, however, that to make a career as an actor in New York would require a far greater knowledge of English than he possessed. Ultimately, it was decided that he should return to Greece and continue his acting studies there. As it turned out, Nikiforos established himself as a major actor with Athens' National Theatre, and to this day remains one of his country's leading artists.

Nikiforos did not wield a strong influence over the composer, however. He did not possess the intellect of a Kinch Horan, nor the extraordinary musical gifts of a Thomas Schippers. What seemed to have attracted Menotti to Niki initially was the boy's essential helplessness. At times, such individuals are psychologically healed by their friendship with Menotti. At others, their problems become intensified.

Some of Menotti's friends claim that the composer's long association with Robert Horan fostered the poet's self-destructive tendencies. For ten years the two men seemed to feed on each other's strengths and weaknesses, but toward the end Horan could not withstand the demons within him. The two had little contact with each other after their meeting in Milan. Horan was put on a plane for New York, en route to California.

When Horan arrived home, he admitted himself into a clinic and undertook extended psychiatric therapy. He taught a class in poetry, prose and drama at the University of California for four years. Menotti did not communicate with him, nor did Horan get in touch with Menotti. But, in 1958, Horan was invited by Menotti and Samuel Barber to be present at performances of their opera *Vanessa,* premiered by the Metropolitan Opera in New York. Also, in the early sixties, Horan had occasion to meet with Menotti during the run of *The Consul* in San Francisco.

"I decided to call him up," said Menotti. "I thought we should see each other again. So I saw him. I was shocked by the change in him. Pain had lined his face, a face which had once been so beautifully serene, and his once mischievous eyes seemed to have become deadened by sorrow. I said to him, 'It's such a crime that you don't write anymore.' At this he said, 'I think I've made peace with myself and I think I could write again.' Then I asked him if he would like to come to Spoleto. He agreed, and I arranged for a ticket."

Horan participated in Spoleto's 1965 poetry readings, which were being organized by the poet Stephen Spender.

"Kinch arrived in Spoleto," continued Menotti, "and he was charming. Everybody adored him. We got him a hotel room and he read his poems and the occasion proved a memorable success. But before the reading, I called his hotel and wanted to invite him to supper. There was no answer. In a while I was told that something was wrong. I rushed to the hotel. We forced his door open, and there he was. He had been drinking on top of suffering from the effects of a virus. I called an ambulance and had him taken to the local hospital, which was run by nuns. When he got there, he began having terrible pains. I remember that the nuns, not knowing what was wrong with him, began giving him wine. They said, 'a little wine won't harm him.' Can you imagine! Finally I took him out of the hospital and gave him my room. I got good nurses to watch over him day and night. He was never left alone for the remainder of the Festival. When the Festival was over, I flew him back to New York, then I put him on a plane to California. At the time, Kinch was about forty-five years old. I called him up a few times after that, but we never saw each other again."

Perhaps no other relationship has had a greater effect on Menotti than his friendship with Francis Phelan, known as "Chip," whom the composer adopted as his legal son in 1974, and who now bears his name.

"Chip is my son, and *his* is a very long story. When I met him he bore the scars of an unhappy childhood, which had somewhat damaged his psyche. Morbidly shy, he used to suffer from excruciating, unbearable headaches which often drove him to excessive drinking and left him in a state of deep depression. I had him examined by many famous specialists. Every doctor gave me a different answer. Not a few of them wanted to open up his head! Finally a wise psychiatrist found the cure. The boy suffered from pent-up resentment; he needed affection, understanding, and a home. That is how he became my son. The headaches have disappeared, the drinking has stopped, and now, if anything, he has become even *too* assertive. Life with Chip is not always easy—but neither is his life with me. He resents my past, and his Irish temper is often terrifying to behold —but he can also be tender and humorous, and surprisingly wise. His shyness and sensitivity make him extremely moody, and that is often misunderstood for boorishness. I wish he wouldn't be so suspicious of almost every friend I have, but it is his intense loyalty that makes him so possessive.

"His life, before he met me, was not uneventful. A skillful skater and an extremely talented actor, he could have made a career for himself in the theater had he not been so uncommonly shy and emotionally unsteady. Surrounded by a group of very eccentric and bohemian friends, he was then leading a rather wild and self-indulgent life which, coupled with too much drinking, threatened to destroy him. However, behind his helpless look and often stuttering speech he hides an astonishing will power. From the day I adopted him, years ago, he stopped drinking altogether—and also stopped smoking—and was able to reorganize his own life and mine with incredible rapidity and efficiency. Of course. since he's Irish, there's a touch of madness in him; but that is perhaps the very quality that makes his personality so appealing to me. He does live in a dangerous world of fantasy, which often leaves him unprepared to face the realities of life. But that very world has lent to his imagination a very personal and charming poetic sense. Once he said, for example, 'A library should always be dark, because the brightest light in a library should be the open page of a book.'

"At the start life with Chip was not devoid of drama, as he was often childlike in his irresponsibility. During the period when he was drinking heavily, he once appeared at the door of Palazzo Campello in the middle of the night all covered with blood. As I opened the door, he fell into my arms in a dead faint. He had crashed his motorcycle and had fallen down a deep ravine, gashing his head horribly. A shepherd going by shortly afterwards had

covered him with a sack, thinking he was dead. But Chip's surprising resistance belies his seemingly delicate frame. In spite of the
hole in his head he was able to drive himself back to the house. It
was almost by a miracle that he was saved. Not much later, we were
Sam's guests in his mountain retreat in the Dolomites, where Chip
loves to go skiing. One evening, as I had scolded him for his excessive drinking, he threw a wool blanket that had been covering his
knees into the fireplace in a fit of anger. The blanket caught fire, and
in a few minutes the whole wooden chalet was up in flames. I ran
outside with Agnese, our housekeeper, only to find that Chip had
not followed us. We were both terrified. For a moment I saw him
run from one window to the other, then disappear. I thought for sure
he had been trapped by the flames. By then the whole village had
assembled in front of the house, the church bells were ringing,
everyone was screaming—and I became convinced that Chip would
be burned alive, as by now no one could possibly enter the house.
As I was shouting his name, I suddenly saw him, standing under a
tree not far away from me, too numb either to move or speak but,
thank God, completely unharmed. These two experiences, which
brought him so near death, made him realize that he had better stop
drinking and pull himself together, and sure enough, on becoming
my son, his whole personality changed. His pent-up feelings are
still apt to explode irrationally over minutiae, but I am getting used
to that. Chip is now my son and I feel for him all the tenderness and
concern that a father feels for a son."

Menotti's adoption of Francis Phelan, while not precisely alienat-
ing all of his friends, nevertheless caused both him and Phelan considerable anguish. Those surrounding Menotti, and ostensibly having
his best interests at heart, considered Chip someone who stood in
the way of all Menotti's other relationships.

Frank Phelan, a tall, handsome man, now in his thirties, offers the
image of special sensitivity and alertness. Possessed of an expressive
face that reflects serenity rather than turmoil, he is soft-spoken and
somewhat diffident. Aware of his sensitive role in Menotti's life, and
understandably suspicious of those infringing upon their privacy, he
was at first reluctant to speak of their friendship. Ultimately he
agreed to reveal something of himself, his background, and his life
with Menotti.

"I grew up in Philadelphia, and I had a rather unhappy childhood," he began. "At the age of fourteen I was already supporting
myself by some professional ice-skating. But I soon became sick of

it and left the ice-skating business to study acting at the Goodman Theater in Chicago. When I turned twenty-three, I came to New York. Amusingly enough, one of the very first jobs offered to me there was the part of Maria Corona's son in the City Center's production of *The Saint of Bleecker Street*. I turned it down, as I was not much interested in opera. Later, Herbert Machiz offered me the role of the young waiter in the Spoleto production of Tennessee Williams' *The Milk Train* [*Doesn't Stop Here Any More*]. But Spoleto sounded like a crazy set-up, so again I turned it down. But I guess I was destined to meet Gian Carlo. A few years later, finding myself without a job, and very much worried about my wild drinking, I applied for a scholarship to go to Spoleto. That's how I met Gian Carlo. I was a bit frightened of him because he was so outgoing. He was a bit too-much, too friendly. He was so wonderful, I thought, 'There's something wrong.' So I got scared, and when he called, asking me to have lunch with him, I refused. When he asked why, I said 'I'm afraid of Italians.' But we did see each other again. You see I was very lost, and he was amazing. From the first, people resented me. It was very difficult. But Gian Carlo taught me to see the world another way. I don't know what I do for him, except that I think I make him happy. Some of his friends think that I pull him around by the nose. But I think they're just jealous.

"In Spoleto things are terrible for Gian Carlo. You could probably cut the staff for the Festival by a third and things would be more relaxed, because you wouldn't have six people doing the same thing, and all fighting to do it. Of course he likes the Festival. These days he still enjoys the silly parts of it, the shops, the restaurants, the receptions. But actually I think he's a little tired of it. It's such an agony to get the productions on and to raise the money. The artists are getting more difficult, and the work is not as good as it should be.

"What's funny is that Gian Carlo has developed a tremendous affection for Spoleto itself—the town. He loves it, he loves Spoleto more than the Festival. He likes the townspeople—although I don't think they are very nice to him. But he feels an obligation toward them. So he'll always be involved in a way. I think what he really should do, and what would satisfy him more than all this Festival business, is to have a theater of his own—a company of singers. I don't really understand the politics of all that. I mean, so many of the people who head opera houses seem such second-stringers. When a man like Gian Carlo comes along, it seems to frighten them. He's tried desperately to get a theater—the Juilliard, the Fenice in

Venice, the Opera Comique. He tried to build a theater in Harlem. It is such a pity that nothing worked out. He shouldn't be running around to everyone else's theater. I talk to him and sometimes he listens to me and sometimes he doesn't. He's a very clever man, so he knows when to listen and when not to.

"I love my life with Gian Carlo. I am very happy. And a bit guilty about it. I travel a lot with him. I've been in many productions of his *The Medium*. Often I go with him to rehearsals and take notes. Gian Carlo is a wonderful director. He is so different when he directs. You get to know a completely different side of him.

"I wish a lot of things for Gian Carlo. I wish his life weren't so spread out. I wish he could be more at ease, to write his music, to have a more harmonious life. I'd like to see his life more concentrated so that he can do his work and not have to bother with things like the Festival.

"I think my job is to organize Gian Carlo's life. I want him to have a repertory company, to have his own opera house. The Spoleto Festival is organized now. It can run by itself."

The extent of Menotti's feelings toward Chip were summed up as he discussed his reasons for his purchase of Yester House: "It is somewhat ironic that after announcing so often to my friends that I would soon retire into a cave and lead a hermit's life, or become some sort of a hospital nurse to expiate my sense of guilt, I should instead end my days in as splendid a retreat as Yester House. But, indeed, I would never have bought Yester had it not been for Chip. It is his choice, his wish, and my last desperate effort to make someone happy. Perhaps it is too extravagant an homage to another human being. But I've come to the conclusion that if you're able in your life to make at least one person happy, you have achieved a great deal."

CHAPTER
19

Yester House was not yet dreamed of in 1966, when Menotti was still very much in the middle of his life as a United States resident, the arbiter of Spoleto, and the peripatetic traveler to all points of America and Europe, busily staging productions of his works. In company with Chip he traveled everywhere, and one such trip took them to Rome, the result of a phone call from the late Anna Magnani. The actress asked Menotti whether he would like to direct her in Jean Anouilh's adaptation of Euripides' *Medea.* Menotti was somehow startled by this unusual request. He had never directed a play before, nor had he ever worked with a stage actress of Miss Magnani's reputed volcanic temperament.

"I told her I would have to think about it. Frankly I didn't much care for the work of Anouilh and had also heard that Magnani was difficult to work with. I called Luchino Visconti to ask him what he thought of the idea. He said, 'Gian Carlo, don't fall into her hands, you'll regret it.' I then called Zeffirelli. He said, 'Gian Carlo, you'll regret it. She'll drive you insane.' I thought, how difficult can she be? After all, she's a wonderful actress. Surely she can't be any more difficult than Marie Powers had been. Finally I decided it would be a challenge and accepted the offer.

"For once in my life I was *really* castrated. I arrived in Rome and quickly saw that Magnani suffered from a tremendous persecution mania, and a terrible inferiority complex, which expressed itself by tremendous aggression. Aside from that, she was incredibly arrogant. I felt I could handle her arrogance, but soon realized I couldn't handle her terrible insecurity. All of this was aggravated by the fact that she was infatuated with an actor in the cast. He was quite young, quite handsome, and it was rumored that he was bisexual. Magnani was very jealous and always on the lookout for men or women who might steal him away. But not only was she jealous, she also had what appeared to be a sadomasochistic relationship with him. It seemed that he loved to be humiliated by her in front of other people.

"Well, we had these incredible rehearsals. We would start a scene. Magnani and her boyfriend were on stage. There they were—confronting each other. He would speak a simple line when suddenly Magnani would stop the rehearsal, turn to me, and say, 'Are you going to let him speak his line like *that?*' I'd say, 'It seemed all right.' And she'd answer, 'All right? Do you think I could answer him, with the delivery he gave? I guess I must be stupid. I guess I know nothing about the theater. I guess I'll have to resign.' She'd start to scream. 'Don't you realize he's reading that line in that way on purpose? Do you know why he does it on purpose? It's because he's not a man!' Well, by this time she was practically foaming at the mouth. All the while, the boy seemed to revel in his humiliation. He'd say, 'But Anna, tell me how to speak the line. Tell me what to do.' And we could all see that he was playing some erotic game. At this point Magnani would turn to me and say, 'Oh, Gian Carlo, I can't work anymore today.' She would then grab the boy by the neck and lead him offstage to a waiting car, which would obviously take them home together.

"Anyway, rehearsals went from bad to worse. By that time I didn't much care one way or the other. She would change managers. She would count money all the time, because she thought everyone was cheating her. She was unbearable. But we proceeded. I asked Rouben Ter-Arutunian to do a set which was absolutely beautiful. He created an island with many layers of wood. It had a sort of cart on top of it, because I portrayed Medea as a gypsy. When we began working on the set, Magnani insisted on wearing very high platform shoes. Can you imagine doing Medea in platform shoes? She refused to wear anything else on her feet. Of course, when she tried to walk up on the island, which rose like a rock, she would fall all over the place. She would scream and pretend she had broken her legs. She would call a doctor. It was horrible.

"Then Magnani started telling me that she was having a lot of personal problems—all of which led to her announcement that she couldn't possibly remember all of her lines. She demanded a prompter. I absolutely refused, saying that in this day and age, one doesn't present a play with a prompter in the wings. Of course, she had her way. So we put a prompter in the wings. Immediately she said she couldn't hear him—especially when she walked to the other side of the stage. We had to get her a second prompter to stand in the opposite wing. Then she complained she couldn't hear the prompters when she stood in the middle of the stage. We had to get her a third prompter, who had to be hidden inside the wooden structure—the island. But even with three prompters, she would repeat some sentences three or four times, trying to remember what was coming next. It was a mess. She kept changing her mind about her costume. I never knew what she would appear in next. She ruined some marvelous lighting effects, because she felt she couldn't be seen properly. She ruined everything. It was a shame, because she *was* a brilliant actress and an intelligent woman. But she was the victim of an insurmountable paranoia, which made her both aggressive and insecure.

"Anyway, the play opened and received surprisingly good notices —and I don't regret the experience. It taught me to beware of glamorous women who hide a razor up their sleeve. Thank God, I escaped unharmed, and Anna and I remained good friends. In spite of it all, we couldn't help liking each other."

One of Gian Carlo Menotti's most inspired efforts came with his 1968 commission from the Hamburg opera to compose a work for children—*Help! Help! The Globolinks!* Menotti had staged Stravinsky's *The Rake's Progress* for Hamburg, and Rolf Liebermann, greatly impressed by Menotti's directorial craftsmanship, now suggested a brand new work for his opera house.

"Knowing that Hamburg was the seat of the avant-garde, I told Liebermann that I would not want to write a long, major, important work, because I knew in advance that it would be booed and hated by the critics. I suggested a one-act work. I thought I would write another one-act opera for children as a companion piece to *Amahl and the Night Visitors.*"

Very different from his Christmas tale, *Globolinks* tells the story of a group of children beleaguered by some dangerous and seemingly indestructible extra-terrestrial beings who can express themselves only by electronic sounds. It is up to a little girl, Emily, to discover that these creatures can be defeated only by real music, and to save the world with the sound of her violin. "Around that period," said Menotti, "I had gone to see the Alwin Nikolais Dance Company in New York and had become absolutely enchanted by Nikolais's sense of theater. I was also very amused by his use of electronic music, which was made to serve his purposes to great effect and without pretensions. So I approached Nikolais and asked him if he would be interested in staging a children's opera with me. He said it all depended on what the opera would be about. 'It is all about you and me,' I said. He laughed, and *Help! Help! The Globolinks!* was born." Indeed, the children are very Menotti, and the Globolinks are very Nikolais. Nor does Menotti claim complete victory over the Globolinks, because at the end of the opera one mischievous Globolink is left outside the curtain, very much alive.

The critical reception of *Help! Help! The Globolinks!* was exceedingly favorable, and on the occasion of the opera's Santa Fe premiere, Harold Schonberg, the music critic for the *New York Times*, wrote a column in which he compared Menotti's latest work with that of Penderecki's *The Devils of Loudun*, which also received its Santa Fe premiere in 1969. Schonberg took occasion to recap Menotti's career up to that moment. "Menotti's career in many respects has been a sad one. He came up in the 1930s and '40s as one of the new heroes of opera. Frankly a romantic, writing in an idiom that went straight back to Puccini and Italian opera, he delighted international audiences with such works as *Amelia Goes to the Ball, The Medium, The Telephone,* and his television opera, *Amahl and the Night Visitors.* In those days, *Wozzeck* was just a vague word. . . . Music critics of the 1930s and '40s were, internationally, an aging lot whose roots were in the nineteenth century and who were happily prepared to accept Menotti's language.

"But after World War II the . . . old critics began to disappear, replaced by a younger lot who had much closer identification with the new speech. All of a sudden, Menotti was considered not only old-fashioned but hopelessly naïve. His operas were contemptuously dismissed. This does not mean they disappeared . . . but, as a composer, Menotti was simply not taken seriously by the tastemakers.

"Many composers shifted their styles to conform to new tastes. . . . But Menotti defiantly continued to buck the trend, even though it got him nowhere, and works such as *Maria Golovin* and *The Last Savage* were stillborn. . . .

"Menotti, not a polemicist, has never fought with his critics. But he must have spent much time brooding about his lack of success with critics and his colleagues. In *The Globolinks,* his newest opera, he has in effect told the pundits of the musical world where to head in. He says he has composed the opera not for them but for children. . . . *The Globolinks* turns out to be polemics in disguise. If Menotti will not engage in direct public controversy with his critics, he will do so in his music. . . .

"While Penderecki aimed for big things and missed them by light years, Menotti has set out to create a lightweight work and hit his goal dead center. *The Globolinks* is more musical comedy than opera . . . but the work does have nerve and charm. It is the best thing Menotti has done in years. . . ."

Practically no one was kind to Menotti's next opera, *The Most Important Man,* premiered by the New York City Opera on March 7, 1971. Although the *Philadelphia Sunday Bulletin* considered it "probably the most important unveiling the City Opera had undertaken since the operas of Ginastera," and while Harold Schonberg in the *Times* found it to be a "noble effort," the opera proved a failure.

Once more Menotti tackled a theme of universal topicality, examining racial conflict with compassion and irony. A black scientist, through an epoch-making discovery based on a secret formula, finds himself about to become the most controversial and important man in the world. But could the white race meekly accept an eventual black supremacy? The unavoidable recognition of the young black genius by even his more enlightened white colleagues is full of hypocrisy and emotional insecurity. The black scientist is finally sacrificed to white fear and pride.

The opera was conducted by Christopher Keene, with sets by Oliver Smith. It was directed by Menotti, and its cast included Eugene Holmes in the title role, with Harry Theyard as the white scientist, and Joanna Bruno as the scientist's daughter. Beverly Wolff sang the role of the scientist's wife.

As with most of his operas, Menotti was hard pressed to finish *The Most Important Man.* In this instance pages of the score were being completed even as the opera was going into rehearsal. Menotti enlisted the aid of both Christopher Keene and Lee Hoiby to collaborate in the orchestration; Arnold Arnstein, long Menotti's official copyist, was particularly pressured to get the manuscript into the hands of the musicians.

This seemingly chronic "last minute" working method was vividly described by Christopher Keene:

"Two pages by two pages, the opera would trickle in. I would get it to the singers and stay up until midnight and teach it to them to make sure they knew it. Finally it came to the point where it literally could not be finished, as everyone could see. Julius Rudel said, 'Let's cancel it.' I said, 'I'm begging you on my promise that we'll get it on.' Well, Rudel gave me another week. So I spoke to

Gian Carlo and told him, 'Let's face it, you can't finish the orchestration in time. I'm going to come up and do it with you.' So I worked with him thirty-six hours nonstop. Somehow it got together, except for the third act. At the world premiere of the opera, I sight-read the third act with the orchestra. *The Most Important Man* was not much of a success for Gian Carlo, nor for the cast, but it literally made my career. It was an enormous personal success for me."

Lee Hoiby also worked feverishly with Menotti on the opera:

"I remember one morning sitting with Keene and Arnstein trying desperately to finish the orchestration, when Menotti said, 'Why do I do this? Why do I get myself into such a situation? Lee, you've been in psychoanalysis for many years, why do people do such things?' And I told him, 'Look, somewhere you must be guilt-ridden, otherwise you wouldn't punish yourself the way you do. Or maybe you hate yourself!'

"Incidentally, it should be made clear that no one does Gian Carlo's orchestration for him. What he does is to indicate on the piano score precisely which instrument does what. He has a kind of shorthand."

Oliver Smith was also enlisted at the last minute. "Gian Carlo had previously offered *The Most Important Man* to two other designers, both of whom declined to do it. So he called me in desperation and said, 'I'm presenting you with a great present. *You* can design the opera for me.' It had already gotten very late in the game, and I had three weeks to do a full-scale opera. No other designer in America could have done it under those circumstances. I don't think Gian Carlo was pleased with the results. I, on the other hand, thought it was a good job. I might add that Gian Carlo has never asked me to do anything for Spoleto, which I resent. Still, I've gotten over that, but I must say it wasn't very generous."

Menotti considers *The Most Important Man* one of his richest works, on a par with *The Saint of Bleecker Street*. "Thematically it has the greater breadth. And it is the most compressed work musically. I'm very fond of it. I also feel the libretto is very strong. But of all my operas it is perhaps the one which needs most careful casting. It requires singers with exceptional acting ability and large dramatic voices."

If *The Most Important Man* did not prove a success with the New York public, and if Menotti would by 1971 have lost a good measure of his popularity, it must be also remembered that the composer's energies were being drained by the Spoleto Festival and by an encroaching apprehension over his diminishing success with the American critics. Important opera houses throughout the world, however, continued to perform his works. The New York City Opera had, in fact, been one of the most faithful adherents to Menotti's art. It had presented his *The Old Maid and the Thief* in its first stage production in 1948, and during that same year gave *Amelia Goes to the Ball.* In 1949 came *The Medium* and in 1952 the first stage production of *Amahl. The Consul* was performed that same year. In 1959 the company presented *Maria Golovin*; in 1965 *The Saint of Bleecker Street.* Five years later it gave a production of *Help! Help! The Globolinks!* and *The Most Important Man* was a world premiere.

Julius Rudel, director of the New York City Opera, commented on his close professional relationship with Menotti:

"We at the City Opera have done all of Menotti's works, with the exception of *The Last Savage* and *The Island God.* I wonder if Gian Carlo will remember it, but after *The Last Savage,* given at the Met, when he was so savagely beaten and brutalized by the critics—he said he'd never write another opera—I wrote him a note saying that not only mustn't he do that, but that I wanted to go on record and say that I would like his next opera. It was the City Opera that commissioned *The Most Important Man.*

"I must confess that when he told me the plot of this new work, I had some misgivings. I felt it was a little behind the times. But I didn't tell that to Gian Carlo. I said, 'Let's see what comes out.' Unfortunately the satirical elements didn't quite come off. It was a bit too much heart-on-the-sleeve for me. Of course, there was the matter of the opera not being finished until the last minute. It's an old story with Gian Carlo. Also there was the matter of trying to find the right designer. I'm not convinced that Oliver Smith was the right one for it. Frankly I still consider *The Medium* and *The Consul* Menotti's greatest works. They are all of a piece and at no point do you find he's gone too far in a situation. Everything is so wonderfully worked out—everything is so logical. Later on he didn't analyze his characters as fully as he should have.

"If his popularity has declined in this country, it's because fads can't be sustained very long. New York is notorious for casting off its idols. It happens in every field. Gian Carlo has been around for forty years. First he was the new Puccini. After a while people got bored with that. But it's like that with Penderecki and with Ginastera. When I opened *Don Rodrigo,* a whole new world seemed to have opened up. I thought we had the 'modern-opera syndrome' licked. But then interest began to flag. Ginastera lost his news value, and perhaps that's what happened with Gian Carlo."

On July 7, 1971, Gian Carlo Menotti turned sixty. On the occasion the *New York Times* asked the composer to reflect on his life. In a mood to lay bare some of his most personal thoughts, Menotti gave the *Times* one of the most revelatory articles in years, published on July 18, 1971. The headline read, "And Where Do You Run at 60?"

"On approaching old age," Menotti wrote, "two ghosts must be abjured: disillusionment and bitterness. For the dreamer I once was, disillusionment is almost unavoidable. For the fighter I still am, the bitter taste of defeat, especially when defeat is considered unjust or treacherous, is apt to poison one's heart and sour one's smile.

"Fortunately, at the age when the gentle shadow of death becomes your constant bed companion, and when every dawn is welcomed as a gift, the merciful hand of indifference begins to erase both old and new scars. My friends may be surprised to hear me speak of disillusionment and bitterness. To them, I am a lucky, successful composer who has every reason to feel happy. But no artist worthy of the name can escape the compulsive search for that platonic perfection, the elusiveness of which is its very essence, and therefore, avoid the bitterness of frustration.

"At best, an artist can find a certain kind of serenity in resigning himself to the curse of imperfection. Even the artist who, like myself, has often been accused of superficiality simply because, to use Jorge Luis Borges's happy phrase, 'they scatter their gifts with indifferent glee,' should not be so easily dismissed by suspicious critics simply as facile. The seeming happy-go-lucky attitude (as in Rossini, Cocteau, or Bernini) is often but a screen for a deeper search. It is as if these artists scatter too heavy a load in order to run faster with their most precious possessions.

"But run where? This is the anguished question that a man of sixty has to ask himself. Perhaps one should not have run so fast or been so negligent in scattering those gifts others then picked up, vulgarized, or misused. Whether or not an aesthetic truth exists, no serious artist can avoid, at least in his youth, the secret hope of being its discoverer. At my age, when one finally realizes how pale a glimpse of it, if any, the jealous gods allow, the artist has to become a drunkard, a madman, or a sage.

"The word 'success' applied to my career becomes ambiguous or even ironic, and I am the first one not to take it seriously. I hardly know of another artist who has been more consistently damned by the critics. Even those critics who have defended my music have done so (with two or three exceptions) condescendingly or apologetically. Recently, a well-known New York critic wrote that he was 'ashamed' of liking my music.

"The insults that most of my operas had to endure through the years would make a booklet as terrifying as *Malleus Maleficarum*. Fortunately, taste in criticism changes as fast as taste in clothes. The almost forgotten *Maria Golovin* is suddenly rediscovered in France as a '*chef d'oeuvre*,' while *Amahl and the Night Visitors*, whose birth was jubilantly greeted on the front page of the *New York Times*, is now damned in the same newspaper as an unbearable piece of maudlinism.

"As for prizes, degrees, and titles, how could one possibly ever take them seriously? What is one to think when a critic who declares you 'a man without talent' receives the Pulitzer Prize—the same prize which was conferred on you twice, supposedly for talent? Even the praise I often receive as a stage director has little meaning for me. For I see at the same time vulgar, tasteless productions in our major opera houses being praised to the sky.

"It is not that I consider myself the only decent opera stage director around, or that I expect opera to be more than it is. On the contrary, many are the productions that have enchanted me and from which I've learned: to mention a few, Luchino Visconti's staging of *Macbeth* in Spoleto and of *Traviata* at La Scala; Zeffirelli's witty production of *Cenerentola*, again at La Scala, and of *Falstaff* at the Metropolitan; Felsenstein's production of Janacek's *The Little Fox* in Berlin or Strehler's terrifying *Angel of Fire* in Venice. But more often than not when I am inside an opera house, I find myself cringing in my seat and thinking that a law should be passed for the prevention of cruelty to dead composers.

"What is the point of fighting for opera as vital theater when the same old, fat opera singers, oblivious to any dramatic sense, go on bellowing high notes to a rapturous and vociferous group of 'opera fans' (not to call them by another name). How can you convince a board of directors that, by building bigger and worse opera houses, rich in bathrooms and restaurants, but poor in acoustics and as intimate as air terminals, they actually endanger the future of opera?

"However, this is not the kind of disillusionment that really hurts. Even my dream that one day I might be able to have my own small opera company in which I could instruct young singers and young stage directors (even my worst enemies recognize my gift for working with young people) has finally and painlessly been abandoned. This kind of disillusionment is easily disposed of compared to the inner one, that of the artist toward his own work. Like my revered operatic masters—Monteverdi, Moussorgsky, Puccini, and Debussy —I, too, once hoped to solve the fascinating problem of *parlar cantando*. Sure enough, although most critics have denied me any kind of originality, *The Medium, The Telephone,* and *The Consul* have bred countless illegitimate children all over the world. But I can hardly claim to have created a school.

"Perhaps my greatest torment has been the inability to capture with a firmer hand the elusive essence of melody, that vein of gold that only a few of us have even been lucky enough to strike. I agree with Stravinsky that music is essentially abstract and cannot express anything except itself. But when one writes for the theater, one must not ignore its tremendous evocative power or the strong emotions that a powerful melody can awaken in the human heart.

"I may be a little disillusioned, mostly with myself, but not bitter. Too many marvelous memories and constant little joys have accompanied the passage of my years. Foremost, is my friendship with children all over the world through *Amahl.* Their innumerable letters still make wonderful reading:

" 'Dear Mr. Menotti: Last night I saw *Amahl and the Night Visitors* and it is the first opera I've ever seen and I think it is the best.'

" 'Dear Mr. Menotti: My sister who is a girl keeps singing the part of Amahl who is a boy. Can you stop her?'

"Or this one, which I received after having announced in a moment of unguarded discouragement that I would abandon the theater:

" 'Dear Mr. Menotti [I spare you the spelling]: Please go on fighting. I have a good story for an opera which I can give you for nothing. It's about Amahl going to New York after Bethlehem and getting sick again. But it's not as gloomy as it sounds.'

"Then, certain unforgettable premieres, such as that of *The Consul* in Israel, or of *The Medium* in Paris. And the joy of working with singers who gave such unforgettable interpretations in my operas: Marie Powers, Patricia Neway, Chet Allen, Richard Cross and many, many others, some of whom have now become very famous.

"And finally, there is the Spoleto Festival—the last, I hope, of my crosses and my joys. Indeed, it has cost me and is still costing me many days of anguish. But it has also enriched my life with experiences which few artists are privileged to have. No dream can ever fully come true, but Spoleto comes close to it. My need during my middle age of feeling needed within a social structure has been fully realized in this once-dead little city now alive with music, dance, and poetry.

"As I open the programs of these past fourteen years, I cannot help being touched by the photographs I see of artists who, because of Spoleto, have experienced with me the dignity of being needed. Who can it be, this young boy who looks like a wild gypsy? Pinchas Zuckerman. And this blond girl who looks as if she were about to rape a cello? Jacqueline DuPre. And this smiling college boy wearing a Mickey Mouse watch? Paul Taylor. And that breathtakingly beautiful girl rehearsing her first *Carmen*? Shirley Verrett. Who are those two self-serious youngsters? Istvan Kertesz and Schippers. And who is that impertinent looking young man eyeing Ezra Pound? Pier Paolo Pasolini. And that smiling boy watching Henry Moore working on the sets of *Don Giovanni*? Charles Wadsworth.

"Hundreds of wonderful memories follow each other. Hilarious incidents and moving stories. It would already take a long book to describe the short odyssey of Spoleto. I look at a piece of paper which hangs in a frame by my piano. It is a message sent to me by the former deputy mayor of Spoleto—a sort of Anna Magnani who fought like a tiger to keep this festival alive. It was written a few hours before she died of cancer and it says in an almost illegible scrawl: 'Dear Gian Carlo, please go on writing beautiful music in honor of God. Addio, Sara.'

"So let opera go the way it wants even if it is in the opposite direction I would like it to go. Let critics jeer at my music. Let audiences acclaim the 'kitsch' and musicologists praise 'soulless' *theoremas*. Although my tyrannical masters—music, theater, and poetry—set me going on a road that looks deserted, I've never lacked a friend when I needed help, or understanding when I've needed comfort. As my young fan says in his letter, 'It's not as gloomy as it sounds.'" *

CHAPTER

20

"Oh, foolish people who feign to feel
what other men have suffered, you, not
I, are the indifferent killers of the
Poet's dreams."

(The Unicorn, the Gorgon and the Manticore)

The written word has always held enormous importance for Menotti. As the author of his own librettos, he has gone to his task as both a playwright and a composer. The delicate balance between words and music is sustained in ways that make clear Menotti's highly poetic sensibilities. His operatic librettos are remarkable for their economy and their dramatic flow. Words inevitably imply action. Menotti seldom stands still to muse or ponder upon a character's thoughts. There is little soliloquizing. Words, music and action are tied one to the other, and they emerge as a unified whole. When Menotti composes, music and text are born at the same time, although it is his habit always to prepare a verbal skeleton before embarking on an opera. This skeleton, however, often becomes unrecognizable once the opera is completed. At times, his texts are carefully prepared and only later submitted to the music. But even here Menotti claims to sing this text as he writes it down, although this instinctive musical approach to words may not be kept in the final product. In the end it is always the music that shapes Menotti's librettos. As he put it, "I have often said that a good opera must be a happy marriage in which the music is the asserting husband, and the words the accepting wife."

Menotti feels that music has a very different tempo than words. It can express a sentiment or an emotion in a few seconds, while the text is laboring to unfold its own inner logic. But it is the musical logic that must be there, no matter what sacrifices are demanded from the text.

"There is nothing worse for an opera composer than to be stuck with a stubborn poet," observed Menotti. "It is partly to avoid the painful process of cutting and modifying my libretti, that I leave the original sketch as skeletal as possible. It has often been heartbreaking to have to cut phrases and scenes from my libretti—phrases and scenes that seem expressive or essential to the action. Still, I am merciless with my texts, often stripping them of their literary beauty, if I feel that by doing so I enhance the musical values. Some of the best lines in *The Consul* still lie unset in my sketchbooks."

Throughout his career Menotti has avidly avoided collaborators for his operas. Any number of composers have approached Menotti to supply them with librettos. Conversely, writers have come to Menotti asking him to write operas based on their texts.

"Francis Poulenc and Bohuslav Martinů both asked me to supply them with librettos, but I had to turn them down," said Menotti. "The only tempting offer came from the Chilean poet Pablo Neruda who wanted me to write an opera with him on his adaptation of Melville's novella *Benito Cereno*. The idea of working with Neruda was quite attractive to me, but I decided against it.

"One of the oddest requests I've had came from Norman Mailer who wanted me to do an opera based on one of his novels. The fact is, many people send me their librettos. They just arrive. Usually they resemble the last opera I've written. For example, after *Amahl* and *The Saint of Bleecker Street* I received dozens upon dozens of religious librettos. After *The Telephone* I received librettos about gadgets. An amusing one took place entirely in a revolving door! It was called *The Turn*."

While the bulk of Menotti's writing is found in his librettos, his notebooks (of which there are scores) are filled with poems, aphorisms, and short stories. Any number of these are worthy of publication, although so far Menotti has chosen not to make them public. The only nonmusical works are his film scripts and plays, and it is perhaps as playwright that Menotti seems most comfortable.

In the mid-twenties, Menotti wrote his first play, *A Copy of Madame Aupic*. Some forty years later he wrote *The Leper*. Both plays have been produced, and each in its way reflects part of Menotti's personality.

A Copy of Madame Aupic is a comedy of manners inspired by Yeats's famous lines:

But one man loved the pilgrim soul in you
And loved the sorrows of your changing face.

It deals with a man who specializes in faking old masters, and
finally convinces himself that he can fake life as well. He creates
what he thinks is the exact living replica of his glamorous former
mistress—a woman whom he has deeply loved and by whom he was
abandoned—from a characterless girl he has met casually. But when
he is confronted with his aging mistress many years later, and finds
her much changed and enriched by the experiences of a tragic life,
he suddenly realizes the futility of his experiment. What he loved
and still loves in her is what has changed and remains changeable.

After trying unsuccessfully to have his play produced in New
York, Menotti locked it away in a drawer and all but forgot about it.
It was unearthed some thirty years later by the playwright Albert
Husson, who presented it in Paris in a French adaptation with
Madeleine Robinson in the title role. It enjoyed a successful run.

The Leper, a far more elaborate and complex play, received its
world premiere at the Florida State University in Tallahassee. The
production was fraught with emotional upheavals on the part of
the playwright. After many years, Menotti's old friend, Chandler
Cowles, agreed to act again as producer. He felt that *The Leper*
needed an out-of-town production before it might be ready for
New York. In Florida the cast was made up of students from the
college drama department and was headed by Francis Phelan in
the title role, and Patricia Neway in the role of his mother.

Principally *The Leper* is a polemic, but one that candidly, and
perhaps for the first time, explores Menotti's own nature. Of all
Menotti's works, *The Leper* is surely the most self-revealing. Superficially it seems to be an indictment of any rebellious or corrupting
minority within the established society, however tolerant that society may be. In other words, Menotti says that in order to function,
the society must tolerate the deviant minority, but only if the minority recognizes its position as such and doesn't defy ethical and moral
laws.

But exactly who *is* the leper? To which minority does Menotti
refer specifically? A careful reading of the play makes it quite clear
that it is pitted mainly against the homosexual, or at least a certain
kind of homosexual. This seems quite surprising, coming from Menotti. Although he has always refused to make any public statement
about his private life, he has often said, when approached on the

subject, "My life is an open book; however, I don't like to leave it around."

The Leper is as open a statement about his private life as he has ever made. As in *The Saint of Bleecker Street,* where he revealed his conflicting spiritual duality by identifying himself with both Michele and Annina, in *The Leper* he expresses a moral conflict by identifying himself in turn with the rebellious leper and with the moralizing queen. The action takes place in the thirteenth century, in a small kingdom bordering on Byzantium. The old king has just died, and his son is not allowed to inherit the throne because he is afflicted with leprosy. It is his mother who rules while he is exiled in a leprosarium outside the walls of the city. Out of spite, and heedless of a famine which is threatening the country, he claims all the palace gold bequeathed to him by his father, and then uses it to corrupt the people. To save the city, his own mother orders him to be killed. Nothing is more revealing than the vibrant speech that the queen makes at the end of act two. Although she does state earlier in the play that "the strength of a government is not measured by what it forbids, but by the amount of freedom it can allow," thus defending the leper's claims, she also makes it clear that the minority must accept its status as such, and earn society's acceptance by making itself useful. It is worth quoting part of the queen's speech, because it explains much of Menotti's guilt, his obsession with wanting to feel useful to society, and his repeated identification of himself with the maimed and the helpless.

THE QUEEN [to the people]: You had the leper exiled as is the custom, but you have trained your dogs to snarl at him, and you have spat at him, and let your children aim your stones at him. No word is filthy enough to point out a leper, no scorn too pitiless, no laughter too indecent. And so you have turned a poor, thwarted boy into a spiteful, vengeful being. You have turned the corrupted into a dangerous corruptor; and you, you who feed his hunger for revenge will be his first victims. You, you who first cursed him, then laughed at the misshapening of his body . . . how quickly you changed your tune at the sound of his money. And now that you have realized he is not only rich, but also generous and clever and amusing, you no longer laugh *at* him but *with* him, and pretend not to see that his laughter hides a hideous grin. Before I could guide him, you all rushed to feed his spiteful vanity with all the precious poisons he could buy. Refusing to make him useful, you made him dangerous. For it is he, the leper, that now rules over your tastes; it is he you all begin to imitate without realizing that he is destroying in you what he envies most. You denied him both love and understanding, and now he's making you into brittle, loveless creatures. You have exchanged your heart for his wit, your honesty for his glitter. And while this city starves, while your children grow cruel and callow, you go on revering these monstrous idols and applauding their indecorous jests—and excuse yourselves by filling your hearts with their barren irony. No, no, he's no longer my son. Little must he prize my esteem, for he did not hesitate to sell it so as to ransom your scorn. Let him have his exquisite court, let him train his jesters. And those of you who want to join his games, be quick—for change is fashionable in a world of decay. But let him know that he no longer has my love. Let him know that as long as I am the queen, he shall no longer be given entry into my city, and that he and his followers will have to celebrate death's carnival inside their suffocating labyrinth, where all that glitters is nothing but the iridescence of putrefaction. I am not a Spartan, nor a censor, nor a merchant. I, too, believe in the flame of fantasy and in the possible genius of an iconoclast. I, too, believe that one man may be right and the whole nation wrong. Those who will stay with me, will not be denied either joy or beauty. But my goldsmith will not be coaxed into fashioning a dish for my dog, nor my musician into soothing the digestion of my tipsy guests. The human heart must be ennobled again.

As it turned out, the Tallahassee production of *The Leper* proved to be something of a catastrophe, and it plunged Menotti into a deep gloom.

Although Menotti felt that Phelan, with his natural vehemence, was perfectly cast as the leper, he was somewhat disappointed in Neway's performance as the queen. He felt that she sentimentalized the role, and, by insisting on delivering some of her most trenchant invectives *sotto voce*, was not enough of a counterfoil to Phelan's violence. He felt that this lack of balance made the play lopsided. "To make things worse," Menotti recalled, "we found ourselves in a theater which was acoustically impossible. No one could understand a word. On top of that, Cowles proposed to invite a hundred New York V.I.P.s for the opening night. My vanity always punishes me. I agreed. And so one hundred of the most blasé people in New York were flown down to Florida for the kill. The university made the added mistake of giving a huge cocktail party for them *before* the play. Naturally, everyone became very high and hazy, and in that state they were all marched into this deaf theater."

Patricia Neway also felt that the circumstances surrounding the performance of *The Leper* were less than felicitous:

"You see, the experience was divided, because Gian Carlo had commitments elsewhere and sort of ran off in the middle of rehearsals. In addition, it was a student production. We didn't have a concentrated professional effort. I think *The Leper* is a very meaningful play, but it suffered a great deal by being presented under difficult circumstances. The kids expected to be trained, but Gian Carlo just came and directed them, telling them what to do. They wanted a great deal more. They wanted a part of his genius.

"As for working with Frank Phelan, we didn't have that many scenes together. Gian Carlo paid a great deal of attention to him— the way he would pay attention to a newcomer. I wasn't pleased with my performance. I felt terrifically under-rehearsed, and Gian Carlo's being away for part of the rehearsals didn't help. In fact, when he went away for ten days, I went home too. I think everybody felt disappointed over the project. And then, to bring down a New York audience for opening night on a chartered plane . . . well, that was one of the biggest mistakes! If I had known about that, I would have screamed. The point is, we weren't ready to be seen. But that's Gian Carlo. He's *so* Italian. He wants to show everyone everything. He wants the parade outside the window!"

Menotti was despondent over the failure of what he considered to be a major effort:

"The local papers gave *The Leper* ghastly reviews, and a lot of people made fun of the play. I got terribly depressed and called Lincoln Kirstein. I asked him to come and see it and give me an opinion. He came down to Florida, and although he's usually very skeptical, he said, 'Gian Carlo, this play is one of your most important works.' He made several very good suggestions. He thought I should change the ending, and simplify the scenery and costumes. Lincoln also said that he would try to get *The Leper* put on at Yale, and then bring it to Broadway."

Although many of Menotti's close friends have resented and condemned the play, and have advised against publishing it, Menotti is determined to see it produced properly. At Lincoln Kirstein's urging, he is correcting the play, and preparing it for publication and performance.

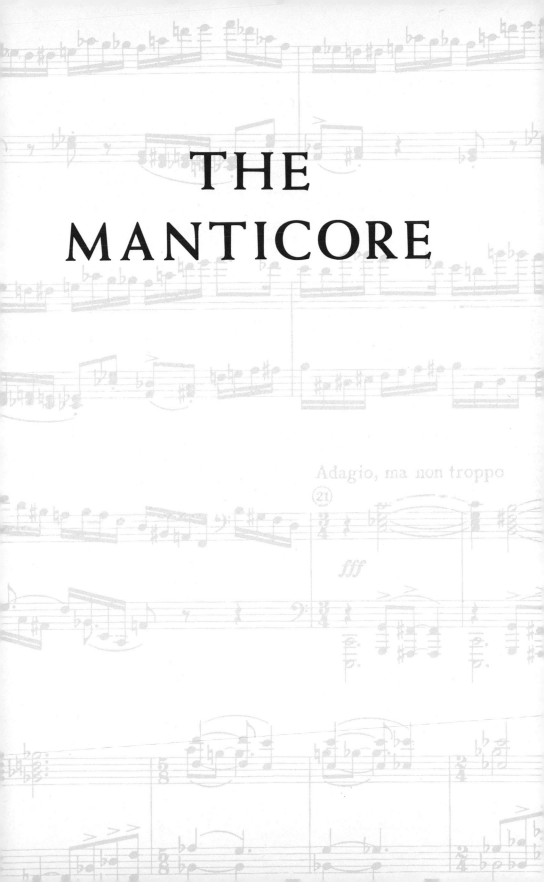

THE
MANTICORE

Do not caress the lonely Manticore.
Do not, unless your hand is gloved.
Feeling betrayed, feeling unloved,
So lost he is in cabalistic dreams
He often bites the hand he really meant to kiss.
Although he's almost blind and very, very shy
And says he loves mankind
Do not caress the lonely Manticore.
His glist'ning back, whenever tapped,
Will quickly raise its piercing quills.
How often, as if in jest
Inadvertently he kills
The people he loves best.
Afraid of love, he hides in secret lairs
And feeds on herbs more bitter than the aloe.
Fleeing the envious, the curious, the shallow,
He keeps under his pillow
A parchment he thinks
Contains Solomon's Seal
And will restore his sight.
And late at night
He battles with the Sphinx.

(*The Unicorn, the Gorgon and the Manticore*)

CHAPTER
21

"For ev'ry love there is a last farewell,
for each remembered day an empty room."

(Vanessa)

With yet another critical failure to haunt him, Gian Carlo Menotti
became more and more convinced that America was irretrievably
turning its back on his work. Disheartened by the reception of his
last major opera, *The Most Important Man,* and by the failure of
The Leper, he sought to work in Europe—in general, a far more
sympathetic milieu.

There is, of course, no question that Menotti also had his share of
dissension in Europe, notably in 1971 when *The Consul* was staged
at the Maggio Fiorentino, which caused one of Italy's most avant-
garde composers, Luigi Nono, to take exception to its presentation.
At the time, Nono's own opera, *Intolleranza,* was scheduled to be
part of this prestigious festival, but he withdrew his work because,
as he stated in *L'Unita,* Italy's official Communist newspaper, "*The
Consul* is a squalid product of the cold war and of anti-Sovietism."
But this furor, taken up by the rest of the Italian press, only underlined the fact that Menotti was deemed a controversial composer
and that his name was very much alive in his native country. *The
Consul,* a work intended as a universal statement against political
repression and inhuman bureaucracy, was used as a pawn by Nono
to air his own political feelings. Known as "The Nono Affair," this
contretemps stirred up intense partisanship and resulted in a flurry
of newspaper articles either condemning or defending *The Consul.*
Heated exchanges in the Italian press even led to attempted can-
cellation of a scheduled production of *The Consul* in Poland, which,
nevertheless, went on as scheduled.

Despite critical failures, the work of Gian Carlo Menotti has received performances all over the world—on both sides of the "iron curtain." According to Hans Heinsheimer, director of publications at G. Schirmer's, Menotti's publishers, only Menotti and Benjamin Britten, of the living operatic composers, enjoy such worldwide acceptance and popularity. (Britten has since died.)

"If Gian Carlo Menotti would not be an insane spender—an absolutely irresponsible spender—he would be a very wealthy man," said Heinsheimer. "His Schirmer royalties alone—not including his ASCAP and Ricordi royalties—would be definitely sufficient for him to make an extraordinary living. He's just as much performed today as fifteen or twenty years ago, and he makes more money every year. *Amahl* is steadily increasing in performances. *The Consul* and *The Saint of Bleecker Street* are regularly revived in America, Canada, and Europe. *The Consul* has been produced in every major theater in Germany, and we have about twenty translations of the opera—including Turkish, Finnish, Swedish, Norwegian, and Japanese. *Amahl* receives approximately 400 performances a year, and so does *The Medium*. *The Globolinks* is a close second.

"But because Gian Carlo puts his money into paying for Yester House or the Spoleto Festival, he is always broke. He's always calling up and asking for five hundred dollars. More than once I've told him, 'Gian Carlo, I cannot give you five hundred dollars, but you have eleven thousand dollars right here waiting for you.' The point is, he is not always aware of the extent of his income."

What troubles Gian Carlo Menotti is not the lack of performances, but that some of these performances have of late been meeting poor critical reception. Even an opera such as *The Consul*, acknowledged as Menotti's masterpiece, received short shrift from New York's music reviewers when it was revived. Menotti was understandably dismayed by the cavalier attitude taken by the New York press over works that had, in previous years, received unstinting praise.

The New York City Opera revival of *The Consul* in 1974, which Menotti came from Europe to direct, elicited grave reservations from the *Times*. In an interview he gave this writer for the *Times* a few weeks later, Menotti made clear his decision on physically removing himself from the country that had once nurtured him:

"I have always felt that my musical home was New York. I have always felt that I had a very faithful audience in America. But this is no longer the case. I mean, when you live in a city like New York, and you know that any new opera of yours will be damned or ignored by the chief music critic of the *New York Times* even *before* it's put on, then naturally, you go somewhere else. After all, I make my living as a composer.

"And so that is why Sam Barber and I have sold Capricorn, which was a very painful decision to make, since it has meant so much to us. Don't forget that Sam and I have known each other ever since we were young students at the Curtis Institute. But once I began traveling all over the world staging my own and other composers' operas, and absenting myself from America for longer and longer periods, both Sam and I felt that the time had come for us to part with Capricorn.

"Of course, the moment we sold the house, Sam regretted it. He's a bit more sentimental than I am. I think he was unprepared for the emotional shock. Nevertheless, we've decided to maintain separate apartments in New York, and of course, Sam has his own house in the Italian Alps."

Thus it was that in 1973 Menotti and Barber sold Capricorn. As Menotti pointed out, Barber was far more affected by the sale than he realized.

"In a way, when we sold Capricorn, I was to blame," said Barber. "But I just couldn't run the place anymore. When Gian Carlo said he was buying a house in Scotland instead, it didn't interest me in the slightest. Giving up your home near New York was difficult enough —but to go and and live in Scotland was something else again. So I suddenly found I didn't have any home. I can't consider my New York apartment my real home. Gian Carlo asked me to come and live in Scotland—to fix up a wing for myself. But you see, it's not really *my* house. It's possibly Chip's house. Yes, it has affected me very much, this business of selling Capricorn. It doesn't seem to have affected Gian Carlo at all. Of course, I have the place in the Dolomites, Santa Cristina, which was a house Gian Carlo discovered. But I can't stay there for more than three months in the summer and a few weeks in the winter. It's just too boring. So, in a way, I'm homeless."

Capricorn was sold to a Polish doctor who studied medicine in Italy. Menotti was delighted that its new tenants were charming and interesting people. Amusingly enough, the doctor and his Italian wife bought the house on the condition that they could also purchase Menotti's piano—which they did. Barber and Menotti retain the ownership of fifty acres of land surrounding the Mt. Kisco house.

Reflecting on this sale, Menotti turned philosophical: "Very frankly, I know I'm entering my old age. I am now sixty-three. Well, once you're seventy, your life is practically over. So I felt that in the last years of my life, I should have a bit of solitude and peace and only concentrate on what I still want to do. I'm beginning to grow some bristles and I'm getting a bit more difficult. I like solitude. I like to be alone. I'm beginning to withdraw. I felt it was the right decision. As I said before, it was Chip who convinced me it was the right move. Otherwise, I would never have had the courage to do it. But aside from all that, I strongly feel that every artist needs to feel surrounded by a certain loyalty . . . an official loyalty. I have defenders of my work in Europe, but not many in America."

Among Menotti and Barber's many friends is the pianist John Browning, who commented on the sale of Capricorn and the subtle rift between the two composers:

"I think at this stage of the game, both Sam and Gian Carlo, each in his own way, are searching for something different. You see, theirs was a great intellectual, musical, and spiritual kind of relationship. But by the very fact that Gian Carlo didn't really live in Capricorn in the last few years, they stopped establishing living patterns. So they grew apart in the little ways that living together implies.

"Frankly, knowing Sam the way I do, I think that he still keeps the light in the window, so to speak. I feel he has been most upset by the breakup of the house and the relationship. Sam is basically a nester. He likes to establish a house, whereas Gian Carlo merely likes to come and enjoy it.

"But there's something more basic. I think that very many people, as they get older, like to surround themselves with younger people because it makes them feel young, despite the fact that, as we all know, it doesn't rub off. Rosina Lhevinne, my teacher, has always said that she can't stand people her own age. I think that perhaps the rift between Sam and Gian Carlo can be explained simply as two people who don't want, by looking at each other, to remind themselves of the fact that they *are* getting older. It could be simply that, because each one of them has young friends, or younger friends. That seems to be the pattern, although Sam is extremely faithful and loyal to his old friends, like Florence Kimball. Gian Carlo looks remarkably young for his age, and he knows this. I think it's important to him to remain as young-looking and thinking and acting as he can. I think it's a very important part of his life.

"I think that Sam is much more philosophical about that. I think that he can accept the sixty-or-over more easily. I don't think that a search for youth is one of Sam's problems. But I think it is one of Gian Carlo's interests. I think that at this point, Sam would rather have companionship and friendship."

Even as negotiations for the sale of Capricorn were underway, and even as Menotti felt disillusioned with his American loyalties, no less than six important American commissions came his way. The first was from an unlikely source: The Ninth International Congress of Anthropological and Ethnological Sciences, which asked Menotti to write an opera that would reflect "a positive view about human difference." The result was *Tamu-Tamu*, which premiered on September 5, 1973, at the Studebaker Theater in Chicago. Menotti also received commissions from the Washington Cathedral, to write a companion piece to *Martin's Lie* which was called *The Egg*, and from the Saratoga Springs Festival, to write his first symphony—*The Halcyon*—for the Philadelphia Symphony Orchestra, under Eugene Ormandy. In addition, he received a Ford grant for a Capriccio for cello and orchestra.

In 1973 Menotti received the prestigious commission to write a bicentennial opera for the Opera Company of Philadelphia. He accepted with alacrity and set about to write a three-act opera, which he entitled *The Hero*. It premiered in Philadelphia on June 1, 1976.

Talking about his latest major opera, Menotti said that it centered on a man who has been asleep for ten years.

"It's not actually a political satire, although it may seem so at first sight. It's a gentle and good-humored indictment of contemporary society's self-satisfaction and greed, and of those leaders who, in order to protect their own interests, choose the mediocre, the expedient, and glorify the innocuous—the man who is asleep and thus cannot bother anyone. It is a plea to Americans to wake up to reality, to abandon self-congratulatory illusions, and to return to their former rugged individualism. Nothing very serious, however. It is an opera buffa, after all."

Also in 1973 The Bel Canto Chorus of Milwaukee, Wisconsin, commissioned a cantata. Entitled *Landscapes and Remembrances*, it premiered in that city on May 15, 1976. It is perhaps interesting to quote a few lines from the last section of this work, entitled "The Sky of Departure": "America, good-bye! Oh, love of my youth. If I return to you, no longer an impatient, anxious lover, but as a wistful, undemanding friend, will you then again open your skies to me?"

Menotti's late operatic works have tended to center on subjects of social and political topicality, none more so than the 1973 opera *Tamu-Tamu*. As with *The Consul* of 1950, *Tamu-Tamu* was inspired by a newspaper clipping, this one a photograph showing an Indonesian family huddling together in terror as soldiers menace them with automatic rifles, about to murder them.

Menotti, struck by the horrified and disbelieving expressions on the family's faces—the utter brutality of the impending act of butchery—asks himself the question: how many of us must bear the guilt for such actions, far away as they may be from us? In other words, for whom does the bell toll? So he imagines that very same Indonesian family bursting into the apartment of a typical western suburban couple, who are bored, self-satisfied, and concerned with their own problems, and the couple's sudden horror at being forced to share the lives of strangers and to witness their martyrdom. In his presentation of the outline to the anthropological congress, Menotti underscored the fact that the action of his opera "does not refer specifically to either Vietnam or Cambodia. It could apply just as well to Africa or India. The soldiers at the end are not American soldiers, but soldiers of a neighboring Indonesian country. The country itself is unidentified. The white couple is not necessarily an American couple; they could just as well be English, French, or Italian."

For the first time, Menotti employed Asian singers whose words were sung in the Indonesian language. Only the white couple sings in English and the score, while thoroughly Menotti-esque, bears an Oriental flavor. The opera was conducted at the Chicago premiere by Christopher Keene (*Tamu-Tamu* would also be given its Spoleto premiere by Keene in the summer of 1975). The leading roles were sung by Robert J. Manzari, Sylvia Davis, Sung Sook Lee, Theresa Teng Chen, Sung Kil Kim, and Sumiko Murashima, among others. The costumes and set were provided by Sandro La Ferla, and the opera was produced for the congress by Ken Myers.

As Menotti put it, "*Tamu-Tamu* was murdered by the Chicago critics." Nonetheless, the *New York Times* considered a new opera by Menotti important enough to send one of its music critics, Peter G. Davis, to Chicago. "*Tamu-Tamu*," Davis wrote, "tells us little that we haven't already learned about Menotti's art. Like all of his operas, it is a vulnerable piece, easily dismissed by those who dislike having their emotions manipulated so flagrantly. Still, it does 'work,' one is engaged after a fashion, and audiences are going to love it."

"*Tamu-Tamu* proved a very difficult production," said Menotti. "Although the anthropologists who commissioned it ran out of money, it was very well done. The musicians and singers gave it a clean and brilliant reading. Of course, I was again very late in presenting the completed work; still, it got done. As for the music, some idiotic critic said it was nothing but fake orientalism. Of course it's fake! It represents *my* version, *my* feeling about oriental music. It doesn't want to be any more authentic than the Spanish music of Bizet, the Japanese music of Puccini, or the Turkish music of Mozart."

Upon the presentation of *Tamu-Tamu,* Menotti returned to Europe, where he undertook to rework the libretto as well as the structure of Samuel Barber's ill-fated opera, *Antony and Cleopatra,* which was the commissioned work that opened the new Metropolitan Opera House at Lincoln Center in 1966. The Met's elaborate production, with sets and costumes by Franco Zeffirelli, and staging by Zeffirelli, proved cumbersome in the extreme. Although there was praise for much of Barber's music and for Leontyne Price who sang Cleopatra and for Thomas Schippers who conducted, critics were of one mind regarding the overall concept. The reviews were so damaging that Barber, plunged in despair, left the country for his retreat in the Dolomites. *Antony and Cleopatra* seemed doomed to obscurity, and it was not until 1974 that an invitation from Peter Mennin, director of the Juilliard School, would bring about its dramatically altered revival. It would also reunite Menotti and Barber, who had not collaborated on a major work since the Metropolitan's production of *Vanessa* in 1958. (*Vanessa* was deemed a masterpiece and brought Barber the Pulitzer Prize for music that year.)

The collaboration proved felicitous. The new version, sung by a student cast and performed by a student orchestra, was not a professional one. Menotti's adroit handling of the opera's somewhat awkward construction and the many musical revisions provided by Barber seemed successful enough to merit professional productions elsewhere. The Juilliard provided its best resources, and both Menotti and Barber received high praise for their joint effort. All the

Juilliard performances were sold out—there were six in all—and Donald Henahan, in his *New York Times* review, called the work a "magnificent . . . rehabilitation."

Menotti's relationship with the Juilliard opera department had begun several years prior to *Antony and Cleopatra*. Peter Mennin, director of the Juilliard School, had approached Menotti with the idea of his heading the opera department, an idea that strongly appealed to the composer, who, throughout his life, wished to be affiliated with an operatic repertory company. When the Juilliard offer came his way, his hopes rose once more, only to be shattered when, in 1971, Peter Mennin suddenly withdrew the proposed appointment. He dispatched a letter to Menotti, informing him that the Juilliard was not able to go forward with its discussions. The reason given was Menotti's schedule of conflicting engagements, which would keep him away from Juilliard too frequently.

Menotti, once more feeling the pangs of rejection and once more retreating into himself, realized that to run his own opera house would perhaps forever remain an unfulfilled dream. Despite bitter feelings, Menotti *did* subsequently accept an invitation from Peter Mennin in 1972 to come to Juilliard and stage and direct the company's production of Donizetti's *Don Pasquale*, and the 1974 Juilliard production of Barber's *Antony and Cleopatra*. The doors were not entirely closed for Menotti at Juilliard.

However, in a *New York Times* interview preceding the revival of *Antony and Cleopatra*, Menotti summed up his feelings—not only about his life and work in America, but also about his deep regret at not finding an acceptable platform from which his store of theatrical knowledge could be disseminated:

"You see, I've always wanted to create a style of production that would prove to the musical world that opera *could* be produced in a different way. I would have formed my own school of lyric theater. I think I'm an excellent teacher. I would have loved to teach students how to stage an opera. I would have loved to work with exciting new singers. I would have loved to prepare one opera at a time, and prepare it perfectly. This is impossible to do within the current system of repertory opera companies. But I'm apparently destined never to do any of these things. This has been one of the greatest disappointments of my life. But perhaps, as Solzhenitsyn says, only stupid people want to teach. Intelligent people want to learn. The older I get, the more bewildered I become. The more I find out about my nature, the more surprised I am by what's inside me, and by what's inside other people. Finally, I've come to the conclusion that a man becomes wise only when he begins to calculate the approximate depth of his ignorance."

CHAPTER
22

"Look at your heart, the secret measure of your soul, which with imperious exactitude beats out the uncontrollable rhythm of your sorrows. The shameless drummer who can shatter your night with desire or freeze your eyes with fear. The running messenger of joy, the frugal dispenser of peace. What mysterious urge first sparks it into motion? For what desperate duty does it hide in its own ashes the last persistent flickers?"

(The Most Important Man)

Old age and the feeling of waning intellectual or creative powers are as absent from the character of Gian Carlo Menotti as are anger, dispiritedness, disloyalty, or joylessness. No matter what his setbacks, Menotti is as resilient as a branch of green wood. The child in him permits for no prolonged anguish or grudge-bearing. Innocence clings to him as fresh moss to a sturdy tree. Menotti may complain bitterly about the injustices that have befallen him, he may rationalize his own vulnerabilities and foibles, but it is never done in a spirit of breast-beating or despair.

The approach of age may sadden Menotti, but it does not seem to frighten him. Mortality does not prey on his mind. Although he threatens retirement from the hectic activities of his life, retirement is decidedly not in sight. These days his life is spent composing and traveling to all parts of the globe where he stages his own works and the works of other composers. He jets from city to city, country to country, bringing his vast directorial experience to the world's best-known opera houses. Together with Chip or on his own he visits with lifelong acquaintances, each of whom is always happy to see him. A man of the world, he may decry his nonstop activities, but beneath it all he thoroughly enjoys the multifaceted dimension of his life.

Conversely, Menotti is essentially a loner, content to spend months at a time sequestered at Yester House, where he composes, reads, and savors the beauty of his surroundings. Removed from the bustle of large cities, away from the frenzy of Spoleto, a calming process takes place. He and his adopted son spend long days occupied at various tasks. Chip is an inveterate nature-lover, spending hours upon hours tending to Yester's huge vegetable and flower garden, supervising gardeners or simply enjoying time out of doors. Menotti will compose, lazily answer correspondence, and perhaps muse over the past.

It was in this period of peace that Menotti found time to reflect upon his life and music, divulging his thoughts and feelings to me. We would sit in his study—the fireplace blazing—and Menotti would fix on a topic of conversation.

On one day his thoughts returned to his birthplace, Cadegliano. He had recently sold his share of the estate belonging to his family.

"I've given up ownership of the house I was born in. It was a much more difficult decision to make than leaving Capricorn, because Italians have a natural attachment for the house they were born in. But I was beginning to have a negative reaction to the Cadegliano house. Actually it started about ten years ago when I attended my brother's funeral. I hadn't been back to Cadegliano in years. They put my brother's coffin in the living room. My whole family and most of the villagers had assembled there. Their dutiful display of sorrow was terribly painful to me, and I tried desperately to withhold my tears. But, with the powerful help of the Catholic church, everything was done to break me down. The Dies Irae sung in the little church where I used to play the organ as a child, the heartbreaking sound of the mortuary bells; my old nurse, bent in two like a starved little monkey, crying in a corner. To top it all, when the coffin was taken to the cemetery and about to be lowered into the grave, an ancient relative of ours swathed in black veils began to recite a long poem which she had written, recalling the youth and childhood of my entire family. Well, I went absolutely to pieces. I couldn't stop sobbing. I said, never, never again will I go to a funeral of someone I love. Since then I've avoided Cadegliano.

"My whole family is dispersed. I haven't seen my brothers Tullio or Piero since I was seventeen. They live in South America. My sister Giosi and I see very little of each other. I do see my brother Francesco, who still lives in Italy, at least once a year, and we do

love each other—but without much commitment, as our lives are so
far apart. I have a particular place in my heart for my immensely
kind niece Ada, and an affectionate relationship with my nephew
Alfonso, a successful psychiatrist in St. Louis. I also feel very close
to two of my grand-nephews: Camillo, whose great ambition is to
become a stage director and who has helped me sometimes as an
assistant, and Skippy, who lives in London and is struggling to become a painter. I am deeply fond of my cousin Josée Bianchini, who
has helped me many times, when I needed her."

If Menotti's contact with his immediate family is slight, his contact with his friends may be said to be even slighter. Although he
often speaks warmly and gratefully of loyal friends such as Wally
Toscanini, Edmonde Charles-Roux, Lincoln Kirsten, Jacques Sarlie,
and the many other people who have stood by in time of trouble,
Menotti's friendships are more rooted in the past than in the present.
In speaking of them, he alluded more often than not to those who
are no longer living.

Of these lost friends he particularly seemed to mourn the death
of a young painter, Milena Barilli. "She was the offspring of an ill-
assorted marriage between a well-known and very eccentric Italian
music critic and the first cousin of the king of Yugoslavia. She was
not beautiful in a conventional way, but her hieratic face, with huge
exotic eyes, had a magnetic power. Very influenced by surrealism,
her painting had a strange quality—a sort of hallucinative fifteenth
century, dreamed by a precocious child. Like me, she was fascinated
by mysticism. We became very close friends and I entrusted her
with the costumes for my ballet, *Sebastian*. Unfortunately, Milena
had an unhappy marriage. One day she called me and said she was
leaving her husband—and asked me if she could come to live in
Mt. Kisco—not at Capricorn, but in a place nearby. So I found her
a funny little house in the village, and we saw a great deal of each
other. Ultimately she returned to her husband and lived in New
York. Just then she was also contracted to do the scenery and costumes for the Theater Guild's production of *A Midsummer Night's
Dream*. Her paintings were becoming fashionable. However, one
day she called me at Capricorn and asked me whether I would take
over her little dog, named Luce. She said it would be happier in the
country. I thought it was an odd request. Two days later, I read in
the papers that Milena had committed suicide. In a self-portrait
that she willed to me, she painted herself as a nun receiving the
stigmata. However, she killed herself before she finished the portrait,

and the nun's hands remained unwounded. The painting now hangs in my studio, and I used it as a cover for my published score of *The Saint of Bleecker Street*. She was a person I loved very deeply indeed."

Of the living, Samuel Barber and Kinch Horan were the friends Menotti spoke of most frequently during his reminiscences at Yester. He had found a box containing many letters he had received from Barber during their early friendship at Curtis. He had reread them and felt moved, amused, and nostalgic over their content. Again and again he voiced his guilt over facets of their life together, in which Barber was the inevitable victim. Half in sorrow and half in jest, he would often exclaim, "I've let Sam down so many times!" "I've disappointed him so much!" "I've made him suffer so!"

Horan crept into our conversations with regularity, and again feelings of ambiguity and guilt colored his words. A sense of sadness and of loss made itself felt as Menotti reiterated his enormous admiration for the young man who had deeply influenced his thinking and who had made him aware of so much. Surprisingly, he never felt compelled to speak in such emotional terms about Thomas Schippers, whose presence in his life seemed equally meaningful. Menotti would only praise Schippers' extraordinary response to his operas—the intuitive kinship he felt toward his music. A certain sense of bitterness seemed apparent even as these words of praise were uttered, and it was obvious that whatever rancor existed between them, to talk about it would perhaps be too painful.

Menotti composes at the piano. At the time of my visit to Yester, he was completing the Cello Fantasy. As I passed his studio door, I would hear piano passages being repeated, altered, reversed. I would hear Menotti hum or sing *sotto voce*. There would be long stretches of silence, then a flow of music, followed by more silence. Sometimes I would hear Menotti pace in his studio and after a few moments hear a new musical line played on the piano. One of our discussions centered on his working methods.

"I loathe to begin a new work," he told me. "Like Tobias, I am always terrified by the prospect of my battle with the angel. Unconsciously I keep postponing the day when I am to embark on a new project. Any excuse is good. I know that once I begin, I am trapped. When that happens, the day, often the night, no longer belongs to me. To begin or finish a work I have to be cornered. That is why I eagerly accept commissions or force myself into a position of having to accept commissions. I am just as loath to relinquish my works and declare them finished. As I said, I have to be cornered to finish a work, and that is why I have so often been accused of 'last minute writing,' and of doing unpolished, slipshod work. I must admit that this frenzied writing does affect the precision with which I convey my thoughts to the written page. But not the main conception and the core of my work, for if some of my works have been written hastily, they have all been planned slowly and carefully. They have all had a long period of incubation. Even some of my most recent works were conceived as long as fifteen years ago. When people marvel at the speed with which I compose, when cornered, they don't realize that most of the music has been in my head for months, and my notebooks are full of music destined for future works.

"What I keep postponing is the agonizing process of freezing on the written page the fluctuations of my thoughts—of robbing myself of the possibility of changing their course. This, of course, has seriously affected the written record of my works. Most of my operas have been published hurriedly, under the pressures of my despairing publishers. At least two of them, *The Globolinks* and *Tamu-Tamu*, were published without my consent. Proofs were not submitted to me—a very serious professional breach on the part of my publishers. Of course, I can sympathize with them. They know that once they submit proofs to me, they may never see them again. *Maria Golovin*, *Martin's Lie*, *The Labyrinth*, and *The Most Important Man* still await final publication. It is not that the publishers are unwilling to bring them out, but because I keep postponing the final version destined for publication. I've taken three years to correct the manuscript of *The Last Savage*!

"I can show you a whole batch of recent telegrams from Schirmer's, urging me to send back the corrected orchestral score of *Amahl*, which they want to publish, as well as the piano score of my *Suite for Two Celli*, which has been on my desk for weeks. Again, I have to be cornered or threatened; and then, to my own surprise, I relinquish the works, which I've guarded so ferociously, and I relinquish them in a curiously offhand way, almost with indifference, as though they no longer belonged to me. And that is why most of my scores are full of imprecisions and full of mistakes, for which I alone am responsible.

"When *Golovin* or *Last Savage* are performed, the musicians and singers work from manuscripts sent to them by the publishers. Of course, conductors go crazy, because there are so many versions. I

mean, the orchestral score has one version, the vocal score has another version, and the orchestra parts a third version! That's why I
have to run after all my operas, because if I leave them the way
they are sent from my publisher, the poor conductor doesn't know
where to begin. One of my biggest projects here at Yester is to polish
my published works, complete and incorporate in them the many
revisions, and finally to proofread a little more meticulously my
many still unpublished works."

When Menotti composes, he does so in a tense and nervous way.
He never sits at his working table or at the piano for more than ten
or fifteen minutes at a time. Before he knows it, he is up and about,
pacing nervously. Years ago it served as an excuse to light a cig-
arette. Having given up smoking, he now likes to munch on either
a nut or a dried fruit, bowls of which are kept in his studio.

"These interruptions, distracting as they may seem, allow me to
view my material with ever-renewed freshness of approach, without,
however, disturbing my power of concentration. I will pace about,
replacing a book or straightening out my desk, but I keep composing
while I'm doing these things. At times, I purposely try to forget what
I've written. Without slackening the creative tension, I try, however,
to cancel from my memory what I have just written down, so that
when I go back to my desk I can look at it with a new eye and hear
it with foreign ears.

"What I try to avoid is to get *so* involved with a passage that it
loses its identity. It is as when you repeat a word too many times, it
suddenly doesn't mean anything anymore. I often compare the artist
to people who have halitosis, admittedly an unpleasant metaphor.
Everyone is aware of it, except the culprit. The same thing is true
for the composer. You are so involved in your work that often you
no longer know what it really sounds like. Anyway, I also use these
frequent interruptions to calm myself, for I get *very* excited when I
am working, and thus risk losing my sense of proportion. More often
than not, I sing along as I write, in an unpleasant falsetto voice. I
have no preference for the time of day I like to compose. When I
was young, I favored the night. Most of *The Consul* was written late
at night. Now I favor the morning. When I write I use a pencil with
an eraser at the end of it.

"Like a good 'dowser,' a composer must learn how to sense when
he has struck water. There are so many composers who are insensi-
tive to this. I mean, they pass right over it and they don't even
know it. It's marvelous with such composers as Wagner or Verdi or

Beethoven . . . they find a good theme, and they *know* that it is pure gold. They can base a whole major work on two or three main themes. And with such assurance! Their divining rod seldom fails them."

Menotti attempted to dissect the essence of his style. Throughout his career, critics have called him "Puccini-esque" and have labeled him a composer in the tradition of operatic *verismo*. They have placed him in this musical niche not in a spirit of condemnation but more in an effort to show that his roots were firmly placed in the soil of nineteenth-century Italian operatic tradition.

"I don't think my music is Puccini-esque. Sometimes I have amused myself by being consciously Puccini-esque. In *The Consul*, for example, I wanted to show the audience how different my music actually is from Puccini. So I wrote a little *hommage* to Puccini in the music for the Italian woman. I did that on purpose. At any rate, it is very difficult for me to talk about my style because I believe that a composer must be more or less unconscious of his style. Characteristics and individual traits are, of course, unavoidable, and they are particularly fascinating to the listener. But they must not be underlined, or cultivated, by the composer. Otherwise, they become senseless mannerisms and unbearable affectations.

"In a sense, the composer must strive toward anonymity and let the music speak for itself. If it is powerful enough, its paternity will become obvious, for man cannot avoid imperfection, and to me, a man's style is the sum of his imperfections. Ideally, beauty is one and the same, and it is the intensity of our effort to obtain it that makes our art more or less moving. I'd rather have my music be recognized by its depth and its breadth than by its idiosyncracies. But as I said before, if an artist is honest enough, he cannot completely hide his physiognomy. Even the great anonymity of Bach betrays his humanity."

Asked what he would consider the most peculiar aspect of his style, Menotti said, "I think that I have contributed to opera a very personal kind of recitative, beginning with *The Medium*, which I consider the fundamental work upon which I base all my other operas. The problem of the *parlar cantando* has always fascinated me. I felt somehow that no composer had yet solved the problem of making people tell and act a story in musical terms. Monteverdi had, of course, tried it, but his recitativi, at best, rarely imply action. They only describe emotions, and only one at a time. Verdi's arias are static comments on what has *just* happened, or contemplations of what is going to happen. His recitativi, except perhaps in *Falstaff*, are but preludes or codas to his arias. Mozart relegates all actions to his recitativi. With very brief and admittedly notable exceptions, his recitativi on the whole are based on similar formulas. Most of his arias are precious jewels, very carefully set, but definitely detachable from their settings, and rarely essential to the action. Wagner's effort toward a vital recitative, both melodic and dynamic, is quite successful at times, but its powerful machinery tends to crush the text, and it lacks the necessary mobility and agility to convey quick changes of feelings, or feelings too vague and too delicate to be underlined. Whatever it says is always proclaimed. Only in Mussorgsky, Puccini, and Debussy, did I find admirable examples of what I myself was looking for.

"The expressive mobility of their melodic line fascinated me. And it is they who pointed in the direction of my search. There is one recitative in particular that made a profound impression on me. It occurs in the second scene of *Pélleas*—Genevieve's reading of the letter beginning with 'Voici ce qu'il ecrit à son frère, Pélleas.' I was fascinated by the simplicity of means with which Debussy was able to express so much. I was spellbound by the evocative beauty of it, and then and there I realized that what I would particularly cultivate in my operas would be the evocative power of melody. I believe that this mysterious entity called melody is a form of memory. Actually, when you discover a melody, you discover something that already exists. Melody is music that you suddenly recognize. It is inevitable. It's already there. Something out of the collective unconscious, as Jung might say. The problem is how to find it, and once you find it, how to gather it without harming or soiling its purity. At any rate, in my operas, it is mostly through clear and simple melody that I try to achieve my dramatic effects. *The Medium* is perhaps the best example of what I am searching for. Because of *The Medium*'s clear and sparse harmonic texture, it all sounds rather simple, and that's what makes superficial critics think that it *is* simple. Actually it was tremendously difficult to keep within the bounds I had set for myself. That is to say, a simple melodic style, mobile enough to adapt itself to almost any kind of dramatic situation, without the help of an elaborate orchestral accompaniment. That is why I consider *The Medium* the most personal of all my works—perhaps the most important in the development of my style.

"Already in *The Consul*, I begin to enrich the orchestral accompaniment, and in *The Saint of Bleecker Street* I do so even more. It is almost always the vocal line which is the guiding spirit of my dramatic works, and very seldom the orchestra. Its lyricism, however, is mostly evocative of some action or conflicting emotions. It is seldom contemplative. It creates action, or it expresses the feelings created by the situation of the moment. Oh yes, I do let my characters sing a little lullaby or a little folk tune here and there, but these 'songs' are really excuses to let me rest awhile from the real struggle. People mistake these 'reposes' for the important parts of my operas. For me, the best music in my works is that which is essential to the drama. The big aria, if one must call it that, in *The Consul* is *vital* to the action. So is the vision scene in *The Saint*. They are not moments of gratuitous lyricism. If I have contemplative moments in my operas, such as the trio at the end of act one in *The Consul,* I try to make those moments as dramatically plausible as possible."

The notion that Menotti's music is steeped in the traditions of *verismo* were heatedly repudiated by the composer. "That's absolute nonsense! Critics point to the verisimilitude of action and language in my librettos; but that's something different from verismo, which strives to be a photographic copy of reality. Yes, my characters are very much alive and quite believable, but there is hardly one of them who escapes symbolic connotations, or is not at the service of an all-embracing idea. I have hardly ever created characters purely as realistic props or for the sake of local color. Certainly my operas are veristic, inasmuch as *The Marriage of Figaro* is a veristic opera, a vivid and real portrait of that epoch—of that life. So is *Carmen,* then. Well, from that point of view, you can call my works veristic. But in my operas, I've always tried to avoid the vulgarizations of, say, *Cavalleria Rusticana* or *Pagliacci*, two operas I frankly detest.

"Some people think that I can set practically anything to music, just as long as it is realistic. Well, they are wrong—because the search for a language that may describe succinctly a real action, without appearing prosaic, is very, very difficult. Not everything can be set to music. If a label must be attached to my style, why not that of 'emotional realism'?"

Although Menotti has never objected to performances of atonal music at the Spoleto Festival, he is basically antipathetic to it and has strong feelings against even such modern masters as Arnold Schoenberg, Charles Ives, and Igor Stravinsky. These sentiments are not simply a matter of blind prejudice, but are couched in definite and cogent beliefs.

"People often make the mistake of considering music more intellectual and profound when it allows for literary or mathematical analysis. But musical logic is self-contained and defies words. It can only be analyzed intuitively. I consider Schoenberg, whom practically everyone reveres as a great intellectual, a very sentimental and self-indulgent composer. In spite of Adorno's ponderous and pretentious claims for him, I find his theoretical books arbitrary and superficial. The difference between a great composer such as Beethoven, for example, and someone like Schoenberg is exactly that of the discoverer of a hidden natural force and the inventor of a fascinating and even at times useful gadget.

"The fact is, music is only intellectual when it has a *musical* logic. For me, Rossini is musically much more intelligent than Schoenberg. His musical wit is a sign of great intelligence. Schubert, in his complete simplicity, is a great intellectual. And so is Chopin. But not Schoenberg or Max Reger or, for that matter, Boulez. They are indeed rich food for mathematicians and musicologists. For me, the intellectual composer is the one who reasons only in musical terms."

Menotti was incensed over an article he read on Charles Ives in the *Times Literary Supplement.* "We now recognize Charles Ives as probably the only American composer whose music has the unambiguous attribute of greatness and, as a composer, [Ives] has a special significance as a link between the old world and the new," wrote the *Times.*

"*Who,* may I ask, is 'we'?" said Menotti. "Surely not the public, who has been constantly indifferent to his music, nor—except for a handful of devotees—the musicians, who hardly ever perform his so-called masterpieces. These makers of myths, these amateur archeologists, are mainly the critics-musicologists of today, who still cannot see the forest for the trees.

"Ives's attempt to create an American style by simpleminded collage of Americana is as naïve as a painter who would claim to have created an African style simply by portraying elephants and palm trees. At best, Ives is an amusing eccentric. Musicologists, of course, have been impressed by his early hit-and-miss use of dissonance. But none of them have remarked on his almost painful failure to use it in an expressive way—in other words, to leave the vague field of experiment and enter the world of art. 'We' may find Ives a great composer. But for the rest of the world, to which I belong, he remains a pretentious, ungraceful amateur. There is hardly a page of inevitable music in his entire output."

"What then should music be?" I asked Menotti.

The answer came quickly:

"Like dance, music is also the expression of the human body. All great music has the inflection of one's breathing and is set in motion, just as the body is, by two fundamental values: tension and relaxation. By weakening and doing away with assonance, the contemporary composer has deprived himself of the very principle of motion. Dissonance has been castrated of its propulsive power. Much of contemporary music reminds me of the erotic excitement of an impotent man. To sing, you must breathe in and out. To walk, you must lift your leg and put it down again. Great music must breathe and must walk.

"There is no melody without normal breathing. There is no musical form without a sense of motion, because it is traced in time. But music must also be given a sense of direction—not only of motion—and it is tonality which gives us a clear point of departure and arrival. Melody and rhythm establish the motion, tonality the space—a space again created by tonal tension and relaxation. Without these principals, music seems lifeless and purposeless. Even the music of Stravinsky, one of the few contemporary composers I admire, has difficulty in breathing and moving. More often than not, in spite of its rhythmic nervousness and melodic mimicry, it remains static. It is very much like a superb athlete, who keeps flexing his muscles and kicking his heels, without ever budging from the same spot."

Throughout his career, Menotti has staged all of his operas—at least all of their premieres. Whenever he can, he will travel far and wide to attend to the direction of his works. During rehearsals he is a punctilious taskmaster. When *The Consul* was revived at the New York City Opera in 1974, he went to the direction as though the work were being given its world premiere. Working with many unfamiliar singers, he was at pains to bring out the qualities that they themselves would intuitively bring to their roles. Menotti has always enjoyed coaching artists not yet world famous. To mold a young singer into a potentially memorable talent is one of Menotti's greatest pleasures. He had done so with Shirley Verrett, Judith Blegen, Patricia Neway, Cornell MacNeil, John Reardon, Gloria Lane, and even the difficult Marie Powers.

On this occasion the role of Magda was sung by Olivia Stapp, her mother by Muriel Greenspon, the secretary by Sandra Walker, the husband by John Darrenkamp, and the magician by Nico Castel.

Again, Christopher Keene was the conductor. With infinite care Menotti instructed each of these singers on the emotional underpinnings of his or her character. It was Menotti himself who acted out each part. He would stand very close to the individual singer, insisting on natural and inevitable actions. As they sang, he would 'grimace' the appropriate feelings. He would move them or walk them toward the appropriate stage places. He would stop them if their diction was in any way unclear. During the highly dramatic opening scene, he showed each singer how to heighten his or her emotional responses to the impending visit of the police. Shedding at least twenty-five years, Menotti transformed himself into a live and agile actor, rushing about the stage, showing people how to express fear, terror, insecurity, hesitation—everything that would make the scene spring to immediate life. "You must think of what you are singing about. Your feelings must be real," he kept telling them, and he would run, fall down, crouch behind chairs, moving swiftly from place to place, and assuming Magda's sense of turmoil as she hides her husband from impending doom. With it all, Menotti never overdid the needed movements. All was steeped in logic and was fitting to the moment.

While this manner of direction might seem simplistic—the show-and-tell syndrome—Menotti always took into account the characteristics of the cast before him. It was not simply a matter of "do this, do that," but "*you* would do this or that." Most fascinating was his constant reminder to the singers, "You must not *think* about what you are doing, you must *feel* it." Again and again, he showed each singer how certain actions would yield expressive results, and timing was always of the essence. With singular deftness, he wedded music to movement. In a sense, he choreographed the events on the stage and, like any good choreographer, attended to the most minute details of movement. Finally it was always the flow of the music that dictated the action. What emerged during the opening night of the City Opera production was an altogether unified and searing sense of ensemble acting and singing.

Menotti reflected on his life as a director of opera:

"I have often said that I am a *metteur-en-scene malgré lui*. I never seriously planned to do any staging, and it was only after watching other directors stage my works that I began wishing to take over the job myself. When I was finally given the chance in *The Medium*, I found out that it all came very easily to me. Curiously enough, when I staged my operas, I divorced myself as much as possible from the composer, and at every new production of the same work, I try as much as possible not to repeat myself and to look at the opera with a fresh eye. However, I never distort my original intentions. I remain faithful to those first intentions, although I often find myself at a loss trying to remember what I had envisioned when writing certain passages, which I then wished either to cut or lengthen.

"Being the composer, I could of course do so, but I never do. I work on those passages until I can recall, more or less, what inspired them in the first place, and that always solves the problem for me. I tried to use the same process when staging other people's works, trying to put myself in the place of the composer, and trying to imagine why he had written a certain kind of music for a certain passage, and I will not give up until I seem to have discovered it.

"Because of my deep reverence toward the works that I like—I'm speaking of other composers—I always shied away from staging their works, but soon I was forced to do it. When the Spoleto Festival found itself on the brink of bankruptcy, I decided that in order to save money on Spoleto productions I had better stage some of the operas myself. I decided on *La Bohème* first, an opera which, because of its popularity, has suffered more than any other from false conventions, and from lazy, unimaginative readings. Thank God it was a huge success, which gave me the courage to face other works.

"My productions have been unequal in quality, of course, but may I proudly say, never have they been conventional or boring. Even my most contested ones, like *Don Giovanni*, with costumes and decor by Henry Moore, was full of *trouvailles*. For example, it was the first time, I believe, that an attempt was made to choreograph the three different dances taking place in Don Giovanni's palace simultaneously—echoing what the orchestra is doing. Or doing a *Boris* with a boy soprano in the role of the Czarevitch, which makes the last scene so much more heartbreaking and so much more real. Or a *Pélleas*, my favorite production and surely my most successful one, done in a pre-Raphaelite frame. It is in the infinite new details—and hidden intentions which I discover in the librettos and in the scores—that I take great pride. For example, so much action is implied in the libretto and in the score of *Don Pasquale* which is *never* realized, and when I conceived of a semi-naked Isolde in the second act, it was justified by the fact that Wagner, in his stage directions, asks Tristan to cover her with his cloak as Mark approaches.

"Undoubtedly *The Rake's Progress* was the most difficult opera I ever staged. This was so because Stravinsky's theatrical rhythm is so different from mine, and his music is often perversely against the grain of the action. But without making a single cut in the music, which I believe is done in almost all productions of *The Rake*, I managed to keep the audience amused and interested."

The days at Yester House would flow one into the other. Time was suspended. The rituals of breakfast, lunch, drinks, and dinner were interrupted by long walks on the grounds. The drawback was the frequent capriciousness of the weather. On one such walk I asked Menotti what it was about the Scottish weather that so appealed to him. "The fact is, I love to compose in cold weather," he said. "In the heat I become very lazy—my thoughts wander. My powers of concentration are much greater in cool weather." And so facing the wind, dressed in our winter sweaters in the middle of August, we'd walk; and when the winds were not so strong, we'd talk. I asked Menotti whether he had ever developed close friendships with any of his interpreters.

"Actually not," he said. "I've always avoided very close friendships with singers and very few of them have ever been invited to my house. I don't know why that is. It's really very strange. I suppose it's because I've had to struggle with them so much that I rarely want to see them again. With Marie Powers it got to be impossible. I resented her very much toward the end because she made me go through such agonies. I felt life was much too short to put up with that kind of eccentricity. And Patricia Neway. She changed so much over the years. I was very fond of Pat—I was very close to her. But then she became terribly didactic. With all that marvelous talent, she tried to become teacherish and very set in her ways. And all the people in *The Saint of Bleecker Street*. I'm friendly with them, but none of them has really become my close friend. Actually I've never been very fascinated by interpretive artists. I'm not a great friend of either pianists, or singers, or violinists. I'm much more fascinated by writers, or painters, or poets. It is the creative process that fascinates me. With conductors it's different. I've become friends with conductors, because you really have to be so involved with them. I mean, when they do a score of yours, you're completely in their hands.

"If I've not become friends with my singers, it's not for lack of gratitude. When they gave of their best, I was always very moved.

That was certainly the case with Marie Powers and Patricia Neway. I was also very moved by Leon Lishner, who sang the policeman in *The Consul.* I was moved by Richard Cross in *Maria Golovin* and Chet Allen in *Amahl.* I loved Gloria Lane as the secretary in *The Consul,* and as Desideria in *The Saint.* What touched me so about these singers was their instinctive understanding of my style. But these are only a few of the singers I loved working with; what about Joanna Bruno, Judith Blegen, George London, Alan Evans, Richard Stilwell, Jack Reardon, and many others? In other words, those that I would call 'Menotti singers.'

"You know, it's very odd, but I've never succeeded in teaching my recitative style to Italian singers. I cannot get any Italian singer to learn it. Americans get it right away and so do the French. But Italians, some of whom have given me brilliant performances, can't master the style. I mean, when they do *The Medium,* it's almost like hearing a different opera."

If Italy created Menotti, his relationship to his country has been nothing if not ambivalent. Italy has treated Menotti like an errant son, and Menotti has not quite forgiven his native country for its all too often halfhearted acceptance of either his gift or his person.

"Italy did not treat me particularly well. During the Fascist years my music was practically banned in Italy, because I refused to join the party. Now I am looked upon with suspicion because I refuse to join the Italian political game. The point is, I have always abhorred professional patriotism. I am anti-Nationalist. I feel that nationalism is one of the greatest evils of our society. It has caused more wrong judgments and more useless bloodshed. Of course, I have a great attachment to Italy because one cannot help feeling sentimental about the country one is born in. Besides that, it touches certain chords in my being that another landscape or another language can't possibly strike. But just as I have never wanted to be overattached to my family, I have not grown overly attached to Italy. I feel that our responsibility is toward all human beings, and that compassion cannot stop at any party line.

"Of course, to the Italians it looked as though I had betrayed them. When I became successful in America, it became a source of irritation to them. Then there are the Italian critics. I am afraid most of them are rather provincial. They repeat what they read in the reviews of their more important colleagues, and these, with a few notable exceptions (such as Montale, D'Amico, Rinaldi, Gori), felt it was highly suspicious for an Italian artist to be discovered in another country, especially a 'barbaric' one like the U.S.A. Some of the most vitriolic reviews came from an Italian critic—Giulio Confalonieri, who started out by crucifying me and years later sent me a letter apologizing for his horrible write-ups and declaring himself a 'Menottiano.' I have also been condemned for being lionized by international 'society,' if there is still such a thing—and the world-wide success of some of my operas is still deemed, by fellow-composers whose music doesn't travel well, the result of clever commercial manipulation of some sort.

"Of course, the last straw was the Spoleto Festival. The Italians fought against it from the very beginning. They tried everything to stop it. The fact that the Festival succeeded was yet another cause for irritation. I suppose the situation is slowly changing. Many of the critics now accept me; still . . . it took a very long time."

The move to Yester seems like a symbolic rejection of not only Italy but of all the countries in which Menotti has gained success. Scotland was alien ground. Menotti's name is hardly known there, his music seldom performed. When Menotti purchased Yester House, his neighbors thought that Menotti was simply a rich Italian. Menotti couldn't be more amused and delighted by the anonymity that came his way. To begin with, the townspeople in nearby Gifford considered his presence in their midst very odd. Little by little, news trickled out that Mr. Menotti (or Mr. McNaughty, as he is referred to in the village) was a famous composer, and many felt rather ashamed that they had never heard of him before. Soon enough, however, they responded to his personal warmth, to the natural affection he showed to their children, and to the generosity of his patronage. In time, he was asked to open flower shows or to appear at official functions. He has endeared himself to the villagers by inviting all their children to a yearly Christmas party at Yester House, where he and Chip organize games, distribute presents, and bring in musicians and turn the occasion into a joyful feast.

Menotti has followed his strong instincts and has chosen a life commensurate with his attitude on how life should be led:

"Of course, I realize how foolish it is to have bought a house as grand as Yester. On the other hand, I dislike doing things halfway. I mean, if I had decided on a very simple house, as I actually *had* before I met Chip, I would have been perfectly happy living in one or two rooms in a forest, with my books and my piano—just the bare essentials. But having decided on a luxurious house, I wanted it to be *very* luxurious. I've been accused of snobbism. Well, it may be so. I mean, if I have to see society people, then I'd rather see real aristocrats—not half-baked society people. When I become lowbrow, then I *really* mingle with the dregs of society. I hate mediocrity.

"But listen, I'm sixty-three! How long can I really enjoy this kind of madness? I've readily accepted my way of living, and I've readily accepted living at Yester, because Yester protects me from a world that I have come to detest—a world of modern cities. I hate that sort of plastic paradise. I hate to see the cities that I have loved defaced by bad architecture, by ugliness.

"Here, at least, I'm very close to nature. I love the wonderful, pure air, the silence, the peace. Oh, I suppose that if I were my own business representative I would probably say, 'Mr. Menotti, what can you be thinking of? You are ruining us! And what about your image?' Well, I care very little about my image. I do what I feel, what I want, what I think is right at the moment, and to hell with what people think. I know that buying Yester is a wildly theatrical gesture. I know I will have to bear the consequences of this last mad act. And if I had planned my old age, I would certainly have planned it more cleverly.

"Actually this last gesture of mine is a foolish disregard for money and wealth, because although I live splendidly, I really live without a penny. Whatever I have, I spend immediately. Very few people believe that, but they will find it out when I die. I have gone on for years and years with two or three hundred dollars in the bank. Of course, as long as people play my music, money comes in. The only reason I can live this way is by continuing to work and not saving anything."

In a strange, quite marvelous way Gian Carlo Menotti is a man of faith. He trusts the unknown—not in a religious way, but in some sort of metaphysical way. He is a man who is mysteriously protected by . . . something. He continues to search for that special sign, for some sanctified occurrence that might bring him back to a strong ecclesiastic belief.

"If I knew I would be 'hit' by faith, I would sell this house immediately. I would leave everything and become a hermit or become a monk. I don't know what I would do, but I would not live like this. Unlike Pascal, I pray to God *not* to give me a sign. Oh, please! I'm too happy the way I am! It's a strange kind of happiness, to be sure. Because I still have this feeling that there is a 'home' (is it the church?) which I have left behind. It gives me a strange and uncomfortable sensation. The fact is, I am a very unquiet and searching person. I believe that truth is nothing but a search for it. As long as you have the desire and curiosity to go on with the search, and are compelled to do so, then you can be reasonably happy. Only when old age or sickness or love prevents you from continuing this search, you are lost.

"Perhaps the reason I enjoy living so much is because I'm continually surprised at being alive."

Enjoyment of life has not deterred Menotti from pondering his own death, but with characteristic aplomb, he looks upon it as something of a theatrical event, which would take the form of the reading of his will. When the moment comes a long list of people will be in for a potentially amusing spectacle.

"I have always felt that a man so often betrays himself in his will —or at least betrays his friendships. So there is a clause in my will in which I name all of the people that I have loved, or who have been nice to me, and to each of them I leave a little thing—either an object or a little money, if they are poor. I tried to remember them all. It is rather amusing, because when I made my will, my lawyer looked at me in dismay and said, 'Mr. Menotti, this is not a will. This is a rummage sale!' "

Gian Carlo Menotti moves and exists within the cumulative complexities of his inner life. They guide him, propel him into action, and in a way render him immune to those forces that might break his spirit or his need for the act of creation. The landscape of his life, with its peaks and chasms, has strengthened a personality whose character remains fixed in hope and optimism.

Menotti has lived with his share of melancholy, despair, and disappointment. He has also tasted happiness and has known the dangerous lures of international recognition. Battered by conflicting emotions, he has survived frequent artistic rejection, the strong envy and jealousy of his fellow composers, the calumnies of the critics.

Menotti is a product of the American dream, but unlike many such products, he has not been destroyed by it. Still productive and still vigorous, Gian Carlo Menotti, with his operatic genius, his instinctive honesty, his clarity of concept, and above all his great humanity, is now entering his full maturity. The works to come will unquestionably enrich the world's musical repertoire, bringing pleasure, fulfillment, and enlightenment to an international public. Menotti's music is being rediscovered with increasing frequency, and the uniqueness of his musical signature continues to announce the unmistakable fact that he is among our major twentieth-century composers—an artist whose singular vision has given the world yet one more reason for whatever claim it may have for survival and dignity.

John Gruen was born in France and educated in Berlin, in Milan, and in America (at the City College of New York and the University of Iowa). From 1960 to 1967 he was art and music critic for the New York *Herald Tribune,* and he has been art critic of *New York* magazine and a feature writer for *Vogue.* He is now a contributing editor to *Dance* magazine and *Artnews,* and a frequent contributor to the Sunday entertainment pages of the *New York Times.* He is also the host of a weekly radio program on the dance. Mr. Gruen, who is currently writing a biography of Erik Bruhn, lives in New York with his wife, the painter Jane Wilson, and their daughter, Julia.

INDEX

Italic numbers indicate quotations